salt sugar smoke

how to preserve fruit, vegetables, meat and fish

DIANA HENRY

MITCHELL BEAZLEY

contents

introduction

Lifelong loves take hold early on. My mum did a lot of baking when we were growing up, and I have a clear memory of sitting on the countertop in our small kitchen as she sliced warm wheaten bread and spread a piece with raspberry jam for me. The jam was made by Aunt Sissy, who wasn't an aunt at all, but an elderly family friend and a tremendous preserver. That jam was better than any fruit I ever tasted fresh. Aunt Sissy's jams were soft set and ran off the bread. They were so loved, we only ate them on homemade bread or in a sandwich. At home, we seemed to be surrounded by great jam and chutney makers and we loved getting jars from them.

So I always appreciated preserved foods, and I have been preserving this or that—chutney, gravlax, pork rillettes (a kind of pâté)—since I was in my mid-teens. But preserving is the kind of cooking you always feel "experts" do. I felt I needed to have an indenture period, to spend, like Aunt Sissy, every day of the summer with kettles on the go. Several years ago I decided to do this. I wanted to improve skills I already had, to understand why I followed certain rules, to make up my own recipes, to feel confident about salting herrings and duck. *Salt Sugar Smoke* is the result of a rigorous exploration and a long journey. For three years, I preserved food every day, often well into the night. My laundry room filled up with jars. The refrigerator became home to slabs of bacon and chunks of beef. I discovered I could go my own way. It may be traditional in Great Britain, where I live, to use equal quantities of sugar and fruit to make firm-set, sweet jams. However, they make soft-set jams in France and lower sugar jams in Scandinavia, so I made the kind of jams I preferred: soft-set and not too sweet.

I am a home cook. I don't have masses of special equipment and I don't do things on a grand scale. A lot of the literature that existed on preserving was off-putting. I didn't want to turn my shed into a smokery. I could never manage—and would never need—to cure a whole pig. I have done everything in this book in a gentle way and didn't spend much on new equipment. I bought an additional kettle, some more wooden spoons, a wide funnel for pouring jams through, a lot of measuring cups, a big plastic box (a storage box from IKEA) to use for brining, and a little stove-top smoker.

Then I started my journey. I had, as the saying goes, a ball. I discovered that preserving made you feel as if you were more than just a cook. There were days when it reminded me of being on my grandparents' farm. It felt as if I was presiding over something natural that had its own momentum, but which I had a hand in. Fish and pork changed because of the application of salt, for example, and I oversaw this and took it to the next stage. There was a tremendous thrill in producing food that was more than a meal. Like a child in a craft class, I have always loved making things, and preserving and curing produced that feeling about a hundred times over. And the food was delicious. People have always preserved because they needed to—it was about survival. However, the reason we still bother to do it at home is because the end products taste so good.

My daily cooking changed. There were so many different condiments on the go that I did a lot of plain meals using these as embellishments: rice and vegetable dishes with chutneys, roasts with relishes, simple cakes with sumptuous fillings of unusual jams. I have always thought that home cooking—especially the quick kind we do a lot these days—is about accessorizing. We have to think of something good to do with a pork chop or a piece of fish.

I want everybody who reads this book to feel they can preserve and do some basic curing. However, to get the best out of it, please read the chapter introductions before you embark on the recipes. They give you the know-how and are there to be referred to. I've tried to keep them simple, while conveying the salient points. Be careful about hygiene, which is essential. Be aware that you are making foods that can spoil, so use your senses to tell you when something is off. The recipes have been tested according to the sterilizing and potting practices followed in Great Britain, where jams and chutneys are not treated in water baths, but, if you are using this book in North America and want to store these products without refrigeration (most will keep in the refrigerator short term), you may want to use the guidelines given for processing your jars in a water bath; this advice has been adapted in the relevant recipes for the American reader. You can also find general information on the process on pages 268–269.

Label and date what you make: When you labour over twenty jars of something, you feel sure you will always know what's in them, but you won't. Remember that some recipes can't be exact, so have extra sugar on hand, for example, when making jellies, in case the fruits release more juice for you than they did for me.

Many books are written these days about how to think about food in a more caring way. Preserving aligns itself with these to some extent, because it is partly about using bumper crops and not squandering abundance. However, this book is not a manifesto. This kind of cooking takes time and is outside the everyday business of getting a meal on to the table. I don't expect everybody to do it. But if you already enjoy cooking, or even if you just have a penchant for making things, preserving is incredibly satisfying.

It could seem grandiose to talk about "what makes a good life" in a book that is simply a collection of recipes. But for me, one of the constituents of a good life is the ability to find pleasure in the small things. A good jam for your toast in the morning. A chutney that is made from apples you gathered last fall. Cutting corned beef that you've made and can feed to friends. These are seemingly unimportant things, and they won't change the world, but the sum of happiness in one's life is often made up of such details. There's a jar of jam on your table. If it is jam that has been made with care, that comes from fruit you picked, that is delicious and starts your day off well, it is much more than just a jam. And—honestly—you can make it.

There are riches there, lad, fortune enough for all the country round, but not a soul sees it!'
Anton Chekhov, *Happiness*

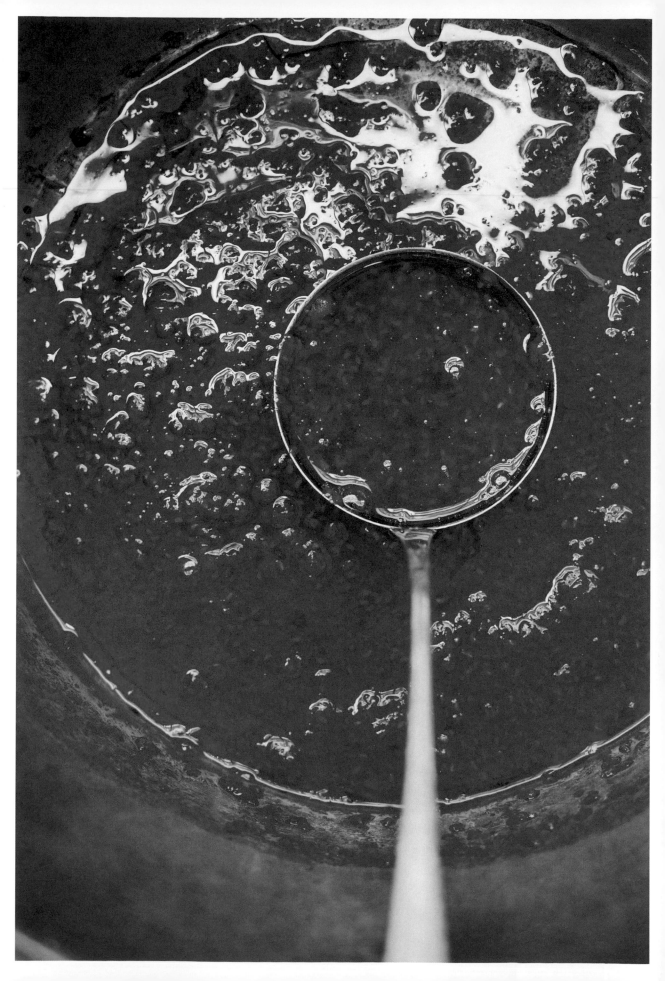

jam

Love can make you do crazy things. I once took an enormous detour while driving to the south of France—making a dogleg through the Loire Valley when I was actually heading for Menton—because of my love of jam. *The Good Hotel Guide* had a description of an eccentric hotel in Chinon whose main pull was an armoire housing thirty flavors of jam.

I fantasized about that cupboard for weeks. The idea of those jewel-colored jars arranged on old wooden shelves was more alluring than the prospect of my vacation on the Côte d'Azur.

Breakfast time at the Hôtel Diderot duly arrived, the armoire was flung open, and there they were: apricot, cherry, red currant, peach, and raspberry, green fig, you name it, they had it. The sight was exhilarating. No-nonsense girls in black skirts and white aprons distributed croissants, tartines, and … just two flavors of jam. We had driven miles and not tasted twenty-eight of the flavors. Manners got me another two, but I was greatly disappointed.

Simone de Beauvoir compared jam making to the capturing of time: "the housewife has caught duration in the snare of sugar, she has enclosed life in jars." I like the idea of stopping a fruit dead in its tracks so you can eke it out little by little (although I certainly wouldn't restrict jam making to housewives). However, preserving is also about capturing and holding onto a season, a particular mood. You can find fall in a jar of pear and chestnut jam, or the fragrance of your Provençal summer vacation in a jar of apricot and lavender. It is one of the most poetic branches of cooking.

It was only relatively late in my culinary life that I started making jam. It seemed a little daunting, reserved for the serious preserver with gleaming equipment and days at her disposal. Once you get started, however, it quickly becomes easy. Now I sometimes make just a few jars at a time; you don't have to have a heavy-duty session.

There are key things to know—how to get a set, how certain fruits behave, how to sterilize jars and equipment—but it's not rocket science. And getting to grips with the science doesn't preclude creativity. The more often you make jam, the more you know what is possible, and you soon start inventing your own flavors. It is also fine, as I learned in Scandinavia, to bend the rules, to make "jams" like fruit purees. Indeed, I make three different kinds of strawberry jam: an old-fashioned sweet, thick jam; another lower in sugar that needs to be kept in the refrigerator; and a final type that is pretty much a sweet puree (delicious, as long as you don't mind it running off your toast). They are all good in different ways.

Jam making has traditionally been seen as the domain of ladies of a certain age. But even if you're the right side of forty, give it a chance. You'll think it's worth it every time your toast pops, and greedy friends, children, husbands, and boyfriends will love it. Here's how …

the essentials of making jam

FRUIT

The fruit you use should be dry, fresh, and just ripe or slightly underripe (you can even make decent jam from rock-hard supermarket apricots). Overripe fruit is lower in pectin and acid (two things jam needs), and also doesn't taste as good in the jar. However, I do make some exceptions. If I have a bag of plums that are too soft to eat (not going off, but not in peak condition), I whack them in a pan and make a jar of jam (usually with less sugar, see below).

PECTIN

Pectin is found in all fruits and some vegetables. Without it, preserves wouldn't set. It is found in the skins, pith, cores, and seeds of fruit and also in the cell walls.

Different fruits contain different amounts of pectin. Strawberries, raspberries, peaches, and nectarines are low in pectin. Apricots, cherries, greengages, and dessert plums are medium. Black currants, red currants, damsons, cooking plums, apples, and quinces are high in pectin. To make jams from low-pectin fruit, you need to add a high-pectin fruit (apple, or lemon juice) or add powdered pectin or liquid pectin. If using powdered pectin, add it to crushed fruit and mix until the pectin has completely dissolved *before* adding the sugar and bringing to a boil for 1 minute. For liquid pectin, add it *after* adding the sugar and bringing the mixture to a boil.

ACID

Fruit also contains acid. This helps release pectin, but it's also necessary for flavor. My favorite jams are made from acidic fruits, because they have a good sweet-tart balance. Lemon juice can be added to low-acid fruits to help the release of pectin and "brighten" the flavor; I often add it after the setting point is reached and before canning to give a jam freshness.

SUGAR

Sugar preserves fruit and allows jam to keep. It also helps pectin to gel and stops it from breaking down while the jam is boiling. However, it inhibits the initial release of pectin and toughens fruit skins, so is always added after the first cooking, once the fruit is soft.

Traditionally, equal amounts of sugar to fruit are used. This gives a firm set and good keeping qualities, but I find the jams too sweet. It is harder to set low-sugar jams (and they must be refrigerated once open), but I prefer a soft set and a fresher flavor. Use granulated sugar rather than superfine sugar, because larger crystals dissolve more quickly.

PROBLEMS

JAM WON'T SET It is too low in pectin or hasn't boiled enough. Boil again with added pectin.

JAM IS HARD OR DRY The jam was boiled too much.

MOLD DEVELOPS Jars may not have been fully sterilized or you didn't can the jam properly.

JAM FERMENTS There wasn't enough sugar, the jam wasn't boiled long enough, the jar wasn't sealed properly, or the fruit was overripe.

the process of making jam

KEEP EVERYTHING CLEAN

All utensils and jars need to be sterilized. This isn't taxing. Funnels and ladles need to be plunged in boiling water. I sterilize jars just before I make jam, so they're hot when I'm ready to fill them. You can boil them, or wash them in soapy water (lids as well) then put in an oven at 340°F, or put them through a dishwasher cycle (unloading while hot and using soon after). If jars will be in a water bath for more than 10 minutes (*see* pages 268–269), they won't need sterilizing.

TESTING FOR A SET

I use a candy thermometer (the setting point for jam is 220°F, although high-pectin fruits can set a couple of degrees lower). A thermometer helps you know if your jam is near ready, but the wrinkle test is the one I rely on, because you get to know the type of set you prefer. For this, put a plate—I keep a metal one—into the freezer when you start making jam. When it's time to start testing (when the rolling bubbles have calmed and the jam looks heavy and glossy), spoon some jam onto the cold plate, refrigerate for a couple of minutes, then push it with a finger to see if it wrinkles. (Take the pan off the heat while you test, or your jam could overcook.) If you want a firm set, the wrinkle will stay in place after you have removed your finger. I can my jams when they *just* wrinkle.

CANNING AND STORING

Put jam in the jars while both jam and jars are hot (jam should be canned at above 185°F) and fill almost to the top. The "headspace," the gap at the top, depends on what you are canning. For complete canning instructions, *see* page 268–269. Seal with screw-on lids, using a dish towel to protect your fingers. Label when cool (it's amazing how you forget what's in them), and store in a dry, cool place between 50°F and 70°F for up to one year. Refrigerate after opening.

REFRIGERATOR JAM AND "NEARLY" JAM

In Sweden, I found what I call "nearly" jam. I stayed on a few farms one year and there were wonderful jams for breakfast. When I asked for recipes, my hosts laughed and explained they just boiled fruit with lemon juice and sugar. Other jams I loved were more firmly set but still lower in sugar than usual. Refrigerate once opened and eat within four weeks.

TIPS

1 Only add sugar after the fruit has softened (except for berries) in recipes without pectin. Heat the sugar gradually, stirring, and only bring to a boil once the sugar dissolves.If using powdered pectin, add it to crushed fruit and make sure it is dissolved, *then* bring to a boil before adding the sugar, return to a boil, and boil for one minute. For liquid pectin, add it *after* adding the sugar and bringing it to a boil.

2 Test for a setting point and remove the pan from the heat while you do so.

3 Skim the jam before canning using a slotted spoon, because the scum looks unsightly.

4 Let jams with large pieces of fruit settle for about twelve minutes before canning. The jam will thicken slightly, so there will be a more even distribution of fruit.

strawberry and passion fruit jam

Passion fruits are wonderful with strawberries because they give them acidity. This is
a luxurious treat. Keep it for filling cakes or spooning onto toast.

Fills 4 (½ pint) jars
1 quart strawberries, hulled, gently wiped
   clean, and large fruit quartered (5½ cups)
10 passion fruits, halved and pulp and seeds
   scooped out

juice of 1 lemon
1 (1¾oz) box powdered pectin
3 cups granulated sugar

1 Prepare a boiling-water canner (*see* pages 368–369) and keep the cleaned jars and lids warm.

2 Put the fruit into a large, deep saucepan and crush with a vegetable masher. Add the lemon juice
and pectin and mix until the pectin has dissolved. Bring to a boil, add the sugar, bring back to a full
rolling boil, and boil for 1 minute, until setting point is reached. This is a soft-set jam, so pull it off
the heat as soon as the jam only just wrinkles (*see* page 11). Skim off any scum.

3 Fill each jar, leaving a headspace of ¼ inch from the top. Process the filled jars in a boiling-water
canner for 10 minutes at sea level (*see* pages 369). Let cool, seal the jars, and label before storing.

"nearly" strawberry jam

I find traditional strawberry jam tastes a bit like boiled candies, so I make this instead in small
batches. It makes a fresh-tasting jam that you can whip up without a boiling-water canner.
Keep it in the refrigerator and eat within four days or so (or make a larger batch and freeze it).

Fills a small jar, enough for about 6 servings
1 pint strawberries, hulled and gently wiped
   clean (2½ cups)

⅓ cup granulated sugar
juice of ½ lemon

1 Chop the strawberries into chunks (leave small ones whole) and put them into a saucepan with the
sugar and lemon juice. Set over medium heat and stir from time to time until the sugar dissolves.

2 Coarsely mash the fruit with a fork or vegetable masher. You want to end up with a mixture that is
part puree, part chunks of fruit. The fruit will be in a a a lot of syrup at this stage, so reduce the heat to
very low and leave to simmer until it's thicker. In all, it will take 20–25 minutes to make. Be careful
not to let the pan burn, and skim off any scum that rises.

3 Pour into a bowl and let cool. This doesn't set, but becomes a chunky, fresh-tasting puree.

traditional strawberry jam

This is regular strawberry jam, made with an equal weight of strawberries and sugar. It is too sweet for me (I love to make the "nearly" strawberry jam, *see* left, when strawberries are in season, and keep it in the refrigerator), but this is jam that will keep. If you make enough, it can last you until strawberries are in season once again. My children love it.

Fills 6 (½ pint) jars
1½ quarts strawberries, hulled and gently wiped clean (7 cups)

juice of 2 lemons
5 cups granulated sugar

1 Prepare a boiling-water canner (*see* pages 368–369) and keep the cleaned jars and lids warm.

2 Quarter any large strawberries and put all the fruit in a large, deep saucepan with the lemon juice. Bring to a simmer; the juices in the fruit will start to run as it is heated. Once the mixture is simmering, cook gently for about five minutes. Press the fruit with a vegetable masher as it cooks to help break the berries down.

3 Add the sugar and stir gently until it is dissolved. Increase the heat and bring the mixture to a rolling boil. Boil for about five minutes, then skim off any scum that rises. Test for a set (use a thermometer or do the wrinkle test, *see* page 11, or do both). If it hasn't reached setting point, return to the heat and keep cooking and testing at two minute intervals until a set has been reached. Remove from the heat, skim off any scum, and let cool slightly (for about 10 minutes).

4 Fill each jar, leaving a headspace of ¼ inch from the top. Process the filled jars in a boiling-water canner for 10 minutes at sea level (*see* pages 369). Let cool, seal the jars, and label before storing.

white peach and raspberry jam

Lovely to look at as it's being made and, of course, fragrant as the scent of raspberries and white peaches blend. You can make it with yellow peaches, but it's not as good. This jam has less sugar than is traditional, so is fresh, fruity, and tart. You can add a sprig of lavender or lemon thyme.

Fills 9 (½ pint) jars
6 white peaches (2lb)
5 cups raspberries

juice of 2 lemons
1 (1¾oz) box powdered pectin
5 cups granulated sugar

1 Prepare a boiling-water canner (*see* pages 368–369) and keep the cleaned jars and lids warm.

2 Plunge the peaches, in batches, into a saucepan of boiling water for one minute. Quickly remove them, run cold water over them, and peel off the skins. Halve, pit, and cut each half into slices. Put the fruit into a large, deep saucepan and crush lightly. Add lemon juice and pectin and stir until the pectin is completely dissolved. Bring to a boil, add the sugar, bring back to a full rolling boil, and boil for 1 minute, until setting point is reached (check on a sugar thermometer and do the wrinkle test as well, *see* page 11), skimming off any scum that rises. Let cool for 10 minutes.

3 Fill each jar, leaving a headspace of ¼ inch from the top. Process the filled jars in a boiling-water canner for 10 minutes at sea level (*see* pages 369). Let cool, seal the jars, and label before storing.

queen henrietta maria's "marmalade" of cherries

Adapted from a 17th-century recipe I stumbled across in Florence White's *Good Things in England*. I couldn't resist: What a regal way to start the day. Interestingly, the original uses only half sugar to fruit, or "peradventure a little more if to keep all the year." This has more, but, if you prefer making just a few jars and refrigerating them, use the Queen's ratio of sugar to fruit.

Fills 15 (½ pint) jars
6 cups cherries (2lb), pitted
5½ cups red currants (1½lb)

4 cups raspberries
juice of 3 lemons
7½ cups granulated sugar

1 Prepare a boiling-water canner (*see* pages 368–369) and keep the cleaned jars and lids warm.

2 Put the fruit into a saucepan with 1¼ cups of water. Bring to a simmer and cook for 12 minutes, until the fruit is tender (as the original recipe suggests, 'bruise the cherries with the back of your spoon'). Add the lemon juice and sugar and cook gently until the sugar dissolves. Increase the heat and boil to setting point (*see* page 11). Skim. Let cool for 12 minutes so the larger bits of fruit will be evenly distributed.

3 Fill each jar, leaving a headspace of ¼ inch from the top. Process the filled jars in a boiling-water canner for 10 minutes at sea level (*see* pages 369). Let cool, seal the jars, and label before storing.

purple fig and pomegranate jam

Unfortunately, it's impossible to retain the jeweled seeds of pomegranates in a jam; the sweet, juicy part just dissolves and you are left with a lot of chewy seeds. However, that doesn't mean you can't capture its flavor. This jam tastes of both figs and pomegranates. Using pomegranate syrup gives it a wonderful tang. The recipe makes a small quantity—that's because I never have such an abundance of figs that I can make loads of it. When you are shopping for pomegranate juice, find one that is pure juice; anything called "pomegranate juice drink" will be sweetened and not produce such a nice result.

Fills 2 (½ pint) jars
8 figs, trimmed and quartered
finely grated zest of 1 unwaxed lemon
    and juice of 2
1 cooking apple, peeled, cored, and chopped

½ cup apple juice
½ cup pomegranate juice
1 (1¾oz) box powdered pectin
2 cups granulated sugar
2 tablespoons pomegranate molasses

1 Prepare a boiling-water canner (*see* pages 368–369) and keep the cleaned jars and lids warm.

2 Put the figs, lemon zest and juice, and apple into a heavy saucepan with the apple and pomegranate juices. Cook on low heat until the fruit is completely soft (about 12 minutes). Mix in the pectin until completely dissolved. Bring to a boil, add the sugar and pomegranate molasses, bring back to a full rolling boil, and boil for 1 minute, until setting point is reached (*see* page 11). Skim.

3 Fill each jar, leaving a headspace of ¼ inch from the top. Process the filled jars in a boiling-water canner for 10 minutes at sea level (*see* pages 369). Let cool, seal the jars, and label before storing.

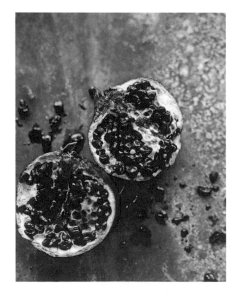

how to use

This is an expensive jam to make, and rich (figs always produce rich, succulent jams that have a dried fruit flavor even when made with fresh fruit). I don't put this straight onto bread but like to spread toast with Labneh (a Middle Eastern yogurt cheese, *see* page 98), spoon some of the jam on top, and sprinkle with pomegranate seeds. It's wonderful for breakfast at the weekend.

You can also make this jam with orange juice and cardamom seeds (use a mixture of orange and apple juice and omit the pomegranate molasses, which is available online), adding a little orange flower water, if you prefer.

raspberry and violet jam

Raspberry jam is one of the most delicious. Turning raspberries into jam intensifies their flavor and, as they have a whiff of the flower, violet is a perfect addition. I don't like it too sweet, so I don't add the traditional quantity of sugar (I also use added pectin; raspberries are low in pectin so it isn't easy to get a set). I try to catch it at the optimum point, I love a soft set but don't want a coulis. With practice, you'll get to judge when the jam is ready.

   Once opened, keep this in the refrigerator. For an easier life, use equal quantities of sugar and fruit, but I think this gives a "boiled candy" flavor. You can add more violet syrup or liqueur, but remember you don't want the jam to be too runny.

Fills 10 (½ pint) jars
5 pints raspberries (3lb)
juice of 1 lemon

1 (1¾oz) box powdered pectin
5 cups granulated sugar
⅓ cup violet syrup or violet liqueur

1 Prepare a boiling-water canner (*see* pages 368–369) and keep the cleaned jars and lids warm.

2 Put the raspberries into a large, deep saucepan with the lemon juice and pectin, and mix until the pectin dissolves. Bring to a boil, add the sugar, bring back to a full rolling boil, and boil for 1 minute, until setting point is reached (*see* page 11). Skim. Stir in the violet syrup. Let cool for 12 minutes.

3 Fill each jar, leaving a headspace of ¼ inch from the top. Process the filled jars in a boiling-water canner for 10 minutes at sea level (*see* pages 369). Let cool, seal the jars, and label before storing.

and also ...

KIEV RASPBERRY JAM

Jam is very important in Russia. They love sweet things so much (hardly surprising when you think how much of their food is sour: all those pickled cucumbers and jars of fermented cabbage), and a well-laid table is a source of great pride. As in the Middle East, jams are eaten with tea, eaten from dishes as if they were desserts, providing spoonfuls of sweetness and luxury, as well as being served with curd cheese or ice cream for dessert. Runny, syrupy jam—*varen'ye*—is the most common in Russia and is distinct from firmer set jams. The following is cooked as instructed by the Princess in *Anna Karenina*. There's a whole tense scene based around making jam, in which the cook is told to make raspberry jam the "new" way, without water. In Russia, they often put a little layer of vodka on top of preserves, so I guess a layer of brandy on the top of this would be perfect.

Put 4 cups of raspberries in a saucepan with ¼ cup of brandy. Gently stir and let rest overnight. Proceed as for raspberry and violet jam, omitting the violet flavouring. Fills 3 (½ pint) jars.

apple and blackberry jam

The good thing about this is that it is largely made from cooking apples—cheap and abundant—yet really tastes of blackberries, although you don't have to use that many. It is full of the flavors of the countryside in England, and the apple brandy is a delicious addition. Russian jam makers used to pour a layer of vodka on top of the jam to protect it. I copied them and watched the booze slowly sink into the jam below. You can use ordinary brandy or applejack.

Fills 8 (½ pint) jars
7 cooking apples, peeled, cored,
   and cut into chunks (2¼lb)
4 cups blackberries

1¾ cups hard cider
a little apple juice, if needed
4 cups granulated sugar
¼ cup apple brandy

1 Prepare a boiling-water canner (*see* pages 368–369) and keep the cleaned jars and lids warm.

2 Put the apple chunks and blackberries into a large, deep saucepan with the cider and slowly bring to a boil. Reduce the heat and let the fruit simmer until it is completely soft, almost like a puree. (Add a little water or, even better, apple juice, if the mixture becomes too dry.)

3 Add the sugar and cook on low heat, stirring to help the sugar dissolve. Turn up the heat and cook until you reach the setting point and skim. Because apples are high in pectin, this jam sets easily; I rely more on the wrinkle test (*see* page 11) than on temperature. You will probably find it reaches setting point with the wrinkle test before it reaches the right temperature. Stir in the brandy.

4 Fill each jar, leaving a headspace of ¼ inch from the top. Process the filled jars in a boiling-water canner for 10 minutes at sea level (*see* pages 369). Let cool, seal the jars, and label before storing.

how to use

This is particularly good on rustic breads made with whole-wheat, multigrain, or spelt flour, or Irish soda bread. It's also wonderful as a filling for a sponge cake made with hazelnuts and light brown sugar. Spread a layer of slightly sweetened crème fraîche mixed with mascarpone on one layer, spoon the jam over it, then put on the top layer. Sift over a dusting of confectioners' sugar before serving.

damson and gin jam

Sometimes it's good to go boozy at breakfast. This is the way to do it (and don't worry about the odd pit in there, although warn whoever's eating it). When damsons are not in season, use tart plums and add the juice of a couple of lemons.

Fills 3 (½ pint) jars
15 damsons (2¼lb)
3½ cups granulated sugar

juice of 1 lemon
2 tablespoons gin, or damson or sloe gin

1 Prepare a boiling-water canner (*see* pages 368–369) and keep the cleaned jars and lids warm.

2 Put the damsons into a large, deep saucepan with 1¾ cup of water and cook gently for 30 minutes, until the fruit is really tender. Add the sugar and lemon juice and stir until dissolved, then bring the mixture to a boil. As it boils, many of the pits from the damsons will rise to the surface; scoop them up with a slotted spoon as they do and get rid of them, along with any scum that rises.

3 Continue to boil until the setting point is reached (use a thermometer and do the wrinkle test, too, *see* page 11). Remove the pan from the heat and stir in the gin or sloe gin. Taste to see if you would like to add a little more (remember that you can't add loads, or the jam won't set!).

4 Fill each jar, leaving a headspace of ¼ inch from the top. Process the filled jars in a boiling-water canner for 10 minutes at sea level (*see* pages 369). Let cool, seal the jars, and label before storing.

greengage and gewürztraminer jam

The idea of pairing greengages with gewürztraminer wine comes from the legendary French jam maker, Christine Ferber.

Fills 3 (½ pint) jars
15 greengages (2¼lb), halved and pitted

1 cup gewürztraminer wine
3½ cups granulated sugar

1 Prepare a boiling-water canner (*see* pages 368–369) and keep the cleaned jars and lids warm.

1 Put the greengages in a large, heavy saucepan with half the wine and bring to a boil. Reduce the heat and simmer until the fruit is soft, then add the sugar and continue to simmer, stirring a little, until the sugar has dissolved. Turn up the heat and boil until the setting point is reached (check on a thermometer and do the wrinkle test, too, *see* page 11), skimming off any scum. Stir in the rest of the wine.

4 Fill each jar, leaving a headspace of ¼ inch from the top. Process the filled jars in a boiling-water canner for 10 minutes at sea level (*see* pages 369). Let cool, seal the jars, and label before storing.

pear and chestnut jam

This is unusual—I don't normally associate pears with jam—but it makes a fragrant, musky preserves. It's based on a recipe from the great French jam maker, Christine Ferber. The apples are there because pears are low in pectin, but they don't overpower the pears. When feeling lazy, I have used canned chestnuts. This works well with a sprig of rosemary or thyme or even a couple of bay leaves instead of the vanilla.

Fills 6 (½ pint) jars
5–6 pears (2¼lb)
3 cooking apples
juice of 3 unwaxed lemons
   plus 2 strips of zest

1 vanilla bean
4¾ cups granulated sugar
18 cooked chestnuts (7oz), cut into big chunks
   (they mostly only need to be halved)
1 (3oz) pouch liquid pectin

1 Peel and core the pears and the apples and cut the flesh into chunks. Put into a large, deep saucepan with the juice of two of the lemons and 1 cup of water. Slit the vanilla bean down the middle and scrape the seeds out with the point of your knife. Add half the bean and all the seeds to the pan. Reserve the other half of the vanilla bean.

2 Slowly bring the fruit to a boil, then immediately reduce the heat and simmer the fruit for about five minutes (depending on how ripe your pears are), until tender. Add 3½ cups of the sugar and cook gently, stirring occasionally to help the sugar dissolve. Cover with wax paper and let sit overnight.

3 Meanwhile, put the chestnuts in a saucepan with ½ cup of water and the remaining sugar and lemon juice. Add the lemon zest and the other half of the vanilla pod. Bring slowly to a boil, stirring to help the sugar dissolve, then heat on a gentle simmer for 15 minutes. Cover with wax paper and let sit overnight, too.

4 The next day, prepare a boiling-water canner (*see* pages 368–369) and keep the cleaned jars and lids warm. Mix together the chestnut and pear mixtures and bring to a rolling boil that cannot be stirred down. Stir in the pectin, and continuing to stir, boil rapidly for one minute, then remove from the heat and skim.

4 Fill each jar, leaving a headspace of ¼ inch from the top. Process the filled jars in a boiling-water canner for 10 minutes at sea level (*see* pages 369). Let cool, seal the jars, and label before storing.

how to use

I think this is so special that I don't often use it on my breakfast toast, but serve it with plain Greek yogurt (for breakfast or a simple dessert) and also spread a layer in a tart shell before adding pears on top to cook. The best thing to do with it, however, is to use it as a filling for an almond or hazelnut cake. Spread a layer of this between two sponge cakes, then top with a layer of cream (or a mixture of mascarpone and crème fraîche). Dust the surface of the cake with confectioners' sugar. Very autumnal …

apricot and lavender jam

This, and the apricot and vanilla jam below, are my favorites in the book. I have to admit I stole the idea for this from one of the best jam makers, Judith Gifford of Tea Together. Her apricot and lavender reminded me so much of hot summer days in France that I would be thinking about having it on my toast as I was going to bed. It is honeyed, tart, and herbal at the same time. Don't be tempted to use more lavender, or it will taste medicinal. Eat it with warm croissants or toasted baguette and you'll almost smell the *garrigue* and hear the cicadas …

Fills 4 (½ pint) jars
2¼lb apricots
3 sprigs of fresh lavender

juice of 1 lemon
1 (1¾oz) box powdered pectin
3 cups granulated sugar

1 Prepare a boiling-water canner (*see* pages 368–369) and keep the cleaned jars and lids warm.

2 Halve and pit the apricots and chop them. Put in a large, deep saucepan with the lavender and lemon juice. Cook the fruit over low heat for about 20 minutes, stirring occasionally. When the fruit is completely soft and partly broken up, add the pectin and stirred until dissolved. Bring to a boil, add the sugar, bring back to a full rolling boil, and boil for 1 minute, until setting point is reached (*see* page 11). Skim. Pick out the lavender sprigs; some of the blossom will fall off but that's fine.

3 Fill each jar, leaving a headspace of ¼ inch from the top. Process the filled jars in a boiling-water canner for 10 minutes at sea level (*see* pages 369). Let cool, seal the jars, and label before storing.

apricot and vanilla jam

The apricots we get here are usually disappointing—unripe, "woolly," tasteless—but heating them transforms even the most unpromising specimens into lovely jam. This is intensely flavored and has a good sweet-tart balance. It is worth using a whole vanilla bean.

Fills 4 (½ pint) jars
2¼lb apricots
3 cups granulated sugar

juice of 1 lemon
1 vanilla bean
1 (3oz) pouch liquid pectin

1 Halve and pit the apricots and put into a large bowl. Add the sugar and lemon juice. Split the vanilla bean along its length and scrape the seeds out with the tip of a knife. Put these seeds, plus the whole bean, into the bowl. Stir everything around, cover with a cloth, and let sit overnight.

2 The next day, prepare a boiling-water canner (*see* pages 368–369) and keep the cleaned jars and lids warm. Put the apricot mixture into a large, deep saucepan and cook over low heat for 20 minutes, stirring. When soft, increase the heat and bring to a rolling boil that cannot be stirred down. Stir in the pectin, and continuing to stir, boil rapidly for one minute. Remove from the heat, skim, and remove the vanilla bean.

3 Fill each jar, leaving a headspace of ¼ inch from the top. Process the filled jars in a boiling-water canner for 10 minutes at sea level (*see* pages 369). Let cool, seal the jars, and label before storing.

mango, passion fruit, and lime jam

Mango and passion fruit are a heavenly match: mangoes slightly lack acidity and the passion fruit (and the lime, too) provide it in the most fragrant way. The color of this jam doesn't stay bright and sparkling, but the flavor does. It gives a good sweet-tart mouthful of the exotic.

Fills 4 (½ pint) jars
8 ripe passion fruits
6 ripe mangoes, peeled, pitted, and
   chopped into chunks (7 cups)

finely grated zest and juice of 8 limes
1 (1¾oz) box powdered pectin
3¾ cups granulated sugar
juice of 1 lemon, or to taste

1 Prepare a boiling-water canner (*see* pages 368–369) and keep the cleaned jars and lids warm.

2 Halve the passion fruits and scoop out the pulp and juice with a teaspoon into a large, deep saucepan. Add the mangoes, the juice of four of the limes, plus the zest of all eight. Add 2 cups of water and bring to a boil. Reduce the heat and simmer for about 15 minutes, until the fruit is really soft.

3 Add the pectin and stir until it is dissolved. Bring to a boil, add the sugar, bring back to a full rolling boil, and boil for 1 minute, until setting point is reached (*see* page 11). Skim. Now stir in the rest of the lime juice and lemon juice, to taste.

4 Fill each jar, leaving a headspace of ¼ inch from the top. Process the filled jars in a boiling-water canner for 10 minutes at sea level (*see* pages 369). Let cool, seal the jars, and label before storing.

summertime berry jam

This is such a delicious jam. You can use whatever mix of summer berries you have: loganberries, raspberries, and fresh currants. You need to include black currants because they have good pectin and acidity. If you don't grow your own, try a farmer's market.

Fills 8 (½ pint) jars
4 cups black currants
3 cups hulled, coarsely chopped
   strawberries

4 cups raspberries (unwashed)
juice of 1 lemon
1 (1¾oz) box powdered pectin
5 cups granulated sugar

1 Prepare a boiling-water canner (*see* pages 368–369) and keep the cleaned jars and lids warm.

2 Put the black currants in a saucepan and add ½ cup of water. Bring to a boil, then simmer for 15 minutes to soften the skins (or they toughen when you add sugar). Add the rest of the fruit, lemon juice, and pectin and stir until the pectin is dissolved. Bring to a boil, add the sugar, bring back to a full rolling boil, and boil for 1 minute, until setting point is reached (*see* page 11). Skim. Let cool for 10 minutes so the fruit pieces settle.

4 Fill each jar, leaving a headspace of ¼ inch from the top. Process the filled jars in a boiling-water canner for 10 minutes at sea level (*see* pages 369). Let cool, seal the jars, and label before storing.

swedish "nearly" jam

Okay, this isn't a true jam, but I have eaten many jams such as this in Sweden and Denmark. They are much lower in sugar than traditional jams—in fact, many just seem like sweet fruit purees—and are deliciously fresh. Of course, these "jams" don't have enough sugar in them to achieve a firm set and they also have reduced keeping qualities, so you need to store them in the refrigerator. In fact, some people in Scandinavia freeze their homemade jams. After staying on farms one summer in Sweden, I came home with loads of jars that had been given to me and defrosted on the journey back to England. I had a wonderful stash of "nearly" jams in my refrigerator. The jam below is based on one of the most unusual I tasted in Sweden. I had it for a Christmas breakfast in a hotel outside Stockholm. I have no idea how they made it—it was partly a marmalade, partly a fruit compote—but I thought about it for a long time afterward, wanted to eat it again, and came up with this years later.

Fills 4 (½ pint) jars
2 organic oranges
10 stems early pink rhubarb (1lb)
juice of 2 lemons

2 tart apples (such as Granny Smith)
½ cup apple juice
1 (1¾oz) box powdered pectin
3½ cups granulated sugar

1 Wash the oranges, then slice them into thin circles. Chop the circles, discarding any seeds you see. Put these into a saucepan with 1 cup of water and bring to a boil. Reduce the heat and simmer until the orange zest is soft. Cover and let sit overnight.

2 The next day, prepare a boiling-water canner (*see* pages 368–369) and keep the cleaned jars and lids warm. Trim the rhubarb and cut it into small chunks. Layer it up in a heavy, deep saucepan with half the lemon juice. Peel and core the apples, cut into little cubes, and toss with the remaining lemon juice. Add the cooked oranges with their cooking water, the apples, and the apple juice to the rhubarb. Add the pectin and stir until it dissolves.

3 Bring to a boil, add the sugar, bring back to a full rolling boil, and boil briefly (less than 1 minute), until you reach 220°F on a sugar thermometer (normal setting point is reached at 219°F). Skim. Let cool for 10 minutes so the fruit pieces can settle.

4 Fill each jar, leaving a headspace of ¼ inch from the top. Process the filled jars in a boiling-water canner for 10 minutes at sea level (*see* pages 369). Let cool, seal the jars, and label before storing.

how to use

This is especially wonderful on Irish soda bread or warmed pound cake, with Greek yogurt or rice pudding.

blackberry and pinot noir jam

My dad used to play a lot of music in the car when I was little and one of my favorite songs was Summer Wine ("Strawberries, cherries, and a angel's kiss in spring/ My summer wine is really made from all these things"). At that age I didn't associate this with alcohol … I just thought it was a drink that contained the essence of summer. And I wanted to have some. Years later, I think I have made a jam as rich and intoxicating as the singer's voice, and not a million miles away from his "summer wine." You can use other wines, but pinot noir has a lovely berry fruitiness that gives real depth.

Fills 6 (½ pint) jars

1 small cooking apple, peeled, cored, and chopped into small cubes
7 cups blackberries (2¼lb)
3½ cups granulated sugar
1 (1¾oz) box powdered pectin
1½ cups pinot noir wine

1 Prepare a boiling-water canner (*see* pages 368–369) and keep the cleaned jars and lids warm.

2 Put the apple into a saucepan with ¼ cup of water. Cook until it is almost completely soft. Put this into a large, deep saucepan with the blackberries, all but 2 tablespoons of the wine, and the pectin, stirring until the pectin dissolves. Bring to a boil, add the sugar, bring back to a full rolling boil, and boil for 1 minute, until setting point is reached (*see* page 11). Skim and stir in the remaining wine.

3 Fill each jar, leaving a headspace of ¼ inch from the top. Process the filled jars in a boiling-water canner for 10 minutes at sea level (*see* pages 369). Let cool, seal the jars, and label before storing.

gooseberry and elderflower jam

A classic pairing—gooseberries and elderflowers echo each other's flavors—this is best made with early, tart gooseberries, home grown or form a farmers market. If you don't have home-made elderflower syrup, you can use store-bought syrup (available online)

Fills 6 (½ pint) jars

2¼lb gooseberries, trimmed
4 cups granulated sugar
⅓ cup elderflower syrup (cordial)

1 Prepare a boiling-water canner (*see* pages 368–369) and keep the cleaned jars and lids warm.

2 Put the fruit into a large, deep saucepan and add ⅔ cup of water. Bring to a boil, then reduce the heat and simmer for about 10 minutes, until the fruit is soft. Add the sugar and continue to simmer, stirring a little to help the sugar dissolve. Bring to a boil and cook for about nine minutes, then test for a set (do the wrinkle test, *see* page 11, and check on a thermometer). As soon as you've reached it, remove the pan from the heat and skim. Let cool for four minutes, then stir in the syrup.

3 Fill each jar, leaving a headspace of ¼ inch from the top. Process the filled jars in a boiling-water canner for 10 minutes at sea level (*see* pages 369). Let cool, seal the jars, and label before storing.

plum, orange, and cardamom jam

Why keep oranges just for marmalade? If you don't like cardamom, you can omit it, or use a broken cinnamon stick. If you use whole spices, fish them out before canning.

Fills 6 (½ pint) jars
4 thin-skinned organic oranges
18 plums (2¾lb)

juice of 2 limes and 1 orange
ground seeds of about 20 cardamom pods
4 cups granulated sugar

1 Prepare a boiling-water canner (*see* pages 368–369) and keep the cleaned jars and lids warm.

2 Slice the oranges into thin circlings, flicking out any seeds you see (discard them), then quarter each circle. Put these into a saucepan with ⅔ cup of water. Bring the mixture to a boil, reduce the heat, cover the pan, and cook until soft (about 20 minutes). Keep an eye on them; you want to end up with the same amount of liquid as you started with, so add more water if you need to.

3 Meanwhile, halve and pit the plums and cut into slices. Put these into a large, deep saucepan with the oranges and their liquid. Add half the lime juice and all the orange juice and cardamom. Bring to a boil, then reduce the heat and cook gently for 15–20 minutes, or until the plums are soft. Add the sugar and simmer gently, stirring to help the sugar dissolve. Once it has, bring to a boil and boil until setting point is reached (*see* page 11).Skim off any scum, then add the rest of the lime juice.

4 Fill each jar, leaving a headspace of ¼ inch from the top. Process the filled jars in a boiling-water canner for 10 minutes at sea level (*see* pages 369). Let cool, seal the jars, and label before storing.

orange and flower water jam

A completely delicious, soft, bitter sweet-scented jam—use on sliced brioche (watch it dribble over the edges). It's fabulous, too, spooned over cream to serve with bitter chocolate cake.

Fills 4 (½ pint) jars
7 organic oranges (2¼lb)
5 cups granulated sugar

juice of 1 lemon
3 tablespoons orange flower water,
    or more to taste

1 Remove the zest from the oranges in broad strips, leaving the pith. Squeeze the juice (you should have 2 cups) and refrigerate. Simmer the zest in water for 10 minutes, until soft. Drain well, cover with fresh water, and soak overnight. Next day, drain and cut into fine shreds.

2 Prepare a boiling-water canner (*see* pages 368–369) and keep the cleaned jars and lids warm. Put the zest into a pan with the orange juice, sugar, and lemon juice. Slowly bring to a boil, stirring to help the sugar dissolve, then reduce the heat and simmer for about 30 minutes. This isn't meant to set firmly, but you can do the wrinkle test (*see* page 11); the mixture should be syrupy enough to just hold its shape once cool. Skim the surface of any scum, then stir in the flower water.

3 Fill each jar, leaving a headspace of ¼ inch from the top. Process the filled jars in a boiling-water canner for 10 minutes at sea level (*see* pages 369). Let cool, seal the jars, and label before storing.

melon, lime, and ginger jam

It was one of my big surprises, in cooking for this book, that it was possible to make a good, fresh-tasting jam with melon. This is very unusual, both fragrant and zippy. And, of course, a little eastern. When I was small, one of my favorite books was a story about two Japanese dolls called Miss Happiness and Miss Flower, by Rumer Godden. The girl to whom the dolls are given tries to make them feel at home in England by building them a Japanese house and giving them every kind of Japanese comfort she can conjure. I imagine this is what she would have given them for an afternoon snack, with green tea on the side, of course.

Use different kinds of melons so that you have a mixture of flesh colors (but not watermelon—it's too wet). Mango works well in the mixture, too.

Fills 9 (½ pint) jars
1 large melon, seeded, peeled, and
    chopped into ¾ inch cubes (10 cups)
    6 cups granulated sugar

½ cup peeled, sliced fresh ginger root
finely grated zest and juice of 6 limes
6 pats of preserved ginger in syrup, chopped
2 (3oz) pouches liquid pectin

1 Put the melon in a bowl, layering it up with half the sugar. Let sit overnight.

2 The next day, prepare a boiling-water canner (*see* pages 368–369) and keep the cleaned jars and lids warm. Strain the sugary liquid off the melon into a large, deep saucepan (hold onto the melon!). Bring to a boil slowly, stirring to help the sugar dissolve. Now boil until the syrup is reduced by half.

3 Tie the ginger in a little cheesecloth bag (use a square piece of cheesecloth). Put this into the pan with the melon, remaining sugar, the lime zest and juice, and preserved ginger. Bring to a simmer and cook the melon for three minutes. Bring to a rolling boil that cannot be stirred down. Stir in the pectin, and continuing to stir, boil rapidly for one minute. Remove the cheesecloth bag and skim.

3 Fill each jar, leaving a headspace of ¼ inch from the top. Process the filled jars in a boiling-water canner for 10 minutes at sea level (*see* pages 369). Let cool, seal the jars, and label before storing.

how to use

A dollop of this is good on a tart ice cream—one made with yogurt, buttermilk, or crème fraîche—but I like it best on plain toasted bread, such as a nice sourdough.

rhubarb, rose, and cardamom jam

Stephen Harris, the chef-owner of The Sportsman in Seasalter, Kent (one of my favorite places to eat), lets rhubarb and sugar sit together to macerate when he is making his amazing rhubarb sorbet. It is an excellent way of drawing the juice and flavor from the rhubarb, so I have used the method here. You don't have to make this with rose and cardamom; you can flavor it with fresh ginger root, orange, or elderflower instead, or make plain rhubarb jam.

Fills 3 (½ pint) jars
20 early pink rhubarb stems (2¼lb)
4½ cups granulated sugar
juice of 1 lemon, plus more if needed
½ cup apple juice

crushed seeds from 10 cardamom pods
½ tablespoon rose water
1 (3oz) pouch liquid pectin

1 Trim the rhubarb and cut into ¾ inch lengths. Put it into a large, deep saucepan, layering it up with sugar as you go. Pour over the lemon and apple juices, cover with a clean dish towel, and let sit overnight. The juices from the rhubarb will be drawn out.

2 The next day, prepare a boiling-water canner (*see* pages 368–369) and keep the cleaned jars and lids warm. Add the cardamom to the rhubarb. Slowly bring the contents of the pan to a boil, stirring a little (but be careful not to break the rhubarb pieces up too much), skimming off any scum. Bring to a rolling boil that cannot be stirred down. Stir in the pectin, and continuing to stir, boil rapidly for one minute. Remove from the heat and add the rose water. Taste the jam. You may want to add a little more rose water, or some lemon for freshness.

3 Fill each jar, leaving a headspace of ¼ inch from the top. Process the filled jars in a boiling-water canner for 10 minutes at sea level (*see* pages 369). Let cool, seal the jars, and label before storing.

how to use

This is not a firm set jam, so you can use it for desserts. I love it with Greek yogurt (the meeting of two mouth-puckering foods), or rice pudding, sprinkled with rose petals for a romantic touch. You can also use the jam, with mascarpone, to fill a cake.

nick's "good morning" breakfast marmalade

Nick Selby is the jam maker (and co-owner) of the London-based deli Melrose and Morgan. He makes my favorite marmalade (this is it), and also gave me intensive marmalade lessons. This is the very opposite of dark and dense. It's soft set, bright and tangy, and wakes you up— the perfect breakfast marmalade. The grapefruit and oranges should weigh 2¼lb in total. I don't usually warm sugar for jams and marmalades, but he does to help it dissolve more quickly. Use organic citrus if you can find it, otherwise scrub the fruits well to remove any wax.

Fills 10 (½ pint) jars
1 pink or red grapefruit
4 blood oranges
3 Seville oranges

⅔ cup lemon juice, plus more if needed
10 cups unrefined granulated sugar,
    warmed in a low oven

1 Wash the fruit. Peel the grapefruit with a vegetable peeler, then cut the skin into fine shreds. Cut all the oranges in half and juice them (keep the skins). Measure the juice, then put it in a large bowl. Add enough water to bring the volume to 10½ cups. Scoop the flesh from the grapefruit and tie it in a cheesecloth bag. Add to the bowl of juice. Shred the orange skins as finely as possible and put them into the bowl, too. Let sit overnight to soak.

3 Cook the fruit mixture the next day in a large, deep saucepan until the shredded skin is completely soft. It will take about 1½ hours. Strain the marmalade through a strainer (keeping the shreds) and measure the liquid, making sure you squeeze all the pectin-filled juice from the bag. You should have about 5½ cups. Fill up with water, or reduce, if you have too little or too much. Return it to the pan, discarding the bag.

4 Meanwhile, prepare a boiling-water canner (*see* pages 368–369) and keep the cleaned jars and lids warm. Add the lemon juice and sugar to the marmalade mixture and heat gently to dissolve. Bring to a boil and skim off any scum. Add the shreds from the strainer and return to a boil. Check for setting point on a sugar thermometer and perform the wrinkle test (*see* page 11). Check for flavor, adding more lemon juice if you think it needs it. Stir, and skim. Let cool for about 12 minutes,

5 Fill each jar, leaving a headspace of ¼ inch from the top. Process the filled jars in a boiling-water canner for 10 minutes at sea level (*see* pages 369). Let cool, seal the jars, and label before storing.

how to use

Because you have to make this when Seville oranges and blood oranges are in season (in January) I guard my stash and rarely use it for anything other than my breakfast toast. However, I do sometimes use it to make an orange syrup (melt several tablespoons with orange juice or water, then let cool until it has a syrupy consistency), to drizzle over chilled rice pudding.

lime and rum marmalade

Based on another recipe from Nick Selby (the jam and marmalade god at London-based deli Melrose and Morgan). Nick doesn't do a rum version, but I find this irresistible. If you're not partial to booze, just omit the rum. You'll need kitchen scales for this recipe.

Fills 10 (½ pint) jars
12 large, juicy limes
6 kaffir lime leaves, bruised

about 8¾ cups (4lb) granulated sugar,
    warmed in a low oven
¼ cup white rum

1 Cut the limes in half and juice them, reserving the juice. Put the skins in a bowl, cover with cold water, and refrigerate overnight.

2 The next day, prepare a boiling-water canner (*see* pages 368–369) and keep the cleaned jars and lids warm. Drain the skins and scrape out the flesh and membranes. Lay this mixture onto a square piece of cheesecloth and tie into a bag with string. Slice the skins into fine shreds and put these into a large, deep saucepan with the cheesecloth bag, lime leaves, 8¾ cups of water, and the reserved juice. Cover tightly with aluminum foil (use a double thickness) and cook gently for 1½ hours, until the shreds are absolutely soft. (You don't want to lose too much water, that's why you cover the pan.) Limes have tough skins, so make sure you are happy with the softness; once the sugar is added, the skins will harden, so do this part carefully.

3 Remove the lime leaves and the bag, squeezing out as much juice as you can from the bag. Weigh the fruit and liquid, then put it back in the pan and add the same weight of sugar. Gently heat the mixture until the sugar has dissolved, stirring a little to help it, then increase the heat and bring to a boil, skimming off any scum. Once it has reached boiling point, test for a set; this jam has a high pectin level so the setting point will be reached quickly. Check on a sugar thermometer but also do the wrinkle test (*see* page 11). If it hasn't reached setting point, put the mixture back on the heat for four minutes and try again. When the marmalade reaches setting point, stir and skim. Stir in the rum. Let the marmalade cool for about 12 minutes (this helps distribute the rind more evenly).

4 Fill each jar, leaving a headspace of ¼ inch from the top. Process the filled jars in a boiling-water canner for 10 minutes at sea level (*see* pages 369). Let cool, seal the jars, and label before storing.

how to use
This is deliciously, exquisitely lime-y ,and, although it's wonderful on toast, it shouldn't be restricted to it. I love a spoonful with sliced fresh mangoes and plain yogurt, or I heat half a jar, adding a little more lime juice and some water, to make a warm sauce for chilled rice pudding. (This works well with either plain lime or a rum and lime version.)

pink grapefruit marmalade

I love pink grapefruits. I can eat them like oranges while I'm sitting watching TV. They are so sweet, yet their sourness still provokes a little shudder. They are increasingly bred to be sweeter, which is why I have added lemon here … you may even find you need two lemons. The color is dazzling. If you want, you can flavor this with juniper or fresh ginger root (crush juniper berries or chop ginger and put into a little square piece of cheesecloth. Tie into a bag and put it in with the shreds while you are cooking them. Remove before canning).

Fills 8 (½ pint) jars
4 large pink grapefruits

juice of 1 lemon
10 cups granulated sugar

1 Prepare a boiling-water canner (*see* pages 368–369) and keep the cleaned jars and lids warm.

2 Cut the grapefruits into quarters and squeeze the juice into a large, deep saucepan. Scrape the membranes—and collect any seeds—and lay them on a square piece of cheesecloth. Tie the cheesecloth with all the membrane and seeds into a bag and add that to the pan. Add the lemon juice with 9¼ cups of water. Cut the peel from the grapefruits into thin shreds, adding them to the pan.

3 Bring the liquid to boiling point, then reduce the heat and simmer gently for two hours, or until the shreds are completely soft. Remove the bag of seeds and set it aside. Add the sugar and cook over gentle heat until it has completely dissolved, stirring frequently to help it along. Squeeze all the juice from the cheesecloth bag of seeds and membrane into the pan.

4 Bring the mixture to a boil. Once it gets to a fast rolling boil, check the time. Start testing for a set about 12 minutes after boiling point has been reached, and at regular intervals after that. Check for a set by using a thermometer and doing the wrinkle test (*see* page 11). Remove the pan from the heat, skim any scum, and let cool for about 10–12 minutes (this helps to distribute the peel throughout).

5 Fill each jar, leaving a headspace of ¼ inch from the top. Process the filled jars in a boiling-water canner for 10 minutes at sea level (*see* pages 369). Let cool, seal the jars, and label before storing.

how to use

It's gotta be spread on toast. Along with Nick's "Good Morning" Breakfast Marmalade (*see* page 35), this is my favorite flavor to wake up to.

vats of sunshine: a history of marmalade

It's almost risky giving a recipe for marmalade. It is the preserve most likely to get people hot under the collar. Some marmalade makers don't make any other preserves; marmalade is their thing. And it's not just a preserve, it's an annual project, undertaken in the dark days of January when the kingly Seville orange is ready for picking. Kitchens are filled with citrus smells—from the first nose-pricking spray that comes from the zest, to the rich, deep scent of cooked peel, juice, and sugar—for days on end. Each cook's output, whether it is pale with fine shreds or thick, chunky and dark, is the only marmalade which that particular cook praises.

Modern marmalade, however you like it, is different from the form it first took. A fruit conserve known as *marmelada* started being shipped to Britain from Portugal in the 15th century. However, it hadn't been anywhere near an orange. It got its name from the fruit on which it was based, the *marmelo*, the Portuguese word for quince. Britain already had recipes for quince preserves, but this was different. It was a firm paste that came in pretty boxes (some were even set in fancy molds) and it still exists in Portugal, although most people in Britain are probably more familiar with its Spanish counterpart, *membrillo*.

C. Anne Wilson, in her thorough history of marmalade, thinks that Portuguese *marmelada* was probably flavored with flower water, which would have made it exotic and different. Gradually "marmalade" became the general name for fruit pastes and preserves (there are recipes in 16th-century cookbooks for apple and pear "marmalades"), but it's difficult to know how or when marmalade became a preserve made only from citrus fruits. The recipe book of a Madam Eliza Cholmondeley (dated around 1677) has one of the first English recipes for citrus marmalade that we know of. Her "Marmalet of Oranges" would produce a thick dark substance, almost as firm as *marmelada*. Some 50 years later, Mary Kettilby, in her book *A Collection of Above Three Hundred Receipts in Cookery, Physick and Surgery*, gives a marmalade recipe that instructs us to "boil the whole pretty fast until it will jelly." A jelly with peel suspended in it? Sounds like the stuff I have in my cupboard.

It's the Scots who are credited with developing marmalade as a spread, and certainly Scottish recipes of the mid-18th century used more water, producing a less solid set preserve. When sugar became cheaper in the latter half of the 19th century, commercial jam making really took off. Marmalade was perfect for winter production, although it was initially a luxury item exported to British homes throughout the Empire. It was the Scots who democratized it, making it affordable to all classes and the bitter-sweet stalwart of the British breakfast table.

I risk the ire of marmalade makers everywhere, but I prefer the soft-set orange blossom-laced stuff on page 29. Marmalade? Well, it wouldn't be served at a sensible Scottish breakfast. It's Middle Eastern, somewhat syrupy, and runs off your toast. However, there are days when the chunky dark stuff seems a bit stern. And in the vast panoply of citrus preserves that take the moniker "marmalade" today, one that harks back to its scented beginnings seems apt.

kumquat and passion fruit jam

This has a wonderful flavor—sweet and tart—and the passion fruit and the kumquats are well balanced. It isn't cheap to make, so I generally do it when I can pick up reasonably priced fruit at a farmer's market.

Fills 4 (½ pint) jars
1¾lb kumquats
juice of 5 oranges (about 1¼ cups)

juice of 1 small lemon
10 ripe passion fruits
4½ cups granulated sugar

1 Cut the kumquats into thin slices (flick out any little seeds you see as you are doing this). Put them in a large, deep saucepan with the orange and lemon juice. Halve the passion fruits and scoop the pulp and seeds from each one. Add to the pan. Bring the contents of the pan to a boil, then reduce the heat and gently cook the mixture until the skins of the kumquats are soft. Cover the pan and let the mixture sit overnight.

2 The next day, prepare a boiling-water canner (*see* pages 368–369) and keep the cleaned jars and lids warm. Add the sugar to the pan and slowly bring the mixture to a boil, stirring a little to help the sugar dissolve. Boil until the setting point is reached (check on a sugar thermometer and do the wrinkle test, *see* page 11), skimming any scum that rises to the surface.

3 Fill each jar, leaving a headspace of ¼ inch from the top. Process the filled jars in a boiling-water canner for 10 minutes at sea level (*see* pages 369). Let cool, seal the jars, and label before storing.

how to use

This is a kind of exotic marmalade, so I keep it to spread on my toast. I'm always sorry when the few jars I make every year run out ...

scarlet bell pepper and chile jam

American preserving books are full of recipes for red pepper jelly. Some are made with an apple jelly base but most of them are clear, because only the juice of the peppers is used. Instead of straining out the cooked peppers, this version incorporates them, so I suppose it is somewhere between a jelly and a jam. It's an absolutely stunning color; the jars of it in my laundry room (where I keep my preserves) glow more than anything else. They are almost surreally bright.

Fills 8 (½ pint) jars
8 red bell peppers, halved, seeded,
  and chopped
8 red chiles, halved and chopped, with seeds

6¼ cups granulated sugar
2½ cups white wine vinegar
3 (3oz) pouches liquid pectin

1 Prepare a boiling-water canner (*see* pages 368–369) and keep the cleaned jars and lids warm.

2 Put all the ingredients, except the pectin, into a large saucepan. Bring to a boil, then reduce the heat and simmer until the vegetables are really tender. Let cool a little, then process in a food processor (not in a blender; you want a chunky mixture, not a completely smooth paste).

3 Put the mixture back into the rinsed-out pan and bring to a rolling boil that cannot be stirred down. Stir in the pectin, and continuing to stir, boil rapidly for one minute. Skim.

4 Fill each jar, leaving a headspace of ¼ inch from the top. Process the filled jars in a boiling-water canner for 10 minutes at sea level (*see* pages 369). Let cool, seal the jars, and label before storing.

how to use

Although I use it all year round, this is particularly great for summer barbecues, because it packs a punch and is great with grilled meats, especially pork. It's also wonderful with plain roasted chicken served with baked potatoes and sour cream or Greek yogurt. I always think of American food when I look at my jars of pepper jam.

jellies, curds, and fruit pastes

This branch of preserving is the one I have most trouble convincing people to try. Those lovely jars of jewelled colors made by red currants, rhubarb, quinces, and rose hips (set them on a windowsill and wonder at the stained-glass effect) are mere frippery to some, and the process you go through to make them (jelly bags hanging from broom handles) seems an effort too far. Fruit pastes (also called fruit cheeses), made from boiling fruit puree to a paste and adding sugar, may be the kind of small delight you stumble across in Keats's poetry, but it's not something you would make today, and curds, well, who wants to stand for 30 minutes stirring fruit juice with eggs and butter? Why do it? Simply because taste always wins …

JELLIES

I made jellies long before I made jams. It was mostly because I didn't like those you can buy (just look at the virulent green color of store-bought mint jelly). For years, all I made was apple jelly flavored with mint, thyme, or rosemary (the process is easy after you do it a couple of times). However, once I figured out that a lot of flavors can be captured in a jelly—smoky Earl Grey tea, fiery chile, fruity port—the kitchen adventures started.

Many jellies are made from apples paired with another fruit (the apples have the crucial pectin needed for a set), but apple jelly also acts as a conduit for ingredients that couldn't be made into jelly on their own. Capturing the flavor of flowers or teas is particularly wonderful. As well as the ubiquitous sandwich filling, jellies are eaten with savory dishes nowadays, but they started off, much like jams, to be eaten with sweet things, and floral jellies are perfect for a summery afternoon (not to mention a romantic ingredient to be used in desserts).

To make jellies, you don't even prepare the fruit, just chop it (skin, seeds, cores, and all) and simmer with water (no sugar) until tender. With berries, use about $1\frac{1}{4}$ cups of water per $2\frac{1}{4}$ pounds of fruit (the berries soon release their juices); with plums and damsons use $2\frac{1}{2}$ cups and with black currants $3\frac{3}{4}$ cups of water $2\frac{1}{4}$ pounds of fruit. Apples, quinces, pears, and other hard fruits should have enough water to cover.

Once the cooked fruit has cooled, spoon it into a jelly bag and suspend over a bowl, using a jelly stand, or hang it from a broom handle set between two chairs (a lot easier than it sounds and surprisingly satisfying). Let rest for 24 hours (no less than 12), so the juice can slowly drip into the bowl. Don't press the bag—it may make the liquid cloudy. (Some recipes made with high-pectin fruit, such as quince, suggest a double boiling and dripping, but that's rare). Measure the liquid, add $2\frac{1}{4}$ cups of granulated sugar for every $2\frac{1}{2}$ cups of juice, bring to a boil, stirring to help the sugar dissolve, get to the setting point (use the same tests as for jam, *see* page 11), and can in warm, dry sterilized jars. You see? It's simple.

CURDS

Curds aren't really proper preserves because they don't have good keeping qualities, but they're wonderful, old-fashioned spreads made with a tart fruit puree or juice, butter, sugar, and eggs. John Betjeman actually summons fruit curd to illustrate the comfort and immutability of afternoons in England, in his poem Indoor Games near Newbury: "Gabled lodges, tile-hung churches/ Catch the lights of our Lagonda/ As we drive to Wendy's party,/ Lemon curd and Christmas cake." It makes you immediately want to toast a "crumpet" and open the refrigerator to look for that jar you know is in there …

Fruit curds were first considered to be "transparent puddings" (according to Mrs. Raffald in *The Experienced English Housekeeper*, published in 1769), not spreads at all. Read the introduction to Raj Nimboo Curd (*see* right), and you'll find that in India they are still sometimes seen this way. The modern form of curds, kept as a preserve, came about in the late 19th century, as food production changed with industrialization.

You do have to be patient to make them, because the mixture is cooked in a bowl set over simmering water (the cooking has to be gentle or the eggs would scramble) until it has thickened—and sometimes this takes as long as 40 minutes—but that balance of rich butter and sharp fruit is a mouth-filling, tongue-tingling wonder and well worth the effort.

FRUIT PASTES

Dense and sweet, these thick fruit pastes (fruit cheese in the UK) usually set in molds. They are cut with a knife to be eaten with cheeses and meat or game. (Fruit butters, more popular in the United States, have a softer set and are spreadable.) At first, fruit pastes were known as "marmalades" (from the Portuguese word for quince paste, *marmelada*) and English recipes for them appeared as far back as the 13th century, but they fell out of fashion in the 19th century, surviving only in the form of fruit pastilles.

Fruit pastes are usually made with fruits that are cheap and abundant (or free), because you don't get much yield for the amount of fruit. Quince, apple, damson, gooseberries, and blackberries are the most common fruits made into fruit paste, and the process is remarkably easy: just chop your fruit (peel, core, and all), add water to cover, and cook gently until completely tender. The hard work comes next. Push the pulpy mass of fruit through a strainer into a large measuring cup. For every 2½ cups of pulp add 1¾–2 cups of granulated sugar. Put both pulp and sugar into a large, deep saucepan and heat gently, stirring to help the sugar dissolve. Once that has happened, continue to cook until the mixture is so thick that when you draw a line through it with your wooden spoon a clear channel is left. You have to stir frequently because it can stick to the bottom of the pan and burn. And you have to be patient—it takes time. I set my fruit pastes in lightly oiled ramekins (small ceramic dishes), then turn them out and wrap them in wax paper or parchment paper.

A friend sets her damson paste in a soup plate (which I recently discovered was an old-fashioned tradition), and lets me know when she is bringing some as a gift, so I can roast some lamb or pork to go with it. Cutting off crimson slices to eat with hot meat is bliss.

gooseberry curd

Curds need to be made with sharp fruits, so tart green gooseberries are perfect. This is one of the best curds you can make and one of the most useful.

Fills 4 (½ pint) jars
3⅓ cups gooseberries, trimmed
1 stick unsalted butter, in small chunks

1¾ cups superfine or granulated sugar
3 extra-large eggs, lightly beaten

1 Put the gooseberries in a heavy saucepan with just enough water to cover. Bring to a boil, reduce the heat, and simmer for about 10 minutes, until tender. Let cool. Put the fruit into a blender and puree, then push this through a nylon strainer.

2 Put the puree, butter, sugar, and eggs into a bowl over a saucepan of simmering water (the bowl must not touch the water). Don't overheat, or the eggs will curdle. Stir constantly with a wooden spoon until it thickens enough to coat the back of the spoon, then immediately push through a nylon strainer again (to remove strands of egg white), pour into warm, dry sterilized jars (*see* page 11), cover, and seal. When cold, refrigerate for up to two weeks. Once opened, eat within three days.

how to use
As with all curds, this is a great cake filling, especially for a rich, almond-flavored cake. Or eat it with poached apricots and fresh raspberries, mixing it with whipped cream and confectioners' sugar.

raj nimboo curd

Vikram Doctor, writing in the *Times of India*, rightly claims lime curd to be superior to lemon. "Lime curd is all about going to the edge," he writes. "Making it almost too sour, before letting the sweetness and creaminess draw you back." Vikram even concludes, with passion, that lime curd is the "Viagra of desserts …" It is as good as blood orange curd for filling a cake, but I also use it to make a chunky banana, mango, and lime fool.

Fills 2 (½ pint) jars
1 cup plus 2 tablespoons superfine or
  granulated sugar

1¼ sticks unsalted butter, cut in pieces
2 eggs and 2 egg yolks, lightly beaten
juice and finely grated zest of 5 limes

1 Put all the ingredients into a bowl over a saucepan of simmering water (the bowl must not touch the water). Don't overheat, or the eggs will curdle. Stir constantly with a wooden spoon until the mixture first melts, then thickens enough to coat the back of the spoon. This can take 30 minutes.

2 Immediately push the mixture through a nylon strainer (to remove strands of egg white), pour into warm, dry sterilized jars (*see* page 11), cover, and seal. When cold, refrigerate for up to two weeks. Once opened, eat within three days.

blood orange curd

Get oranges with a good red interior; some are disappointingly pale. Most recipes for curds suggest cooking for 10 minutes, but it does take longer. Don't give up, it thickens eventually.

Fills 1 (½ pint) jar
4 egg yolks, lightly beaten
⅓ cup superfine or granulated sugar

⅓ cup blood orange juice
2 tablespoons lemon juice
6 tablespoons unsalted butter, cut into small cubes

1 Put all the ingredients into a bowl, stir together, and set over a saucepan of simmering water (the bowl must not touch the water). Stir with a wooden spoon until it first melts, then thickens enough to coat the back of the spoon. This can take 30 minutes. Don't overheat, or the eggs will curdle.

2 Push through a nylon strainer, then put the curd in warm, dry sterilized jars (*see* page 11), cover, and seal. Cool, then refrigerate for up to two weeks. Once opened, eat within three days.

how to use

A great cake filling. Spread mascarpone on the bottom layer, spoon on the curd, place on the top layer, and dust with confecioners' sugar.

passion fruit curd

Passion fruits are expensive, but making this curd is an excellent way to capture their flavor.

Fills 1 (½ pint) jar
8 passion fruits
⅔ cup superfine or granulated sugar

3½ tablespoons unsalted butter,
    cut into small chunks
3 eggs, plus 3 egg yolks, lightly beaten

1 Halve the fruits and put the pulp and seeds in a food processor. Pulse-blend briefly to separate seeds from pulp. Push through a nylon strainer into a bowl. Keep half the seeds and discard the rest.

2 Put the fruit pulp, sugar, butter, and eggs into a heatproof bowl over a saucepan of simmering water (the bowl must not touch the water). Stir with a wooden spoon until the mixture coats the back of the spoon. This can take 30–40 minutes. Don't overheat, or the eggs will curdle. Push through a nylon strainer and add the reserved seeds.

3 Put the curd into warm, dry sterilized jars, cover,and seal. Let cool, then refrigerate for up to two weeks. Once opened, eat within three days.

how to use

This is particularly good—because it's quite tart—with mascarpone or crème fraîche on mini meringues. Add sliced mangoes (drizzled with lime juice) or chunks of poached rhubarb (a fantastic combination).

rose hip jelly

Rose hip jelly is slightly a labor of love because you have to do a lot of picking, but an afternoon's work can leave you with as much as 5½lb of rose hips. Wear gardening gloves to protect your hands, because they're very prickly, and use pruners or scissors. I find it easier to snip off the rose hips with their stems than to pull off individual berries (rose hips are the plant's berries). This prevents them from getting bruised, too. You need to cook rose hips soon after they are picked (no more than 24 hours), because they spoil quickly. Apart from the wonderful jelly they produce, the sight of apples and rose hips in a saucepan (and the wonderful smell) makes it worth the work.

It's a pity we don't use rose hips more. (In Sweden, rose hip juice is so common you can buy it in supermarkets.) They have a distinctive sweet, musky taste, they're good for you (packed with vitamin C, which is why rose hip syrup was available to give to British children after World War II, when citrus fruits were in short supply). And they're free!

Fills 4 (½ pint) jars
1¼lb rose hips

7 cooking apples (2¼lb)
about 4½ cups granulated sugar

1 Pull all the rose hips off their stems and wash. Throw away any that are bruised, damaged, or overripe (overripe fruits will be soft and mushy). Cut the apples into big chunks; there is no need to peel or core them. Put them in a large saucepan with the rose hips and add enough water to cover. Bring to a boil, then reduce the heat and simmer gently for 45 minutes to one hour. I crush the rose hips every so often to help them break down (their skin is tough). The fruit should be soft and pulpy. Let cool, then spoon into a jelly bag suspended over a bowl. Let sit overnight (at least 12 hours).

3 The next day, prepare a boiling-water canner (*see* pages 368–369) and keep the cleaned jars and lids warm. Discard the pulp and measure the juice. Put the juice into a large, deep saucepan with 2¼ cups of sugar for every 2½ cups of juice. Heat gently, stirring from time to time, until the sugar dissolves. Boil for 10–15 minutes, until setting point is reached (Check on a thermometer and do the wrinkle test, *see* page 11). Skim off any scum.

4 Fill each jar, leaving a headspace of ¼ inch from the top. Process the filled jars in a boiling-water canner for 10 minutes at sea level (*see* pages 369). Let cool, seal the jars, and label before storing.

how to use

In Britain, we have mainly used rose hip jelly with game (especially venison), but it's also good with roasted pork, cheeses, and as a sweet jelly (delicious on warm, crumbly biscuits). I've been delighted to find that, in northern Italy, it is paired with cured meats. I had a salad of speck with bitter leaves, rose hip jelly, and rye bread, which was one of the best things I've ever eaten—a real interplay of fruit with fat, sweet with bitter—and the product of different types of preserving. I now serve rose hip jelly with prosciutto, especially in winter when there are no fresh figs.

JELLIES, CURDS, AND FRUIT PASTES

apple and lavender jelly

Apple acts as the base for many flavored jellies, both sweet and savory. They are so high in pectin that they produce a jelly that sets easily, and their flavor doesn't dominate when you mix it with other things. You can make plain apple jelly, but herbs and spices allow you to have a whole array of flavors to use with different meats: lavender and rosemary for lamb, sage for pork, for example. I prefer savory apple jellies made with cider vinegar (so they have a sweet-acid tang) but some people prefer them sweet. Properly sweet ones to be served with muffins and biscuits (like the Fireside Jelly below and the Rose Petal Jelly, *see* page 54) are made with water (add enough just to cover the apples) instead of vinegar.

Fills 8 (1 pint) jars
5½lb cooking apples
3 sprigs of fresh lavender, plus 8 small sprigs

5½ cups cider vinegar
about 6½ cups granulated sugar

1 Cut the apples into chunks—no need to peel or core them, but remove any bruised sections—and cover with 6½ cups of water. Add the lavender. Bring to a boil, then reduce the heat to a simmer and cook until the apples are completely soft (about 45 minutes).

2 Add the vinegar and cook for another five minutes. Pour the mixture into a jelly bag suspended over a large bowl, and let sit overnight. Do not press the apples or you'll get a cloudy jelly.

3 The next day, prepare a boiling-water canner (*see* pages 368–369) and keep the cleaned jars and lids warm. Measure the liquid from the apples. For every 2½ cups, you will need 2¼ cups of sugar. Put the liquid into a large, deep saucepan with the sugar and heat gently, stirring to help the sugar dissolve. Bring to a boil and boil until the setting point is reached on a thermometer (and do the wrinkle test, *see* page 11). Skim off any scum.

4 Fill each jar, putting a sprig of lavender in each and leaving a headspace of ¼ inch from the top. Process the jars in a boiling-water canner for 10 minutes at sea level (*see* pages 369). Let cool, seal the jars, and label before storing. While it is setting, shake it so the lavender doesn't stay at the top.

also try

APPLE AND THYME JELLY, APPLE AND SAGE JELLY, APPLE AND ROSEMARY JELLY

Make as for Apple and Lavender jelly, substituting thyme, sage, or rosemary for the lavender.

and also …

FIRESIDE JELLY

Make as for Apple and Lavender Jelly, but omit the vinegar. To the apples, add a cheesecloth bag containing the zest of 1 orange, 1¼ inches of fresh ginger root, grated, and 1 cinnamon stick. Put a piece of cinnamon in each jar. Wonderful on toasted muffins. Fills 5 (1 pint) jars.

Amazing that Goude finds women
so willing to be redesigned by him,
to comply with his fantasies. He's

involved painting her blue-black,
cropping her hair like a marine and
giving her Joe Di Maggio's shoulders

obsessed with fashion – and has taken
flak for it. There might be more for
his description of Grace Jones, whom

medlar jelly

Medlars are strange. The smell as they cook is like wet wood. They're not to everyone's liking, but they are such unusual fruits that it's hard to resist turning them into a preserve—if you can find them (supplies are limited in the United States) or have a medlar (*Mespilus germanica*) tree. You can't cook them until they are "bletted," which basically means very ripe. When you get the fruit, lay them in a bowl in a single layer and let them get very soft before you cook them. The jelly is usually a lovely pale russet, but I've had batches that were more golden than red.

Fills 1 (1 pint) jar
2¼lb bletted medlars
about 2 cups granulated sugar

juice of 2 lemons
1 (3oz) pouch liquid pectin (optional)

1 Put the medlars into a saucepan with 2½ cups of water and simmer for about 40 minutes, or until completely soft. Make sure the water doesn't reduce too much, filling it up if necessary. Spoon the fruit pulp into a jelly bag suspended over a bowl and let sit overnight.

2 The next day, prepare a boiling-water canner (*see* pages 368–369) and keep the cleaned jars and lids warm. Measure the juice that has dripped out and throw away the pulp. Add ½ cup of granulated sugar for every ½ cup of juice.

3 Put the juice and sugar into a saucepan with the lemon juice. Bring to a boil slowly, stirring from time to time to help the sugar dissolve. Boil the liquid hard until the setting point is reached (check on a thermometer and do the wrinkle test, too, *see* page 11). If you find that the mixture is not getting to setting point, with the mixture at a rolling boil that cannot be stirred down, stir in the pectin. Continue to stir, boil rapidly for one minute, then remove from the heat and skim off any scum.

4 Fill each jar, leaving a headspace of ¼ inch from the top. Process the filled jars in a boiling-water canner for 10 minutes at sea level (*see* pages 369). Let cool, seal the jars, and label before storing.

and also …

CIDER JELLY

This is a cinch—you don't even have to cook apples. It's a savory jelly and is great with Italian-style sausages. The recipe is for 2 (1 pint) jars.

Prepare a boiling-water canner, jars, and lids as above. Put 2½ cups of hard dry cider, ½ cup of cider vinegar, a strip of orange zest, a sprig of rosemary, and 3½ cups of granulated sugar into a large saucepan and bring slowly to a boil. Stir from time to time to help the sugar dissolve. When the sugar has completely dissolved, bring to a rolling boil that cannot be stirred down, add 4 (3oz) pouches of liquid pectin, continue to stir, and boil rapiding for one to two minutes, then test for a set (*see* page 11). Ladle it into warm, dry jars (leaving the zest and rosemary behind), as above and process in a boiling-water canner, also as above.

rose petal jelly

I have such a passion for roses and their scent that I've tried a lot of recipes for this over the years. In the Middle East, they make it just with petals (no apple base), but it doesn't set well.

This is a gorgeous preserve to make. The process of turning petals into a deep red or purple paste makes you feel as if you are making paint or dye. The resulting jelly absolutely reflects the color of the roses you use. You need to find unsprayed rose petals; I found a neighbor who was happy to let me have enough to make this, so ask around for a source. It will be easier to get hold of them than you think.

Many varieties of rose look wonderful but are really low in scent; you need to find roses whose fragrance makes you swoon.

Fills 4 (½ pint) jars
7 cooking apples (2¼lb)
about 3⅓ cups granulated sugar

2½ cups dark red or pink, perfumed rose petals
rose water, to taste (optional)

1 Wash and chop the apples coarsely—without peeling or coring—and put in a large, deep saucepan. Cover with 1 inch or so of water, bring to a simmer, and cook the fruit until it is completely soft.

2 Spoon the pulp and juice into a jelly bag hanging from a jelly stand, or suspended on a broom handle between two chairs set over a large bowl. Let the juice drip overnight.

3 The next day, prepare a boiling-water canner (*see* pages 368–369) and keep the cleaned jars and lids warm. Measure the amount of juice that has dripped out and for every 2½ cups of juice, measure out 2¼ cups of sugar. Take half the rose petals and pound them in a mortar and pestle with about one-quarter of the sugar (it just acts as an abrasive and helps to release the color of the petals), then put these, the apple juice, and the remaining sugar in a large, deep saucepan. Heat gently until the sugar dissolves, then add the reserved rose petals and increase the heat. Boil fast until the setting point is reached (check on a sugar thermometer and do the wrinkle test, *see* page 11). Skim off any scum. If it doesn't have a strong rose taste, add rose water.

4 Fill each jar, leaving a headspace of ¼ inch from the top. Process the filled jars in a boiling-water canner for 10 minutes at sea level (*see* pages 369). Let cool, seal the jars, and label before storing.

how to use

This is for romantic, slightly otherworldly dishes. Use it to fill a sponge cake (adding whipped cream and strawberries or raspberries), or top meringues with crème fraîche and a dollop of rose petal jelly before sprinkling with berries, or mix it into cream to serve with fruit, or bake figs or peaches, halved and stuffed with a little dollop of it, until tender.

It's also good on plain white bread and you can make wonderful little sandwiches with brioche, mascarpone, and rose petal jelly. Once made, simply dust them lightly with confectioners' sugar, sprinkle with some fresh petals, and serve as part of a summery afternoon treat.

white currant jelly

White currants produce a wonderful, pale golden jelly that looks exquisite; it reminds me of the glow that pearls make on skin. The fruit is difficult to find, so try a farmer's market or grow your own (but first check your local Cooperative Extension to make sure it's not banned in your area).

Fills 3 (½ pint) jars
9 cups white currants (2¼lb), stems removed

about 2½ cups granulated sugar
juice of 1 lemon

1 Put the currants into a large, deep saucepan with 1¼ cups of water. Bring slowly to a boil—mash the fruit with a vegetable masher to break it up a little—then reduce the heat and cook gently for 30 minutes. Ladle the pulp into a jelly bag suspended over a bowl and let sit to strain overnight.

2 The next day, prepare a boiling-water canner (*see* pages 368–369) and keep the cleaned jars and lids warm. Measure the juice and add 2¼ cups of sugar for every 2½ cups of liquid. Put the juice and sugar into a large, deep saucepan with the lemon juice and heat gently, stirring to help the sugar dissolve. Bring to a boil and boil rapidly until the setting point is reached (check on a sugar thermometer and do the wrinkle test as well, *see* page 11). Skim any scum from the surface,

4 Fill each jar, leaving a headspace of ¼ inch from the top. Process the filled jars in a boiling-water canner for 10 minutes at sea level (*see* pages 369). Let cool, seal the jars, and label before storing.

how to use

This is very good with savory foods—washed rind cheeses and prosciutto, for example—as well as with sweet things. It's delicious to eat it when white currants are in season, so you can serve sprays of the fresh fruit alongside. Fill a sponge cake with whipped cream, white currant jelly, and fresh white currants, or serve the fresh fruit and the jelly with English muffins for an afternoon snack.

damson and juniper jelly

You can make this with other spices, such as cinnamon, cloves, fresh ginger root, or star anise. Damsons have such a strong, deep flavor (like a plummy merlot), it's worth making this jelly.

Fills 9 (½ pint) jars
5 cooking apples
3¼lb damsons

about 7½ cups granulated sugar
15 juniper berries, crushed

1 Remove any damaged sections from the apples, then chop into chunks (no need to peel or core them). Put into a large saucepan with the damsons. Add enough water just to cover and bring to a boil. Reduce the heat and cook until completely tender, stirring now and then (it takes about 45 minutes). Put the fruit puree into a jelly bag, hung over a large bowl. Let sit for at least 12 hours.

2 Prepare a boiling-water canner (*see* pages 368–369) and keep the cleaned jars and lids warm. Measure the juice. For every 2½ cups, add 2¼ cups of granulated sugar. Put these into a large, deep saucepan. Lightly crush the juniper berries, tie them in a square piece of cheesecloth, and put it in the pan. Heat gently, stirring to help the sugar dissolve. Bring to a boil and boil rapidly until setting point is reached (do the wrinkle test, *see* page 11). Skim off any scum and remove the bag.

3 Fill each jar, leaving a headspace of ¼ inch from the top. Process the filled jars in a boiling-water canner for 10 minutes at sea level (*see* pages 369). Let cool, seal the jars, and label before storing.

golden-flecked chili jelly

This recipe is the result of meanness. I love chili jelly, so I decided to make my own. It's very pretty, golden with rust-colored flakes.

Fills 4 (½ pint) jars
10 cooking apples (3¼lb)
about 3⅓ cups granulated sugar

juice of 1 lemon
3 teaspoons dried red chili flakes

1 Chop the cooking apples coarsely—no need to peel or core—and put them into a large, deep saucepan with 4 cups of water. Bring to a boil, reduce the heat, and simmer for 30–40 minutes or until really soft. Put the pulp into a jelly bag, hang it up, and let drip over a bowl overnight.

2 The next day, prepare a boiling-water canner (*see* pages 368–369) and keep the cleaned jars and lids warm. Measure the juice and add 2¼ cups of sugar for every 2½ cups of juice. Put into a large saucepan and slowly bring to a boil, stirring occasionally to help the sugar dissolve. Once it has dissolved, add the lemon juice and chili flake. Return to a boil, boil rapidly until you reach setting point (check on a thermometer and do the wrinkle test, *see* page 11), and skim. Cool for 10 minutes so the flakes disperse.

3 Fill each jar, leaving a headspace of ¼ inch from the top. Process the filled jars in a boiling-water canner for 10 minutes at sea level (*see* pages 369). Let cool, seal the jars, and label before storing.

rhubarb jelly

This is great with roasted pork or lamb, especially if you add rosemary (*see* directions on page 51).

Fills 3 (½ pint) jars
3 cooking apples
15 pink rhubarb stalks (1½lb), trimmed

about 2½ cups granulated sugar
juice of 1 lemon

1 Cut the apples into chunks—no need to peel or core—and cut the rhubarb into chunks, too. Put the apple into a large saucepan with just enough water to cover. Bring to a boil, reduce the heat, and cook until almost completely soft. Now add the rhubarb and cook gently until the rhubarb is soft. Pour into a jelly bag over a bowl and let sit overnight.

2 Neat day, prepare a boiling-water canner (*see* pages 368–369) and keep the cleaned jars and lids warm. Measure the liquid. For every 2½ cups of juice you will need 2¼ cups of sugar. Put the fruit juice, lemon juice, and sugar in a large, deep saucepan. When the sugar dissolves, bring to a rapid boil. Test for setting point with a thermometer and the wrinkle test (*see* page 11). Skim off any scum,

3 Fill each jar, leaving a headspace of ¼ inch from the top. Process the filled jars in a boiling-water canner for 10 minutes at sea level (*see* pages 369). Let cool, seal the jars, and label before storing.

passion fruit jelly

This isn't cheap to make but it is very special.

Fills 2 (½ pint) jars
2 large cooking apples
14 ripe passion fruits

2 cups apple juice
about 2¼ cups granulated sugar
juice of 1 lemon

1 Chop the apples and put them in a saucepan with just enough water to cover. Bring to a boil, reduce the heat, and simmer until almost soft. Now halve 10 of the passion fruits and add to the pan with the apple juice. Return to a boil, reduce the heat, and simmer for five minutes. Pour into a jelly bag over a bowl and let sit overnight.

2 The next day, prepare a boiling-water canner (*see* pages 368–369) and keep the cleaned jars and lids warm. Measure the juice. For every 2½ cups of liquid you'll need 2¼ cups of sugar. Put these into a large, deep saucepan and slowly bring to a boil, stirring to help the sugar dissolve. Boil for two minutes, then skim off any scum. Add the pulp and juice from the remaining passion fruits with the lemon juice. Boil for a minute, then test for setting point with a thermometer and do the wrinkle test (*see* page 11). Let cool for five minutes.

3 Fill each jar, leaving a headspace of ¼ inch from the top. If the seeds float to the top, leave for four minutes, then gently stir each jar with a sterilized spoon. Process the filled jars in a boiling-water canner for 10 minutes at sea level (*see* pages 369). Let cool, seal the jars, and label before storing.

earl grey tea jelly

Strangely I really dislike Earl Grey tea to drink, but love it to cook with. The smoky, floral scent is wonderful in an ice cream or pannacotta and I love this jelly with duck or game, especially pheasant. Be sure to use good-quality tea with a strong scent.

Fills 5 (½ pint) jars
10 cooking apples (3¼lb)

about 4½ cups granulated sugar
3 tablespoons loose leaf Earl Grey tea

1 Chop the cooking apples really coarsely—no need to peel or core—and put them into a large, deep saucepan with 4 cups of water. Bring to a boil, then stew the apples for 30–40 minutes, or until they are really soft. Put the pulp into a jelly bag, hang it up, and let sit to drip over a bowl overnight.

2 The next day, prepare a boiling-water canner (*see* pages 368–369) and keep the cleaned jars and lids warm. Measure the juice and add 2¼ cups of sugar for every 2½ cups of juice. Put both into a large, deep saucepan and slowly bring to a boil, stirring to help the sugar dissolve. Boil rapidly until you are nearly at setting point (use a thermometer to check, *see* page 11), then remove from the heat.

3 Put the tea in a bowl with ½ cup of boiling water and let steep for 15 minutes. Add this to the apple juice in the pan, pouring it through a strainer, and boil again, this time going right to setting point (do the wrinkle test, *see* page 11). Skim off any scum.

4 Fill each jar, leaving a headspace of ¼ inch from the top. Process the filled jars in a boiling-water canner for 10 minutes at sea level (*see* pages 369). Let cool, seal the jars, and label before storing.

and also …

GREEN TEA JELLY

Make as above but this time use 3 tablespoons green tea leaves, adding the juice of 2 limes along with the green tea.

how to use

The Earl Grey jelly is wonderful with pheasant and duck and can be melted to a syrup and poured over ice cream.

Green tea jelly is delicate and doesn't work with savory foods (unlike the Earl Grey tea jelly). I like it with toasted brioche.

JELLIES, CURDS, AND FRUIT PASTES

quince and star anise jelly

Smoky and autumnal with just a whiff of anise, this is delicious with ham, pork, duck, or pheasant. Don't use any more star anise than suggested or it will taste medicinal. It might seem a hassle to cook the fruit twice, but it really does help extract more juice. The jelly is a wonderful glowing russet color.

Makes 1 (1 pint) jar
4lb quinces
2 cooking apples

finely grated zest and juice of 3 unwaxed lemons
about 2½ cups granulated sugar
2 star anise, plus extra for decoration (optional)

1 Wash the quinces, removing the little black part at the bottom and rubbing off any downy covering. Chop the quinces and apples coarsely into big chunks (no need to peel or core) and put into a large, deep saucepan with 10½ cups of water and the lemon zest and juice. Bring to a boil, then reduce the heat and simmer, covered, for one hour (use a double thickness of aluminum foil if you don't have a lid). Stir from time to time to make sure that the fruit doesn't stick to the bottom of the pan. The liquid shouldn't reduce too much, so add some more if needed. When the fruit is completely soft and mushy, let it cool a little. Spoon the pulp into a jelly bag suspended over a large bowl and let drain overnight.

3 Next day, put the resulting liquid in the refrigerator. Put the pulp from the jelly bag into a saucepan and add 4 cups of water. Bring to a boil, then reduce the heat and simmer for about 30 minutes. Again, strain this through a jelly bag overnight.

4 The following day, prepare a boiling-water canner (*see* pages 368–369) and keep the cleaned jars and lids warm. Discard the pulp from the jelly bag and measure the new liquid plus the liquid that you refrigerated the previous day. For every 2½ cups of juice add 2¼ cups of sugar and put both into a large, deep saucepan.

5 Tie the star anise in a piece of cheesecloth. Now hit it with a rolling pin to break up the spice. Put it in the pan, too. Heat gently, stirring from time to time to help the sugar dissolve, then boil it rapidly for 10 minutes or until setting point is reached (check on a sugar thermometer and do the wrinkle test, *see* page 11). Skim off any scum and take out the cheesecloth bag of star anise.

6 4 Fill each jar, adding a star anise for decoration, if desired, and leaving a headspace of ¼ inch from the top. Process the filled jars in a boiling-water canner for 10 minutes at sea level (*see* pages 369). Let cool, seal the jars, and label before storing.

quince paste

Membrillo, or quince paste, requires some patience, but it is so worth it and is delcious with cheese and crackers. Use a terrine or individual ceramic ramekins or other molds.

Makes 1 (1 quart) terrine
5 quinces (2½lb)

about 4½ cups granulated sugar
sunflower oil, for the jars or molds

1 Wash the quinces, removing the little black part at the bottom and rubbing off any downy covering. Chop them and put them in a heavy saucepan with enough water to cover. Bring to a simmer and cook until completely soft and pulpy. It will take about 30 to 40 minutes.

2 Push the pulp through a nylon strainer into a clean bowl. When you have strained it all, measure it. Put the puree into a large, heavy saucepan and, for every 2 cups of puree add 2¼ cups of sugar. Bring gently to a boil, stirring until the sugar has dissolved.

3 Reduce the heat and simmer gently for 1–1½ hours, until it is really thick; be careful because it can spit like a volcano. You need it to be so thick that, when you scrape your spoon across the bottom of the pan, it leaves a clear channel before closing up again. It should also start to come away from the sides of the pan as you stir, forming a thick mass.

4 Brush a 1 quart terrine with the oil. This will help you unmold the quince paste. Alternatively, greasing individual ramekins or molds. Pour the mixture into the terrine or molds. Cover with plastic wrap and chill in the refrigerator for about four hours, until loosely set.

5 Run a knife with a thin blade around the sides of the terrine or molds to invert the paste onto a plate, then wrap in wax paper and plastic wrap to store in the refrigerator for up to three months.

and also ...

DAMSON PASTE

Make as for quince paste, using 2¼lb of damsons (you can't pit them because the pits won't budge until the damsons are cooked. The pits will come out when you strain the fruit). Measure the resulting puree. Add 2¼ cups of granulated sugar for every 2½ cups of puree.

The resulting paste is a glorious dark purple color, which is lovely with cheeses (especially blue cheeses), pâté,s and roasted lamb or pork.

sauces, pastes, mustards, and vinegars

This probably looks like the miscellaneous chapter, the place where I've put everything that doesn't fit anywhere else. In fact, this is one of the most useful sections in the book and, for a cook, "useful" recipes are to be cherished. The recipes here produce containers, bottles, and jars that will make a difference, provide the basis of an easy meal, or transform half a dozen pork chops. They are generally kept on the top shelf of my refrigerator in crowded ranks of tapenade, anchoïade, and chili sauces and pastes.

Tapenade and anchoïade, both Provençal pastes based, respectively, on ripe, inky black olives and salty anchovies, are for healthy lunches (with good bread, hard-boiled eggs, and radishes) or to make roasted lamb more than just lamb (tapenade makes a good stuffing, and spoonfuls of anchoïade pushed into slits in the flesh will season the meat from within).

The chili sauces come in varying shades of red and are ready to do their transformative work. They may all be based on chiles, but their flavors couldn't be more different. The Mexican adobo paste is smoky and woody, and it tastes the way a double bass sounds. At the other end of the scale, the Thai sweet chili sauce is sweet and perky. I turn out big batches of it, so bright it makes you feel as if you're making paint. The harissa is multifaceted—there's cumin, caraway, and coriander in there—and as complex as a Moroccan souk. What makes them useful is the fact that they can be marinades as well as condiments. Spread harissa (thinned with olive oil and lemon juice) on lamb chops before broiling, and serve with a chickpea or spicy mashed potatoes and parsnips. Paint Thai sweet chili sauce (adding lime juice and crushed garlic) on chicken thighs before roasting, and keep the adobo for big, meaty pork chops (adobo is simply the classiest cooking sauce you can have around).

Some have a reasonable shelf life if refrigerated, others don't keep for more than a week. They are not true preserves, but they still have their place here because they can be made in advance and stored. Cook a batch, give some to friends, and use your jar quickly (especially Thai curry pastes, which taste better fresh). They're easy to make and the flavors—sometimes zingy, sometimes dark and deep—make them much more delicious than any you can buy.

There's a designated place for vinegars in my kitchen, too. How could I need five different vinegars? Because they produce dressings as different to each other as a wool suit is to a silk dress. Elderflower vinegar brings fragrance to a summer salad of avocado, tomato, and melon; maple vinegar brings depth and sweetness to a wintry salad of rice, pecans, and duck.

Regard this chapter as a box of culinary accessories. Keep a few of them in your refrigerator—and at the front of your mind when you go food shopping—and they'll help you to answer the question, "What on earth will I cook today?"

georgian plum sauce

I included a recipe for Georgian plum sauce, *tkemali*, in my first book, *Crazy Water, Pickled Lemons*, but this is slightly spicier and the addition of wine vinegar means it keeps longer. It's a little sweeter than the traditional Georgian version, but I prefer it not too tart. It's one of my favorite sauces, so I don't feel guilty about providing it again. Its uses go beyond Georgian food.

Fills 1 (½ pint) jar

8 plums, halved and pitted

2 tablespoons packed light brown sugar, or to taste

good pinch of salt

¼ cup red wine vinegar

3 garlic cloves, crushed

2 teaspoons hot Hungarian paprika

juice of ½ lemon, or to taste

2 tablespoons chopped mint

3 tablespoons chopped cilantro

1 Put all the ingredients for the sauce, except the lemon juice and the herbs, into a saucepan and add ¼ cup of water. Bring to a boil, stirring a little to help the sugar dissolve, then reduce the heat and simmer for about 30 minutes, until the mixture is jammy and the plums are soft.

2 Puree the mixture (or if you prefer it coarser, you can leave it as it is). Stir in the lemon (taste to see if you would like more lemon or sugar, then adjust it accordingly), then the herbs. Put into a sterilized jar (*see* page 11) and seal with a vinegar-proof lid. Cool, then refrigerate for up to a month.

how to use

In Georgia, this is served with *tabaka*, a dish of chicken that is flattened and fried under a weight. The other traditional Georgian use is to mix it with kidney beans (they should be well seasoned, so add more of the herbs used in the sauce and crushed garlic, too) to serve as part of a spread of zakuski (*see* page 229). It's also very good with lamb kebabs or spicy roasted lamb, and with pork.

My favorite use for plum sauce, however, is to serve it with chicken—whole or separated into pieces—which I've marinated in a mixture of plain yogurt or buttermilk, crushed garlic, cayenne pepper, lemon, salt, and pepper for 24 hours. Make sure your chicken is covered in the marinade, and turn it a couple of times while it's marinating. Shake off the excess marinade and roast the chicken, then sprinkle it with walnuts chopped with raw garlic and fresh cilantro or parsley. Pomegranate seeds look wonderful sprinkled over it, too. Serve cucumber with dill and bulgur wheat or spelt on the side, with plenty of the plum sauce.

harissa

The classic Moroccan chili sauce. I make it in small amounts because you need only a little at a time, but you can double the quantities if you think you'll use it within four months. Some are made with roasted peppers and tomatoes, but I like a pure chile flavor. There are even versions with dried rose petals, but I honestly can't detect them, they have too many chiles to fight with.

Fills 1 (½ pint) jar

2½ teaspoons caraway seeds
2½ teaspoons coriander seeds
2½ teaspoons cumin seeds
5 fresh red chiles, halved and seeded
5 dried guajillo chiles, soaked in
   warm water, drained, and seeded
   (reserve the liquid)

8 garlic cloves
leaves from a small bunch of cilantro
juice of 1 lemon
1¼ cups olive oil, plus more for storing
¾ teaspoon salt, or to taste

1 Toast the caraway, coriander, and cumin seeds in a dry saucepan. Heat them for three to four minutes, until they start to release their fragrance. Pound in a mortar and pestle.

2 Put the spices with all the other ingredients into a food processor and puree. You should get a thick, but not solid, paste. Add a little of the chile soaking liquid to help you get the right texture.

3 Put into a small sterilized jar (*see* page 11) and pour a film of oil on top. Store in the refrigerator— make sure it is always covered by a layer of oil—and use within four months.

pickled chiles

You can add spices or herbs to this (coriander seeds, bay leaves, dill), but I like to keep a plain jar of them. Serve with mezze, or add to casseroles. The vinegar is great for hot vinaigrettes.

Fills 1 (1 quart) jar

2¾ cups white wine vinegar
½ cup granulated sugar

2 tablespoons salt
8 oz chiles: green, red, or a mixture

1 Put the vinegar, sugar, and salt into a saucepan and heat, stirring to help the sugar dissolve.

2 Slit each chile along its side, from tip to stem (don't cut right through) and pack into a sterilized jar (*see* page 11). Pour the vinegar solution over the chiles and weigh them down; the vinegar must cover them.

3 Seal with a vinegar-proof lid. Store in the refrigerator and let the chiles sit for two weeks before using. They'll be good for four months if you keep them under the level of the vinegar.

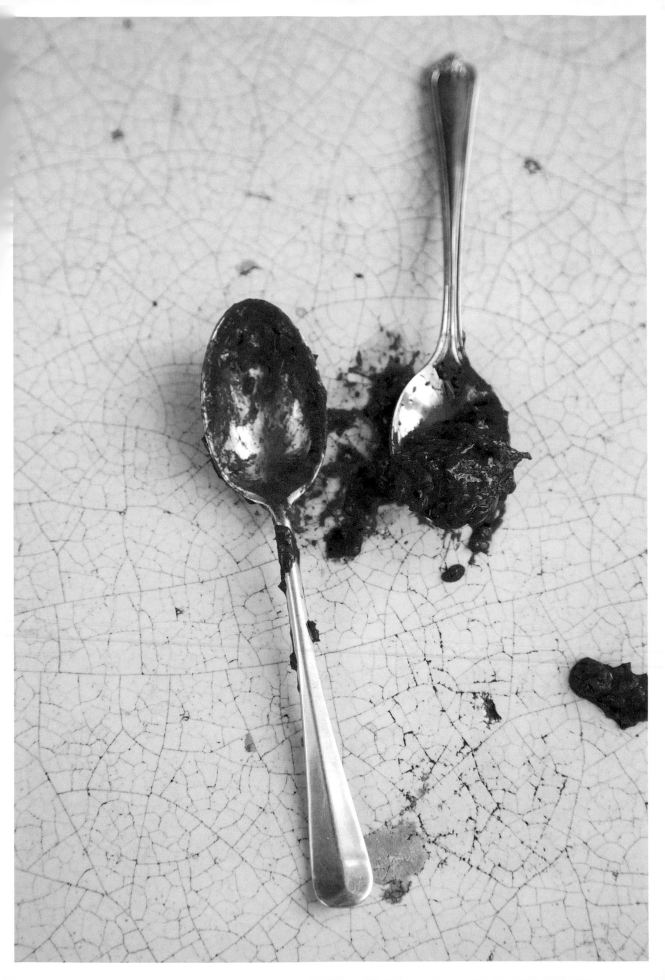

west indian hot pepper sauce

I go through a lot of West Indian hot sauce (it's my standby sauce for pepping up and bringing heat to dishes), so I was intrigued to see how a noncommercial version would taste. After a bit of research, this wonderfully golden orange sauce is what I produced. And it's great, really worth making and takes just 15 minutes. Beside it, the sauces you can buy taste metallic and thin. Be careful, however, because it is very hot. It's not a dipping sauce or a condiment but a sauce to add—as you might add Tabasco—to bring heat to dishes.

Fills 2 (½ pint) jars

1 small green papaya, peeled, seeded, and chopped
6 scotch bonnet chiles, halved
1 onion, finely chopped
4 garlic cloves, finely chopped
1 inch fresh ginger root, chopped
1 tablespoon salt
2 tablespoons mustard powder
1 teaspoon turmeric
1 teaspoon ground cumin
1½ tablespoons honey
1¼ cups malt vinegar

1 Put everything into a saucepan and bring to a boil. Reduce the heat and simmer for 15 minutes, or until soft. Cool and puree.

2 Put into sterilized jars (*see* page 11) and seal with vinegar-proof lids. Keep refrigerated for up to six weeks.

chipotle sauce

Mexican recipes sometimes call for "chipotles in adobo." Dried chiles are available in Mexican grocery stores and online, so you can make your own. It's simple. Chipotles lend a wonderful smoky flavor. You can use these in chili con carne or other Mexican stews: a braise of pork or lamb with chorizo, black beans, and these chiles is fantastic. If this recipe seems too much to use in three weeks, you can just halve the quantity.

Fills 2 (½ pint) jars

1½oz dried chipotle chiles, stem removed, halved lengthwise
1 onion, finely chopped
⅓ cup cider vinegar
2 garlic cloves, finely chopped
¼ cup ketchup
¼ teaspoon salt

1 Put all the ingredients into a saucepan with 2½ cup of water and bring to a boil. Reduce the heat to low and cover. Cook for an hour, then uncover and cook for another 30 minutes.

2 You can either puree the chili sauce now, or keep it as it is. Put it in sterilized jars (*see* page 11) and seal with vinegar-proof lids. It will keep in the refrigerator for three weeks.

thai sweet chili sauce

So much better than anything you can buy. It doesn't have that cloying flavor of commercial jars, but barks at you with a biting, fresh taste. Refrigerated, it lasts almost indefinitely.

Fills 1 (pint) jar

6 large fresh red chiles, 3 of them seeded, coarsely chopped

2 inch square piece of fresh ginger root, peeled and coarsely chopped

finely grated zest of 3 limes and juice of 2

12 garlic cloves, peeled

1 large bunch of cilantro leaves

1½ cups granulated sugar

¼ cup Thai fish sauce

½ cup white wine vinegar

1 Puree the chiles, ginger, lime zest and juice, garlic, and cilantro in a food processor to a paste.

2 Put the sugar into a heavy saucepan with ⅓ cup of water and place on medium heat until the sugar dissolves. Increase the heat and boil until the syrup becomes a caramel color. Stir in the paste, fish sauce, and vinegar—the caramel will spit, so be careful—and simmer for two minutes. Let cool. Pour into a sterilized jar (*see* page 11) and seal with a vinegar-proof lid. When cool, refrigerate.

how to use

Use as a sauce for anything Eastern that you can dip. It's also great with a veggie breakfast (roast mushrooms, guacamole, fried egg, hash browns), and to add a kick to braises.

turkish pepper paste

This has such a sweet, front-of-the-mouth peppery flavor and can be made so quickly that it's well worth the effort. It's also different to the other chili sauces.

Fills 2 small (½ cup) jars

2 large red bell peppers, halved, seeded, and chopped

2 red chiles, halved, seeded, and chopped

1 tablespoon granulated sugar

1 tablespoon olive oil, plus more for drizzling on top

½ teaspoon salt

1½ tablespoons white balsamic vinegar

1 Put all the ingredients into a food processor and process to a puree.

2 Scrape the mixture into a nonstick saucepan and bring to a boil (watch it, because it gets there really quickly). Reduce the heat and simmer for 15 minutes. The paste should be thick.

3 Pack it into hot sterilized jars (*see* page 11), pour a film of oil on top, and seal with vinegar-proof lids. Let cool, then store in the refrigerator. It will last for two weeks.

tigers and lime leaves

Thai curry pastes are a boon, because they're the complex part of an almost-instant meal. Complex not because they are difficult to make—the hardest thing is gathering the ingredients onto your countertop—but because they combine layers of flavor. Very few other ingredients have to be added to them to form a dish.

Both of the paste recipes here make enough for a couple of curries and will keep in the refrigerator for about two weeks (but I prefer them when they're less than five days old). It just doesn't make sense to make a smaller quantity, because it's hard to blend in the food processor. (So have two Thai curries within two weeks, or give half to a friend when you make a paste.)

As for food processors, serious Thai cooks believe pounding the ingredients gives a better result and that you should add the ingredients sequentially, starting with the coarser ones that are harder to break down. You need to do a lot of pounding because the paste must be fine. I must say I am all for convenience. The fresh taste makes it worthwhile preparing your own paste (commercial versions just don't have the same zing and zip), so why make it such an arduous task that you never do it? I nearly always make my pastes in the food processor.

Curry pastes are personal. Those below have been made to please me—and they'll be changed when I cook with them—so tweak as you desire. You won't know if these are to your taste or not until you cook with them, too. Then you might decide there's too much lime, or that you'd prefer using lime leaves instead of zest, and you may find them too hot. It's like reading a play in a book. A play has to be staged to be judged properly. A curry paste has to be made into a curry.

thai green curry paste

Fills 1 (½ pint) jar
8 lemon grass stalks
8 green chiles, halved, deseeded and chopped
6 garlic cloves, peeled
generous 1 inch fresh ginger root or galangal, coarsely chopped
4 shallots, coarsely chopped

big bunch of cilantro (about 2¾oz)
juice of 2 limes
zest of 2 limes (if you can get kaffir lime leaves, use about 4 of those instead)
ground black pepper
½ teaspoon salt
1 teaspoon shrimp paste (optional)

1 Discard the tough outer leaves from the lemon grass (they are woody). Chop the rest. Put this into a food processor with all the other ingredients plus 3 tablespoons of water, and process to a paste. You'll need to stop every so often, to scrape down the sides of the processor and process again.

2 Put into a sterilized jar (*see* page 11) or plastic container, set a sheet of plastic wrap on the surface of the paste, and cover with a lid. Keep in the refrigerator. It will be fine for two weeks, although I prefer the flavor when it's less than one week old.

thai jungle curry paste

Hot, hot, hot!

Fills 1 (½ pint) jar

¼ teaspoon ground coriander,
   or coriander seeds
¼ teaspoon ground cumin, or cumin seeds
3 lemon grass stalks
2 red chiles, coarsely chopped
2 red Thai chiles, coarsely chopped
2 green Thai chiles, coarsely chopped

6 garlic cloves, peeled
generous 1 inch fresh ginger root or galangal,
   coarsely chopped
4 shallots, coarsely chopped
⅛ teaspoon turmeric
1 teaspoon paprika
¼ teaspoon salt
½ teaspoon shrimp paste (optional)

1 It's best to toast and grind the coriander and cumin freshly if you can. Just put them in a dry skillet, toast for 30 seconds or so (you will smell their aroma as they toast), then grind in a mortar.

2 Make the paste exactly as for the green curry paste (*see* left).

3 Put into a sterilized jar (*see* page 11) or plastic container, set a sheet of plastic wrap on the surface of the paste, and cover with a lid. Keep in the refrigerator for up to two weeks.

how to use

The simplest way to use these is just to add spoonfuls to simmering stock or coconut milk. After that (and the addition of the more substantial ingredients, such as chicken or vegetables) the curry is made more complex with seasonings—a little sugar, Thai fish sauce, more lime—all added to taste. This kind of curry is the easiest you can make.

The other way is to first sauté the paste. This can be done in oil. You cook the paste over high heat for a minute or two, until you really smell the herbs and spices—it's an exciting part of cooking if you are doing it with your own homemade paste because the kitchen becomes infused with the smell—the chile may even catch in the back of your throat, although the green ingredients (lime leaves or zest) softens it. Pastes cooked in oil are then seasoned again, and stock and the chunky main ingredients are added.

It is the final seasoning that completes the dish. Thai cooking is a balance of hot, sour, salty, and sweet, and different dishes show these qualities in varying but balanced proportions. So your base paste is finished off with more lime leaves or lime juice, Thai or holy basil or fresh chiles. And your taste buds are as crucial as the pastes you have already stashed away in your refrigerator.

constance spry's chile sherry

An ingenious and very useful addition to your panoply of flavorings, from the redoubtable
Mrs. Spry. A dash of this hot sweetness is excellent, as she suggests, in a braise, curry, or sauce
(try it in a creamy sauce to go with pork chops). I sometimes use a drop in an Eastern-flavored
vinaigrette, too. You can also make this in a jar and add a couple of handfuls of golden raisins or
regular raisins so you have some plump, boozy dried fruits that are bursting with heat; they're
great for a spicy sweet-and-sour salad or a hot beef braise.

Fills 1 (¾ quart) bottle
6 long red chiles (or a handful of small
   Thai chiles if you want it really hot)

3 cups amontillado sherry

1 Wash and sterilize an old wine bottle (*see* page 11). Make a little slit in the side of each chile.
Put them through the neck of the bottle—it should be completely dry—then pour in the sherry.

2 Cork or put a screw cap on the bottle and let sit for a few weeks before tasting. It will get hotter
in time. Store in a cool, dark place; you can fill up the sherry from time to time. I like amontillado
sherry because it's not too sweet, but I can see that a sweeter chile sherry would have its uses, too.

pimenta malagueta

The Brazilian pepper sauce. Use the liquid for seasoning (as you would use Tabasco, for
example, for adding to casseroles, or tossing through pasta), and even the chiles themselves.

Fills 1 (1 quart) bottle
350g (12oz) Thai chiles
about 1¼ cups white rum

2¾ cups olive oil
1¼ cups white wine vinegar

1 Pick through the chiles, throwing away any that are damaged or bruised. Wash the chiles in the
rum, then discard the rum (they do this in Brazil, where they think that using water makes the chiles
rot), and carefully shake them dry. Make a tiny cut in the side of each one.

2 Put the chiles into a sterilized (*see* page 11) one-quart bottle (old liquor bottles are good because
they have clear glass). Gently heat the olive oil to about 105°F and pour it over the chiles. Let cool,
then pour in the vinegar. The chiles have to be submerged. Seal with a vinegar-proof lid and let sit
for a month in the refrigerator before using. This keeps for a month in the refrigerator.

adobo

Wow. That's the only response to this. Adobo is a Mexican paste made from dried chiles, herbs, and vinegar and will, once you've tried it, become one of the most useful things in your refrigerator (and it will change your experience of pork chops forever). There are a lot of different versions—some people add cloves, others bitter orange juice instead of vinegar—and the type of chile used varies, too. This is my own version, but feel free to adapt it as you want. I particularly like sherry vinegar in this (although a Mexican would not use it), because it adds a wonderful, deep "woody" flavor. Brown sugar isn't usual either but, again, it adds depth.

This amount gives you enough paste to make two Mexican-flavored meals for six people.

Fills 1 (½ pint) jar
5 dried chipotle chiles
4 dried ancho chiles
1 teaspoon cumin seeds
1 teaspoon coriander seeds
½ teaspoon allspice
1¼ inch piece of cinnamon stick

1 teaspoon dried oregano
5 garlic cloves, roughly chopped
2 shallots, roughly chopped
1½ teaspoons salt, or to taste
2 teaspoons dark brown sugar, or to taste (optional)
2 tablespoons red wine vinegar
⅓ cup sherry vinegar

1 Toast the chiles in a dry skillet; you don't want to char them—just make them more pliable (the heat softens them). Discard the stems and the seeds from all the chipotles and half the anchos.

2 Put both types of chiles in a small saucepan and cover with water. Bring to a boil, then remove from the heat and leat soak for 30 minutes. Strain the chiles, reserving the soaking liquid.

3 Toast the whole spices in a dry skillet until they are fragrant (about 40 seconds). Now put all the ingredients into a food processor and process to a puree, adding enough of the chile soaking liquid to get it to the consistency of a paste. Taste for seasoning and adjust if you think it needs it.

4 Put into a sterilized jar (*see* page 11), seal with a vinegar-proof lid, and keep in the refrigerator. It will be fine there for several weeks, but you'll have used it way before that …

how to use

Spread this over chicken parts or big pork chops. Ideally, marinate overnight, but I often let them sit for just 30 minutes. If you are using chicken, cook for about 40 minutes at 350°F. For pork chops, roast for 20 minutes at 375°F. In both cases, cover with aluminum foil after 15 minutes, because the paste can burn. Transfer to a warm serving dish and spoon the thick juices over the top. Serve with wedges of lime, guacamole, green salad, and boiled white rice.

You can also use adobo as a sauce, adding a generous amount (about half of this recipe) to the braising liquid in a casserole of pork and chorizo.

mustards

A dab of mustard can make all the difference. In fact, it can make the meal. I sometimes wonder, when I am cooking a difficult recipe on a weekend, why I am doing it. I think of dishes I love: roasted chicken, pork schnitzel like my mum used to make, and realize that they're just meat with a dollop of mustard on the side. Mild Dijon. Hot English. These are sometimes enough.

They knew this in medieval Europe. Because mustard grows in Europe, it makes it one of the cheapest spices, and medieval courts often employed a "mustardius," an official who oversaw the growing and preparation of mustard. In Britain, its production developed in the 16th century around Tewkesbury, and the British are unique in drying and then milling the seeds into a powder that can be stored and mixed with water. (One of the best-known brands was produced by Keen and Sons of London, hence the British phrase "as keen as mustard").

Only one of the mustards below is made from scratch: the grain one. The others are based on mustards that are already made. Why bother? You get to control the flavorings, you get to play around and make a mustard that is great with lamb (the anchovy one) or with a hot dog (the Creole one). And once you have made the grainy mustard, you can use that as a base and develop mustards of your own. Try to think of mustards as you would any other preserve or paste: you know how to make the base, so go off on your own tangent from there. The only thing you always need, besides mustard seeds, is vinegar. That's what preserves the seeds' heat.

whole-grain honey mustard

The real McCoy; your own mustard from scratch. And it's easy. You can use this as a base and try other spices or vinegars, or use brown sugar or maple syrup instead of honey.

Fills 3 small (½ cup) jars

⅔ cup yellow mustard seeds

⅔ cup white wine or cider vinegar, plus more
   if needed

¾ teaspoon ground cinnamon

1 teaspoon ground ginger

¼ cup honey, or to taste

2 garlic cloves or ½ teaspoon garlic powder

salt

1 Put the mustard seeds, vinegar, and spices in a bowl and let them soak overnight.

2 The next day, using a mortar and pestle (or a food processor), pound this mixture to a paste with the honey and garlic. Add more vinegar, as needed, to get to a mustard-type consistency, and season with salt to taste.

3 Put into small sterilized jars (see page 11), then cover and seal with vinegar-proof lids. Refrigerate for up to three weeks.

anchovy mustard

Great with steak (anchovies are delicious with meat). You can add a small crushed garlic clove.
I sometimes mix this with cream and drizzle it on steak or, sparingly, over roasted cod or salmon.

Fills 2 small (½ cup) jars
2 egg yolks
⅔ cup Dijon mustard
generous 2 tablespoons sunflower oil
    or light olive oil

10 anchovy fillets, drained of oil and pounded
1 tablespoon finely chopped parsley or tarragon,
    or a mixture

1 Put the egg yolks and mustard in a bowl and, working with a wooden spoon or an electric mixer running slowly, beat together while slowly adding the oil. Beat in the anchovies, too. Stir in the herbs.

2 Put into sterilized jars (*see* page 11), then cover and seal with lids. It will keep in the refrigerator for one week.

hot sweet creole mustard

This packs a punch—the horseradish is very strong—and is best with big hunks of beef or pork.
It's also great on hot dogs at a summer barbecue, but do watch the heat.

Fills 1 small (½ cup) jar
½ cup Dijon or grainy mustard
2 teaspoons freshly grated horseradish
2 teaspoons paprika

2 teaspoons hot sauce (*see* page 72 for West Indian
    Hot Pepper Sauce, or buy some)
2 tablespoons packed dark brown sugar

1 Simply mix all the ingredients together and put into a small sterilized jar (*see* page 11), then cover and seal with the lid.

2 Keep in the refrigerator. It will be fine for up to three weeks.

new york sweet cranberry mustard

This is inspired by a mustard served at New York's Home restaurant, a fabulously comforting place. I have made it slightly sweeter. It's perfect at Christmas, when you're making all those turkey and ham sandwiches and want cranberries with a kick.

Fills 1 (½ pint) jar

¾ cup dried cranberries

⅔ cup apple juice or orange juice

2 cups fresh cranberries

3 tablespoons granulated sugar

¼ cup honey

1 tablespoon olive oil

1 small red onion, finely chopped

1 tablespoon red wine vinegar

1 tablespoon grainy mustard

sea salt

freshly ground black pepper

1 Put the dried cranberries in a saucepan and add enough apple juice or orange juice to cover. Bring to a boil, then remove from the heat and let sit to plump up for 30 minutes.

2 Put 1 cup of water and the fresh cranberries in a saucepan and bring to a boil. Reduce the heat and simmer until the cranberries have burst (about five minutes), then add the sugar and honey and stir until dissolved.

3 Heat the olive oil in a small skillet and sauté the onion until soft and golden. Add the vinegar and mustard and cook gently for another five minutes. Mix this with both types of cranberries and any remaining soaking liquid from the dried cranberries, and season to taste.

4 Process in a food processor using the pulse button (if you want it really smooth, you can then press the mixture through a nylon strainer, but I leave it chunky). Put in a sterilized jar (*see* page 11), then cover and seal with a vinegar-proof lid. Let cool, and keep in the refrigerator for up to two weeks.

how to use

This is obviously a good thing to have around at Christmas, and it's good with cold cooked ham, too. Russians eat cranberries with red meat, so don't rule it out with cold rare roasted beef. Its selling point is that it is both hot and sweet.

mostarda di frutta

Ever since I looked at a vast array of mostardas—some with mixed fruits, others with just single fruit, such as pears, figs, or apricots—on the shelves of an old deli in Siena, I have wanted to make it. Mostarda glows. I'm also amazed that such a condiment—it seems almost medieval in the way it combines sweet fruits with hot spices—has survived.

Over the years, I have tried this or that version—following recipes that suggested you could do it quickly—and ended up with a spicy jam. If you want real mostarda, it takes time. This is probably the recipe that thrills me more than any other in the book and it took the most testing. You can find mustard oil—made from mustard seeds—in Indian grocery stores. Use it sparingly. In fact, it will burn your hands; actually, you shouldn't even smell it. I'm not kidding, it's lethal stuff. (Keep it away from little hands.) In Italy they use mustard essence.

Fills 2 (1 quart) jars
2¼lb fruit (pears, apples, quinces, apricots, underripe figs, kumquats, melon; use just one fruit or a mixture)

a little lemon juice, if using pears or apples
6 cups granulated sugar
1 cup honey
1 tablespoon mustard oil (or to taste, but be careful)

1 Peel, halve, and core any pears, apples, and quinces, then cut into cubes. Squeeze lemon juice over pears and apples to stop them from discoloring. Put the quinces in a saucepan and cover with water. Bring to a boil, reduce to a simmer, and cook until just tender. Apricots should be halved and pitted, figs halved. If using kumquats, prick them all over with the tip of a sharp knife, blanch for two minutes, and drain. Repeat three times each time for two minutes—changing the water, to reduce the bitterness.

2 Mix together the sugar, 7⅔ cups of water, and the honey and slowly bring to a boil, stirring to help the sugar dissolve. Add the fruit and simmer for 10 minutes, then remove from the heat. Put a plate on top of the fruit to weigh it down, cover with a dish towel, and let sit for 24 hours.

3 Remove the fruit with a slotted spoon and return the syrup to a boil for 10 minutes. Return the fruit. Bring just to a boil, remove from the heat, weigh, cover with a dish towel, and let sit for 24 hours.

4 You have to go through this process of removing the fruit and boiling each day for another three to five times, to evaporate the water that the fruit leaches into the syrup. Eventually, it will get to the stage where you can feel the fruit is absolutely imbued with syrup, and the syrup has a lovely viscous weight. Go through the process carefully; it's not difficult, you just have to watch it like a hawk. If the syrup starts to caramelize (because of a hot spot in your saucepan), that's a disaster. You have to decide when you can stop boiling every day. Take it too far and it will set like boiled candies. The syrup should never become as thick as honey. If you think you've taken it too far, add water immediately and gently stir. (If you've eaten mostarda, you'll know the texture you're looking for.) Let cool.

5 Put on rubber gloves and carefully stir in the mustard oil. Taste only when it is mixed well, and add a little more than you think you need, because it mellows in time. Put into sterilized jars (*see* page 11) and refrigerate for up to ten days. Now make a bollito misto, and some salsa verde, and invite your friends. You'll glow as much as much as the mostarda.

patience and old wine: how vinegars are made

Vinegar may seem like an unimportant ingredient in cooking. When do we ever use more than a few spoonfuls, unless we are making chutney? But, like lemon, vinegar can be used to lift a dish, to pull its components together, or to balance out sweetness and give depth. Flavored vinegars—easy to make as vinegar absorbs the tastes of other ingredients—give even more. They can bring a shadow of an ingredient to a dish. You can use saffron-steeped vinegar to make a gilded mayonnaise, a drop of rose vinegar in a summery vinaigrette to use with strawberries and melon, or tarragon vinegar in a creamy dressing for a salad of chicken, cherries, and almonds. And a slug of sweet maple vinegar drizzled over slices of roasted pumpkin, or added to a slow braise of pork and apples, will bring a nutty, burned sugar edge. Vinegars help you to create layers of flavor, and to play around with the subtleties of taste, too.

This chapter has recipes for flavored vinegars, but it's easy to make vinegar itself, and your own will be less acidic and have more depth than store-bought bottles. Don't use them in chutneys—their finer points would be lost—but it's worth using your own to make flavored vinegars. Basically, vinegar develops as the result of fermentation of bacteria in alcohol into acetic acid. The word may be *vin aigre*, or "sour wine," but just leaving the collected dregs of your wine glasses to turn sour will not result in great vinegar. You need a culture of *Acetobacter aceti* to do that, and there are different strains. You can be sure you have the right kind by adding a batch of "live" vinegar to the wine you want to ferment. Live vinegar contains a vinegar "mother," a harmless jellylike layer that forms on the top. It doesn't sound pleasant, but you need it.

Most books instruct you to get the "mother of vinegar" from a friend. Yeah. We all have a friend like that … In fact, you can buy this mother of vinegar from wine-making suppliers. To make vinegar, put 3 cups of mother of vinegar and 1 bottle of red wine (one you would drink, horrible wine makes horrible vinegar) into a large sterilized glass jar (*see* page 11). Cover the opening with cheesecloth, put it in a dark place, and let sit for a couple of weeks. Remove the cheesecloth and sniff; it should smell more vinegary than winey. Taste to see how different it is from when you first put it in the jar. Cover with the cheesecloth and let sit for another week or two, then taste again. You can use it now if you like the flavor, or let it sit for longer; it will keep developing—it's a living thing. When you're happy with the taste, pour off some of the vinegar—leaving behind any sediment. If it's cloudy or has little parts of the mother floating in it, filter it through a coffee paper. The flavor will develop as it ages, and the vinegar with the mother, left in the jar, can be used as a base for more vinegars. The vinegar can last for up to six months, but if the mother or the vinegar has a bad smell, discard both of them right away.

There are a lot of definite, confident flavors in this book—hot chile, dark fudgey sugar, sour lemon, airily fresh dill—but here is an ingredient that, although sharp, can create the most muted effects. Vinegar is one of the most surprising ingredients. It's worth using a range of vinegars, and noting just what they can do for your cooking.

elderflower vinegar

Elderflowers make an exquisite vinegar, tasting of grass and muscat. It's almost impossible to buy, so it's well worth making your own and very easy. It's important to pick blossoms that are very fresh—you don't want any that are yellowing or wilting—and use them immediately. After about six hours, the blossoms develop a slightly sickly sweet smell.

Fills 1 (¾ quart) bottle
very fresh elderflowers

3 cups white wine vinegar, plus
more if needed

1 Pick over the elderflowers, getting rid of any bugs. Cram as many elderflowers as you can—using only the blossom—into a sterilized jar (*see* page 11) and pour the vinegar over them. Push the flowers under the vinegar (use more vinegar if you have to) and let sit for three weeks in a cool, dark place.

2 Strain off the vinegar through a cheesecloth-lined nylon strainer. Pour through a plastic funnel into a sterilized bottle, seal with a vinegar-proof lid, and label. It will keep for up to six months.

how to use

Salads of vegetables and fruit are frowned on now—they're a 1980s throwback—but Joyce Molyneaux made a delicious version when she cooked at The Carved Angel in Dartmouth, England. It was avocado, melon, and strawberries, sliced and drizzled with an elderflower vinegar dressing. I prefer raspberries to strawberries.

tarragon vinegar

You can make other herb vinegars using exactly the same method—try chives, flat-leaf parsley, or thyme—but tarragon is the one I have most call for and it's very hard to find in stores.

Fills 1 (¾ quart) bottle
3 cups white wine vinegar

6 bruised white peppercorns
5 sprigs of very fresh tarragon

1 Put all the ingredients into a sterilized jar (*see* page 11), then let sit for a month in a cool, dark place.

2 Strain through a cheesecloth-lined nylon strainer, then pour through a plastic funnel into a sterilized bottle, seal with a vinegar-proof lid, and label. It will keep for a year.

how to use

Essential for making béarnaise sauce. I also use it to make a creamy, slightly sweet vinaigrette with which to dress a summer salad of chicken, cherries, and almonds.

sweet black currant vinegar

Fruit vinegars got a bad image in the 1980s. They came into vogue with nouvelle cuisine (along with kiwis and raspberry coulis) and were used indiscriminately. When fashions changed, they came to be pilloried. But they are very useful. A drop can add both tartness and fruitiness to braises, and they're also very good in vinaigrettes for certain dishes. This black currant recipe is sweet and sour, but you can make completely tart ones (*see* page 87).

Fills 1 (½ pint) bottle
4 cups black currants

1¼ cups cider vinegar
about 2 cups granulated sugar

1 Put the black currants into a bowl and cover with the vinegar. Crush the fruit (use a vegetable masher) and let sit to flavor the vinegar for about five days in a cool, dark place.

2 Put the fruit and vinegar into a jelly bag over a bowl and let sit overnight. Measure the liquid (throw away the fruit pulp in the bag). For every 1¼ cups of fruit vinegar add heaping 1 cup of sugar.

3 Put into a saucepan and heat gently, stirring a little to help the sugar dissolve. Boil for five minutes or so after the sugar has melted, skimming the scum from the surface. Let cool completely, then pour into a sterilized bottle (*see* page 11) and seal with a vinegar-proof lid. It will keep for up to six months

maple vinegar

Sweet and autumnal, I got the inspiration for this in a fascinating little book called *Ideas in Food* by Aki Kamozawa and H. Alexander Talbot.

Fills 2 (¾ quart) bottles
1½ cups maple syrup
1¾ cups mother of vinegar
   (*see* pages 86)

⅔ cup dark rum or bourbon (they produce different
   flavors, so try both at different times)

1 Mix everything with ½ cup of spring water (not tap water) in a glass jar. Cover with cheesecloth and replace the lid, half on (air needs to get in). Let sit in a cool, dark place for four weeks.

2 Taste. Once you can no longer taste alcohol, bottle and seal with vinegar-proof lids. You may feel you want to use it now; it depends on the flavor, which will deepen with time. It keeps for six months.

how to use

Drizzle over pumpkin or chicken halfway through roasting for a sweet-sharp glaze, or mix with warm fried apple slices to go with roasted pork. It's also great in vinaigrettes for nutty-tasting grains, such as quinoa.

SAUCES, PASTES, MUSTARDS AND, VINEGARS

sweet fig vinegar

It is rare to find yourself with cheap figs, but occasionally I can pick them up right at the end of the day from a street market or in a Middle Eastern or Turkish grocery store. They make a sweet vinegar that has something of a marsala or a tawny port about it. You can replace some of the cider vinegar with balsamic vinegar to get a wonderful rich result, but you need to cut down the amount of sugar if you do that.

Fills 1 (¾ quart) bottle
8–10 ripe fresh figs
¼ cup chopped dried figs

1¾ cups cider vinegar
about 2¾ cups granulated sugar

1 Quarter the fresh figs and put them into a large jar with the dried fruit. Pour the vinegar over the figs. Crush the fruit using a vegetable masher, then cover and let sit in a cool, dark place for about a week. Mash the fruit a little a couple more times. The vinegar will turn a fantastic color.

2 Suspend a jelly bag over a bowl and pour the fruit and vinegar into it. Let drip overnight. The next day, measure the liquid and for every 1¼ cups of vinegar add heaping 1 cup of sugar. Put both into a saucepan and bring to a boil, stirring to help the sugar dissolve. Once at a boil, cook for five minutes. Let cool, then pour into a sterilized bottle (*see* page 11) and seal with a vinegar-proof lid. It keeps for up to six months.

how to use

This makes a wonderful vinaigrette to serve with a salad of roasted or smoked duck breast, particularly if it contains a fruity component. A dash is also good in a fig ice cream, especially if you make your vinegar with some balsamic.

chinese-style plum sauce

Great with duck, of course, and also with pork. I make this sauce in small batches and store it in the refrigerator.

Makes 2 (½ pint) jars

15 red-skinned plums (preferably with red flesh, too; 2¼lb), pitted and chopped

2 cups red wine vinegar

1 teaspoon salt

1 teaspoon dried red chili flakes

3 star anise, tied up in a piece of cheesecloth

½ cup dark soy sauce

⅔ cup firmly packed light brown sugar

1 Put the plums, vinegar, salt, chili flakes, and bag of star anise into a heavy saucepan and bring to a boil. Reduce the heat and simmer until the fruit is completely soft; this takes about 20 minutes.

2 Push the plum puree through a nylon strainer into a clean saucepan. Add the soy sauce and sugar and bring slowly to a boil, stirring to help the sugar dissolve.

3 Reduce the heat and cook on very low heat for about 45 minutes. The mixture should be thick (like the plum dipping sauce you get in Chinese restaurants). Pour into warm, dry sterilized jars (*see* page 11), then cover and seal with vinegar-proof lids. It will keep in the refrigerator for two months.

zhoug

Careful, this is bitingly hot. A relish from the Yemen, you need to taste a smidgen before using it so that you can serve accordingly. The Yemenis believe that a daily dose of zhoug keeps illness away and strengthens the heart. I like that.

Fills 2 small (½ cup) jars

seeds from 8 cardamom pods

¾ teaspoon caraway seeds

4 fat garlic cloves

1 teaspoon flaked sea salt, or to taste

4 green chiles, halved and seeded

1 red Thai chile, halved and seeded

½ tablespoon ground cumin

2 cups cilantro leaves

¼ cup flat-leaf parsley leaves

⅓ cup olive oil, plus more for pouring on top

juice of ½ lemon, or to taste

1 Pound the cardamom seeds, caraway seeds, and garlic with the salt until you have a coarse paste. Put this into a food processor with both types of chiles, the cumin, cilantro, and parsley and, with the motor running, add the olive oil. Add the lemon juice and mix together.

2 Taste to see if you want to add any more salt or lemon juice. Put into sterilized jars (*see* page 11), pour olive oil on top to cover, and seal with vinegar-proof lids. Refrigerate; it will be fine for about two weeks.

tapenade

This—a classic Provençal olive spread—is my standby lazy appetizer. There are other versions (I also do one that contains tuna), but this has a good, pure olive taste. The flavor brings to mind that quote of Gerald Durrell's, that olives taste "as old as cold water." I think they taste the way ink smells. If you use Niçoise olives—they are the best for this—they are impossible to pit with an olive pitter, so just cut the flesh from around the pit. Laborious, but worth it.

Fills 3 small (½ cup) jars

2½ cups pitted good ripe black olives
   (try to get Niçoise)
1 (2oz) can anchovy fillets in oil, drained
1½ tablespoons capers,
   rinsed and patted dry
2 garlic cloves, crushed
1 teaspoon Dijon mustard
black pepper
leaves from 1 sprig of thyme
½ tablespoon chopped flat-leaf parsley
1 tablespoon brandy
about ⅓ cup extra virgin olive oil,
   plus more to cover

1 Put all the ingredients, except the oil, into a mortar and pestle or a food processor (a food processor will be much easier). Process or pound to a coarse paste, adding oil as you work.

2 Scrape it into sterilized jars (*see* page 11), pour a layer of olive oil over the top, and cover. It will keep in the refrigerator for about 10 days.

how to use

This is great as a no-hassle appetizer—serve it with bread, hard-boiled quail or hen eggs, radishes, anchovies, and salami—or take it on picnics. It's also wonderful spread on croûtes, topped with goat cheese, and broiled until golden. I stir dollops of it into pasta or warm new potatoes to toss with roasted tomatoes and steamed green beans, too.

anchoïade

Another classic Provençal "paste." If you like anchovies, it's completely addictive. You can go be traditional and pound everything together with a mortar and pestle, or use a food processor. It's very satisfying to watch the anchovies "melt" into a paste. There are a lot of versions of anchoïade; many include olives, and one startling recipe, which appears in my book *Crazy Water, Pickled Lemons*, even contains dried figs and orange flower water. I have also read of "anchoïade" that is nothing more than anchovies melted in warm olive oil and used as a kind of sauce for baked or broiled fish.

Fills 3 small (½ cup) jars
2 (2oz) cans anchovies in olive oil
3 garlic cloves, chopped
⅓ cup blanched almonds, toasted

2 tablespoons chopped parsley
finely grated zest and juice of ½ unwaxed lemon
freshly ground black pepper
about ¼ cup extra virgin olive oil

1 Drain the anchovies, reserving the oil. Put everything, except the anchovy oil and the olive oil into a blender, or crush it all in a mortar and pestle (especially if you prefer a chunkier mixture). Process until well crushed.

2 Measure the anchovy oil and add enough extra virgin olive oil to make it up to ⅔ cup. Reserve about 3 tablespoons, and slowly add the remaining oil to the anchovy mixture to make a paste.

3 Put the anchoïade into sterilized jars (*see* page 11) and spoon a layer of oil on top. Seal and keep in the refrigerator. It will last for about two weeks.

how to use

This is wonderful on little toasted croûtes with drinks, or serve it with Tapenade (*see* page 93), radishes, hard-boiled eggs, and bread for a very simple appetizer.

under oil

You see them on vacation in Italy, in small shops, presided over by mamas who look as if they made them that morning, and you are almost always seduced into buying them. Foods preserved in oil are really useful for the way we eat now; keep some jars of roasted peppers and grilled eggplants stashed away and you have an instant dinner for yourself, or the basis of an antipasti spread for friends.

However, they're not just convenient: foods steeped in an olive oil bath taste luscious. They are flavored with the oil in which they have soaked, and the oil, in turn, takes on their flavor. Oil softens the texture of many ingredients, too, and storing in oil is a particularly good preserving method for expensive foodstuffs: wild mushrooms, asparagus spears, and artichoke hearts, for example, are all worth treating in this way. It extends their life and recognizes and venerates their specialness.

Oil is not strictly a preservative, but it acts as an air excluder. You probably already use it to protect food without thinking about it … I keep preserved lemons under a layer of oil, and pour a film of it on top of pesto I'm not going to use immediately. The Romans used oil this way—Apicius wrote about it—sometimes mixing it with honey (another ingredient that's hard for air to penetrate). Oil protects the food that it surrounds by preventing deterioration, but only to a degree. The food usually needs to be treated another way first; it might be salted, cooked, marinated, or pickled in vinegar. There's a multitude of recipes, some using mostly oil, others vinegar with a substantial layer of oil on top. These preserves do not have a long shelf life: keep them only for the period of time suggested in each recipe, and always put them in the refrigerator. A layer of oil should always cover the contents of the jar, too.

What kind of oil should you use? It depends on how luxurious you want your preserve to be and whether a distinctly flavored oil suits what you're preserving. I would never use an expensive single estate extra virgin olive oil; these have their own subtleties and nuances and would be wasted if overwhelmed by other flavors. I go for a blended extra virgin olive oil for something like wild mushrooms; the mushrooms will give the oil a new, delicious dimension and the oil itself is powerful enough to stand up to the meaty flavor of the fungi. With roasted peppers, I generally use plain olive oil. I never use bland sunflower oil or peanut oil, however, because one of the side benefits of making this kind of preserve is that you get flavored oil as well as the food in the jar. It's best if the oil has a good flavor of its own to start with, so that way you can use it for salad dressings, braises, and risottos. These are preserves that keep on giving …

labneh in olive oil

Labneh is simply yogurt "cheese" made by draining Greek yogurt in cheesecloth. You can then eat it as it is or flavor it and keep it in olive oil, as in this recipe. Making your own cheese may sound like a lot of work but it is really easy, very versatile, and has a great tangy, fresh flavor.

Fills 1 (1½ quart) jar

FOR THE LABNEH AND OIL
4 cups Greek yogurt
1 teaspoon salt (optional)
olive oil
dried chiles, sprigs of tarragon, thyme, or
    rosemary, black peppercorns, and slivers
    of garlic (all optional)

FOR SPICED LABNEH
2–3 tablespoons ground cayenne, paprika, or ground
    sumac (or a mixture of these)

FOR HERBED LABNEH
handful of chopped tarragon, flat-leaf parsley,
    chives, cilantro, or mint (or a mixture), plus more
    sprigs for the jar (optional)

1 Line a strainer with a double layer of clean cheesecloth and set it over a bowl. Mix the yogurt with the salt, if using (it's entirely a question of taste). Transfer the yogurt to the fabric, then tie it up like a bag and make a loop from which to hang it using kitchen string.

2 If it's cold weather, suspend the bag somewhere cool, such as in the garage, over a bowl. If it's hot, suspend it over a bowl in the refrigerator (tie it to one of the racks). The yogurt will lose excess moisture over the next 24–48 hours, leaving you with a firmer mixture, a little like cream cheese. Help it by giving the bag a squeeze a couple of times a day.

3 Unwrap the labneh; the fabric leaves a lovely pattern. Break it into chunks a little larger than a walnut and gently roll into balls with wet hands. Keep as they are, or sprinkle each with cayenne, paprika, or sumac (or a mixture) for spicy labneh, or roll them in herbs if you want herbed ones.

4 Pour some olive oil—about 1 inch deep—into a sterilized jar (*see* page 11). Start putting the cheeses in, adding more oil as you work so the balls don't stick together. Pour in oil to cover completely and add any other flavorings, sprigs of herbs, or whole spices. Cover, refrigerate, and let sit for two days.

5 Bring the labneh and its oil to room temperature before serving (just scoop out however much you want, with some of the oil, and put in a bowl to warm up). The labneh and oil will keep for two weeks in the refrigerator and you can use the oil for salad dressings or for drizzling over warm vegetables.

how to use

I make labneh so often that I barely notice the effort (a big container of Greek yogurt goes into my shopping basket every week). The reason I do this is that it is so useful: fresh, it can be spread on toasted sourdough and topped with roasted peppers or tomatoes (a good lunch). And the little balls in this recipe make an instant lunch or appetizer (all you need is a few more little Middle Eastern ingredients and flatbread). Its rich, tart creaminess goes well with both starchy and sweet ingredients.

moroccan-flavored olives

You are not curing these—olives have already been cured when you buy them—but there are many ways of giving olives extra flavor and bite. These are hot with Harissa (*see* page 70). Black olives can be treated in the same way, or you can use a mixture of the two.

Fills 1 (1 pint) jar

2¾ cups unpitted green olives in brine
½ teaspoon cumin seeds
½ teaspoon coriander seeds
½ teaspoon black peppercorns
4 teaspoons Harissa (*see* page 70)
½ small red onion, minced
½ roasted red pepper (*see* page 103), minced
1 celery stick, finely diced
2 bay leaves, crumbled
4 garlic cloves, sliced
finely grated zest of ½ organic orange
juice of ½ lemon
1 cup olive oil

1 Drain the olives and rinse under running water. Using a small sharp knife, make a slit in each one; or you can put the olives in a bowl and crush them with the end of a rolling pin or a pestle—the idea is to break the skin so that it can absorb the other flavors.

2 Put the olives in a sterilized jar (*see* page 11). Toast the cumin and coriander seeds in a dry skillet. Put in a mortar with the peppercorns and crush. Add to the olives with the other ingredients. Stir with a sterilized spoon and seal. Refrigerate (always keep a layer of oil on top) and use within one month.

olive verdi condite

Olives that taste of Sicily.

Fills 1 (1 pint) jar

3 cups unpitted green olives in brine
½ small red onion, minced
1 celery stick, with some leaves attached, diced
2 garlic cloves, finely chopped
1 tablespoon dried oregano
1 small dried chile, crumbled
2 tablespoons white wine vinegar
2 tablespoons chopped Oven-dried Tomatoes (*see* page 105)
about 1 cup olive oil

1 Rinse the olives under running water and pat dry. Make slits in the flesh of these with a small sharp knife or, for a milder flavor, leave them as they are. Put the olives in a sterilized jar (*see* page 11). Add everything else except the oil and stir with a sterilized spoon. Pour enough oil over the olives to cover.

2 Keep in the refrigerator (make sure there is always a layer of oil on top) and use within one month.

Note: You need to take these and the olives above out of the refrigerator before serving them, because the oil sets and becomes cloudy when chilled; this isn't harmful, but it isn't nice to eat solid olive oil.

persian marinated olives

Fresh and green tasting, these are unlike most marinated olives, and they make a good contrast to a bowlful of inky black ones. They are especially nice as part of a mezze spread, with barrel-aged feta and pink Middle Eastern Pickled Turnips (*see* page 242)—the colors are fantastic.

Fills 1 (1 pint) jar

5 cups unpitted green olives in brine
1 small unwaxed lemon
4 garlic cloves, sliced
about 6 sprigs of dill, chopped

3 tablespoons chopped flat-leaf parsley
3 tablespoons chopped cilantro
2 green chiles, halved, seeded, and finely sliced
juice of ½ lemon
¼ cup extra virgin olive oil, plus more to seal

1 Make a little slit or cross in each olive (laborious, but it's the only way you can get the flavorings through the flesh). Cut the lemon into thin slices, then cut each slice into four.

2 Mix all the ingredients together, then put into a sterilized jar (*see* page 11), or if you will be eating them soon, just put them into a small bowl. Cover and refrigerate for at least 24 hours to marinate. Keep refrigerated and eat within one month (but cover with more oil to keep them this long).

provençal olives

My favorites. They just taste so much of Provence. Take a bowlful into your yard—or sit by a sunny window—with a glass of rosé, close your eyes, and eat. You should be able to go, for a just a little while, to the countryside around St. Rémy or Arles.

Try to get really good olives to start off with, those moist black ones that almost taste of ink. You don't have to cut the flesh—that just helps the flavors to penetrate—you can skip this step, especially if using small olives (the flesh on small olives can seem "hacked" at if you slash it).

Fills 1 (1 pint) jar

4 cups ripe black, wrinkly "moist" olives
2 garlic cloves, minced
1 dried chile, crumbled
leaves from 2 sprigs of thyme, or chopped
    needles from 1 sprig of rosemary

½ teaspoon fennel seeds, crushed
2 bay leaves, crumbled
8 black peppercorns, lightly crushed
juice and finely grated zest of ½ unwaxed lemon
about 1 cup olive oil

1 Follow the directions for Olive Verdi Condite (*see* page 100), cutting each olive if you want to, then mixing with all the other ingredients. Put into a sterilized jar (*see* page 11) and seal.

2 These will keep in the refrigerator for one month (make sure there's always a layer of oil on top).

roasted peppers in olive oil

These are very easy to do when you have the oven on for other things. Just stick the bell peppers in, follow the (quick) recipe, and you have half the basis for another meal ready to go.

Fills 1 (1 quart) jar
3 red bell peppers
3 yellow bell peppers
2 teaspoons dried oregano (preferably wild)

salt
freshly ground black pepper
½ cup white balsamic vinegar
about 1¾ cups extra virgin olive oil

1 Preheat the oven to 400°F. Put the bell peppers—whole—in a roasting pan and roast in the oven for 25–30 minutes. They should have begun to char, but not too much. You don't roast these as much as you would if you were making soft roasted vegetables to eat instead of to preserve, because if the peppers get too charred they just collapse.

2 Put the peppers in a bag (it makes the skins easier to slip off as the peppers sweat) and let cool. Pull away the stems, tear the peppers in half (this will be easy), and remove the seeds. Carefully peel the skin from the pepper halves, then tear the flesh into broad strips (there are natural breaks in the skin and the peppers will just come apart along these. These natural breaks produce nicer looking strips than using a knife does).

3 Put the peppers straight into a hot, dry sterilized jar (*see* page 11) with the oregano and seasoning and pour on the vinegar and about ¼ cup of the oil. Stir gently with a sterilized spoon to combine. Cover right up to the top with more oil—it's crucial that the peppers are completely immersed— and seal with a vinegar-proof lid. Let to cool, then keep in the refrigerator. Once you've opened the peppers, continue to keep them in the refrigerator, making sure they are always covered with oil, and eat within one month. As always with produce stored in olive oil, take the jar out of the refrigerator to come to room temperature before using. The oil tends to "set" around the vegetables when chilled, so you need it to warm up.

how to use

This is for an antipasti spread (and a good thing to have stashed away for an impromptu meal), or serve the peppers with burrata or mozzarella and a salty anchovy dressing (great with the sweetness of the peppers).

The peppers are also good in a sandwich with mozzarella and avocado, the bread soaked in oil from the jar. Use the oil to make dressings, too, or for sautéing onions; it develops a sweet peppery flavor.

oven-dried tomatoes

These are delicious, but only really worth making if you have a bumper crop of tomatoes from your own plants (or someone else's), or they would be expensive. It's hard to be exact about the quantity you end up with, because it depends on the size and juiciness of your tomatoes.

Fills 1 (¾ quart) jar
4½lb tomatoes
4 teaspoons sea salt
freshly ground black pepper
4 teaspoons superfine or granulated sugar

1 cup white balsamic vinegar
   or white wine vinegar
½ cup olive oil (you may need a little more)

1 Preheat the oven to 212°F. Halve the tomatoes and scoop out the seeds with a spoon. Put the halves, cut side up, on wire racks set in roasting pans (the tomatoes shouldn't touch each other). Sprinkle each with salt, pepper, and sugar. Let sit for 15 minutes so the flavors can penetrate, then turn over.

2 Put the tomatoes in the oven. The length of time it takes to dry them depends on the size and juiciness of the tomatoes, but take a look after three and a half hours to see how they are doing. (I usually find that large plum tomatoes take more than four hours.) They should be shrunken but still a little plump, and without any brittleness.

3 Carefully take them off the rack (they can stick a little, so try not to tear them). Let cool a little, then put them in a wide, shallow bowl, pour the vinegar over, and let sit for an hour.

4 Put the tomatoes with the vinegar into a warm, dry sterilized jar (*see* page 11) and fill up with the olive oil; the tomatoes must be completely covered. Seal with a vinegar-proof lid, refrigerate, and use within within three weeks.

wild mushrooms in olive oil

This makes a precious haul of wild mushrooms go a long way; instead of eating them in all at once, you can stretch them out for a few weeks, and the olive oil seems to emphasize their meatiness. You can use a mixture of mushrooms, but it's best to deal with an assortment of a similar size (remembering that chunky mushrooms will need longer to cook than little chanterelles). You can also use interesting cultivated mushrooms in the mixture, such as shiitake, oyster, and cremini. Do not pick wild mushrooms unless you know they are safe.

Fills 2 (1 pint) jars
2 cups white wine vinegar
2 cups dry white wine
3–4 garlic cloves, sliced
1 teaspoon black peppercorns
1 tablespoon salt

4 sprigs of thyme
1lb assorted fresh wild mushrooms
   (or a mixture of wild and cultivated mushrooms)
2 strips of unwaxed lemon zest
1 bay leaf
about 2 cups extra virgin olive oil

1 Put the vinegar, wine, garlic, peppercorns, salt, and half the thyme into a saucepan and bring to a boil. Reduce the heat and simmer gently for 15 minutes.

2 Carefully clean the mushrooms using paper towelsand a mushroom brush if you have one (it is best not to wash mushrooms in water if you can avoid it, because they are little sponges). Put the mushrooms in the vinegar solution and simmer for about a minute for small delicate mushrooms, longer for larger, denser fleshed ones. Scoop the mushrooms out with a slotted spoon and drain them well (discard the garlic and thyme).

3 Lay the mushrooms on a clean dish towel—spreading them out—and let dry. This is really important because mushrooms absorb a lot of liquid and then eventually release it again. You don't want liquid to leach out of them and dilute the olive oil, because the mushrooms will rot and the olive oil will look murky.

4 When they feel dry, put the mushrooms into warm, sterilized jars (*see* page 11) with the lemon zest, bay, and the remaining thyme. Heat the oil in a saucepan to 165°F and pour it carefully over the mushrooms; they must be completely covered. Put the end of a sterilized spoon in among the mushrooms to move them around and make sure there are no air pockets. Seal with vinegar-proof lids, refrigerate, and refrigerate for two weeks before eating. These will keep well for several weeks.

how to use

Offer these as part of an antipasti spread, or on warm chargrilled bread that you've rubbed with garlic and drizzled with extra virgin olive oil.

goat cheese in olive oil

This is not so much preserving as enhancing flavor, and a very popular way of treating goat cheeses in Provence. The oil softens the cheese and the cheese infuses the oil, making it tangy and slightly sour. You can omit the chile and orange—it depends how much you want extra flavors—and use rosemary instead of thyme, or lemon instead of orange.

Fills 1 (1 pint) jar

9oz goat cheese, either small logs or small individual cheeses

1 tablespoon mixed peppercorns (black, pink, and white), lightly crushed

3 sprigs of thyme

3 garlic cloves, halved lengthwise

1 small dried chile (optional)

2 thin strips of organic orange zest (optional)

1½ cups extra virgin olive oil (not too strong)

1 If you are using logs, cut the cheeses into disks. Put the disks or whole small cheeses into a sterilized jar (*see* page 11) and add all the other ingredients. The oil must completely cover the cheese.

2 Let marinate in the refrigerator for two to three days (and as much as a week) before using. The cheeses will keep, chilled, for two weeks from when you first put them in the jar.

how to use

These make a good appetizer, just sitting in your refrigerator ready to go (although bring to room temperature before serving). Offer with a green salad (dressed with olive or nut oil vinaigrette) and nut bread.

foudjou

There is a range of wonderful French cheese spreads, made at home and kept for spreading on croûtes. This is delicious with a tomato or lentil salad. You need a soft goat cheese without a rind and I like a strongly flavored hard cheese.

Fills 1 (½ pint) jar

5½oz soft goat cheese

3¼oz hard goat cheese

2 teaspoons thyme leaves

1 tablespoon brandy or eau de vie

2 tablespoons extra virgin olive oil (preferably Provençal, but something light and fruity)

pinch of salt

freshly ground black pepper

1 Mash the soft cheese in a bowl. Finely grate the hard cheese and add it with the thyme. Mash with the alcohol and half the oil. Season. Pack into a sterilized jar (*see* page 11) and pour the rest of the oil on top.

2 Seal and refrigerate. Let sit for two weeks before eating, and return to room temperature to serve.

grilled eggplants in olive oil

It might seem strange to store eggplants in oil, but something happens to them when you prepare them like this. The time spent in their olive oil bath makes them even softer and more deeply flavored than when you simply grill or broil and serve them immediately. The other plus is that you have a jar of homemade goodies ready to serve as part of a table of antipasti.

Fills 1 (1 pint) jar
2 eggplants
sea salt
olive oil, for grilling

1 cup extra virgin olive oil, plus more if needed
leaves from 2 sprigs of thyme
2 tablespoons white wine vinegar,
   or white balsamic vinegar

1 Cut the eggplants lengthwise into slices about ¼ inch thick. Layer these in a colander, sprinkling with salt as you work, then let sit for 30 minutes. The salt will draw out some water. Rinse the slices under cold water and pat each one dry.

2 Brush both sides of the slices with olive oil and heat a ridged grill pan until really hot. Grill the eggplants in batches, cooking on both sides, until golden and soft. (You have to adjust the heat all the time; it needs to be hot enough to give the slices a good color, then you need to reduce the heat so that they can cook to softness.) Set aside each batch as you cook them.

3 Put the extra virgin olive oil into a saucepan with the thyme and heat gently for about four minutes. Reduce the heat and add the vinegar and eggplants. Bring everything to a boil, then immediately remove from the heat. Let cool.

4 Take the eggplants from the oil and put them into a sterilized jar (*see* page 11), packing them in tightly. Strain the oil to remove the thyme, and add the oil to the jar. The eggplants need to be completely covered, so add more oil if you need to. Seal with a vinegar-proof lid and, when cool, put the jar in the refrigerator. Keep it refrigerated and make sure the eggplants are always covered with oil. Use within a month.

how to use

Keep the eggplants in the jar and serve them alongside other preserved goods—mushrooms or roasted peppers in oil, or any of the Italian pickles in the Chutneys, Relishes, and Pickles chapter (*see* pages 206 to 267)—plus bread, olives, and Italian cured ham and salami.

spiced feta in olive oil

We don't really value feta cheese as highly as we should. Go and look for it in a Turkish food store and you may find as many as five different types sold from huge containers instead of the prepacked supermarket type. The difference between the two is huge. Some are more creamy, others more salty. And, once it's marinated, it is even more of a revelation. You can vary the spices and herbs, although I nearly always include chile. The olive oil "sets" around the feta because it's being stored in the refrigerator, so let it come to room temperature before serving.

Fills 1 (1 pint) jar
¾ cup olive oil
juice of 2 lemons
leaves from 2 sprigs of thyme
½ teaspoon dried red chili flakes

½ teaspoon fennel seeds
½ teaspoon black peppercorns
½ teaspoon white peppercorns
9oz feta cheese, broken into chunks

1 Mix the olive oil with the lemon juice, thyme, and chili flakes. Put the fennel seeds and both types of peppercorns in a mortar and crush them lightly so that the spices are bruised and partly broken. Add to the oil mixture.

2 Put the feta into a sterilized jar (*see* page 11; make sure it is not piping hot—let it cool to warm or the feta will start to melt), and pour the oil and lemon mixture over it. Seal and keep in the refrigerator. Make sure the feta is always covered with a layer of oil and eat within two weeks.

how to use

It's great to have a jar of this, because you can easily mix it with dips (hummus, taramasalata, spiced carrot puree, baba ghanoush) and bread to make dinner for one, or serve it as part of a spread of mezze.

smoked

We are irrevocably drawn to the smell of wood smoke. Perhaps it's a primeval thing: the smell of something that warms us and, in the past, has cooked our food. It draws you outdoors and makes you want to tramp around in the undergrowth. It's a smell of good times, too: a camp fire smouldering at the end of a summer evening on the beach. I can't resist visiting smokeries wherever I find one. The scent is so intens—imbued in the very walls—that you leave with your hair and clothes redolent with it.

To bring that smell of smoke into your own kitchen or backyard is special. But don't worry: I'm not going to suggest you convert a garbage can into a home smoker and I haven't turned a corner of my garage into one (there'd be nowhere to put the children's bikes). Still, I hope I can encourage you to think it is possible to smoke food at home.

Why bother when you can buy it? Well, hot-smoked food—which is what this chapter is mainly about—is difficult to find, and expensive. It's now easier to find hot-smoked salmon than it was, but can you find hot-smoked scallops or sausages? And just imagine what it's like to eat your own warm, hot-smoked sausages around a camp fire. It's an exciting and satisfying process, too. If you like the thrill of do-it-yourself food production, smoking ranks alongside making your own bresaola.

The emphasis on constructing your own equipment was what turned me off home smoking in the past. I wanted to eat smoked food, but I didn't want to drill holes in some old piece of metal I had lying around the backyard. A lot of home smokers love this, but it may not be safe if there are any residue chemicals. I've been smoking in a gentle way, using an inexpensive stove-top smoker or a regular wok. However, if you like to barbecue and have a covered grill, you can use it for smoking by putting a drip pan filled with water under the meat on the grill, inbetween two piles of briquettes (start with a pile of 50 briquettes in the center, and when they turn to gray ash, divide them into two piles). Keep the grill vents open but close the lid, and add another ten briquettes every hour to keep the temperature stable.

Smoke is a complicated substance, made up of more than two hundred components, some of which inhibit the growth of microbes, while others retard the oxidization of fat. This is what makes it a preservative. However, we don't need to smoke food to preserve it anymore. We do it for the flavor it imparts ... that of smoldering wood.

You can cold smoke or hot smoke food. Cold smoking produces food that can be eaten raw (such as smoked cheese) or that needs additional cooking, such as smoked haddock. The food is smoked for a long period at a low temperature. It takes attention and experience to do it well and safely, and specialty equipment.

Serious smokers often cold smoke meat and fish before hot smoking them to impart a stronger smoky flavor, but it isn't essential. Hot smoking is an easier place for the home smoker to start. It can produce food that is fully cooked and easier to store. However, if you are hot smoking with a wok or stove-top smoker, they won't get hot enough to fully cook the food. Use them to smoke the food for flavor, then finish it off in the oven or under a broiler to complete the cooking process—you'll also have the pleasure of a golden, crispy skin.

Fish for preserving is smoked at 90°F for the first two hours, then at 150°F for four to eight hours, depending on the thickness of the fish, with ½ inch thick pieces needing four hours, 1 inch pieces needing six hours, and 1½ inch pieces requiring eight hours. Smoke the fish until an internal temperature of 150°F is reached on a food thermometer for 30 minutes (but 160°F would be even better), or cook the fish in the oven at 160°F for 30 minutes after smoking—you'll need to do this if using a wok or stove-top smoker. All poultry dishes require an internal temperature of 165°F to be safe; whole pieces and cuts of meat (beef, pork, and lamb) need an internal temperature of 145°F; and ground meats should be smoked until an internal temperature of 160°F is reached on a food thermometer. The temperature of the smoker or grill should stay between 225 and 300°F.

Salting is the first stage in the smoking process. Smoking is partly about drying, and salting starts this off. Nearly all foods for smoking are salted before being smoked, either in a brine (salt solution) or with a coating of dry salt. (The exceptions are cheese and food that has already been processed.) Fish and meat are firmer after salting and well-seasoned, too.

For hot smoking, I use a basic brine made up with ½ cup of non-iodized salt and 4 teaspoons of sugar in 4 cups of water. This is a 40 percent brine and lower than many other cookbooks suggest. Because you are smoking for flavor instead of to extend a food's keeping qualities, you can hot smoke after a light brining. (The normal recommendation for hot smoking is one part salt to seven parts water, or ½ cup salt to 3½ cups water.) You will get to know yourself, the more you experiment with smoke, what you like best and what works for you. Experienced smokers dry-salt salmon for hot smoking, instead of brining it, because they think it gives a better result.

I always add some sugar, although you can vary the quantity or use maple syrup or honey instead. This is where you start the flavoring—the part that gives your home-smoked food its own special stamp—so herbs and spices can be added now, too.

Once the food has been salted, rinse it briefly and put it in the refrigerator to dry. How long you leave your meat or fish like this before smoking will affect both its saltiness and how well the smoke flavors the flesh. You'll find that the food develops a slightly tacky coating—a "pellicle"—which attracts smoke.

If you are smoking in a wok, simply put 1 tablespoon of wood sawdust in the bottom. Line the wok with aluminum foil and put a metal rack inside. Put the food to be smoked onto the rack, leaving space in between if you are cooking several pieces so that the smoke can circulate. Cover tightly with a lid (if it doesn't sit tightly, you may have to put a band of scrunched-up foil around where the wok and lid meet), and put on your extractor fan. Set the wok over medium heat. Within a couple of minutes you will smell the smoke and see the first wisps. When this happens, reduce the heat to low and let the food to hot smoke. Check after the allotted time and either continue to smoke if the food isn't cooked through (check with a food thermometer—see above for temperatures—inserting the thermometer into the thickest part of the meat, away from any bones), or finish the cooking by roasting or broiling.

Food is always smoked over a hardwood, the most common examples being oak, hickory, and maple (small amounts of juniper wood or rosemary can be added in the later stages of smoking for aroma and flavor). The wood shouldn't have been treated with chemicals or in any other way, and do not use softwoods. You don't need to use wood chips (they are often expensive), I use sawdust or shavings from a local wood supplier.

Actually, you don't need to smoke over wood at all, because you can do it over tea, rice, and sugar. This takes a little longer to "catch" than wood (about five to seven minutes as opposed to three to four). Try it with teas that have smoky flavors, such as lapsang souchong or Earl Grey. Use 1⅔ cups of tea leaves, ¼ cup of superfine sugar, firmly packed ¼ cup of light or dark brown sugar, and ½ cup of raw rice. Mix these together and put in the bottom of a wok or smoker just as you would with wood. Smoke as normal, starting over medium heat, then reducing it to low once you can smell the smoke.

Hot-smoked food can be eaten immediately (faced with a warm hot-smoked sausage, I defy anyone to wait) or refrigerated for the specified time. Or if you have used a grill and cooked it completely by hot smoking, you can store it in the freezer. Hot-smoked food can be eaten at room temperature, or gently reheated, wrapped in aluminum foil, in a low oven.

It's hard to be completely specific about smoking times (that thermometer will tell you) and even about flavor, so the recipes in this chapter are simply guides. You will get to know, the more you do, how long it takes for a certain thickness of fish to be hot smoked, whether a piece of chicken will be too salty if you leave it for four hours instead of two after brining,

whether it is better to brush a glaze on halfway through the smoking time or just before smoking starts. The permutations for flavor are endless: do you prefer dill or fennel with the hot-smoked trout, star anise or five spice in your soy-smoked salmon? This is all in your hands. Once you have the basics, you can go on your own adventures.

Try your hand at smoking food and you won't look back. It's a real thrill to be able to hot smoke six fillets of salmon and have them looking burnished and beautiful, ready to serve with roasted beets and horseradish sauce as soon as your friends arrive for dinner. Or to have home-smoked chicken in the refrigerator that you can use to rustle up a salad. (If you like the flavor, you'll find it is cheaper in the long run to buy a little stove-top smoker and do it yourself than to buy hot-smoked food.)

hot-smoked mackerel with spanish flavors

This is a stunning looking dish—rust-hued and burnished—that will have you looking at smoked mackerel in a completely different way. I love the double layer of smokiness, one from the wood and the other from the smoked paprika. You can use a smoker, grill, or wok.

Serves 2

FOR THE BRINE
½ cup sea salt
½ cup firmly packed light brown sugar
3 garlic cloves, crushed
10 peppercorns, bruised
2 teaspoons smoked paprika
6 sprigs of thyme
2 bay leaves

FOR THE FISH
2 mackerel, cleaned and gutted
½ tablespoon olive oil
1 teaspoon smoked paprika
sea salt
plenty of ground black pepper
4 sprigs of thyme
1½–2 tablespoons oak sawdust

1 Put all the brine ingredients into a saucepan with 4 cups of boiling water and stir to help the salt and sugar dissolve. Let cool completely.

2 Wash your mackerel, making sure that you get rid of any signs of blood inside. Make three slashes in the flesh of the fish on each side. Put the mackerel in a nonreactive container and pour the brine over it—the fish must be completely covered—then refrigerate for an hour. Remove from the brine, rinse the fish briefly, then put onto a clean, dry plate and refrigerate to dry out for about three hours.

3 Mix together the olive oil, smoked paprika, salt, and pepper. Rub this mixture all over the mackerel, inside and out. Put in the refrigerator and let marinate for another three hours. If you have somewhere cold where you can hang the fish to dry (a garage safe from cats in the colder months, for example), thread string through the fish and hang them there instead.

4 Remove the fish from the refrigerator and divide the thyme among the cavities. Put the sawdust into a wok. Set a metal rack over that, big enough to take the mackerel. (Try a round cake rack, or improvise with metal skewers.) Arrange the fish on it, leaving room for smoke to circulate around. Put the lid on; it should fit tightly. If it doesn't, make a seal using aluminum foil. Set over moderate heat. Once the first wisps of smoke appear, reduce the heat and smoke for 15 minutes. Check the fish is cooked with a food thermometer and transfer to an oven, at 160°F, to finish cooking if necessary.

5 Let sit in the wok for another 15 minutes, then cover and refrigerate; it tastes better after 12 hours, but eat it within 24 hours. You can eat it warm from the wok, but the flavor will be more delicate.

how to use

Eat with caper berries, bread, and a tomato salad, or with warm waxy potatoes tossed with finely chopped shallots and a saffron vinaigrette.

hot oak-smoked salmon

This is a one of the most straightforward recipes for hot smoking. There are no added flavorings, just salt, sugar, and smoke.

Serves 4
about 3 tablespoons fine sea salt
2 tablespoons packed light brown sugar

4 salmon fillets of an even medium thickness
  (about 5½oz each)
1 tablespoon oak sawdust or shavings

1 Mix the salt with the sugar and sprinkle it evenly on the fish fillets. Refrigerate for 10 minutes (thick steaks can take up to 30 minutes). Rinse the fish under running water, then pat dry and return to the refrigerator for three hours so the salt can permeate better.

2 Put the sawdust or shavings in the bottom of a smoker (or grill, *see* page 113) and insert the drip pan (the little pan underneath the rack that comes with the smoker). Line the drip pan with aluminum foil (it makes for easier cleaning, you can just throw the foil away). Put the wire rack on top, arrange the fish on the rack (leaving room around each fillet), then slide the lid on. (Use a wok as described on page 114 if you don't have a smoker or grill.)

3 Set the smoker over medium heat. As soon as wisps of smoke start to appear, or you can smell the smoke, reduce the heat to low and smoke the fillets for about 20 minutes.

4 Turn the heat off and wait until you can't see any more smoky wisps, then open the smoker and check that the fish is cooked through with a food thermometer. It should be opaque and not at all glassy looking. If it isn't cooked through, you can put the heat on again or you can finish the fish off by steaming. You can eat this immediately or wrap it in plastic wrap and, once cool, refrigerate for up to two days. If you want to serve it later and have it hot, you can reheat it, wrapped in foil, in a medium oven.

how to use

I usually go the Scandi route with this, serving with roasted beets (a mixture of crimson and golden beets if you can get them) drizzled with buttermilk, and warm new potatoes tossed with dill. Swedes also cook hot-smoked salmon in a gratin with cream and spinach (cook the spinach and squeeze out the moisture, then chop and season).

maple hot-smoked salmon

This is delicious, flaked, on top of corn cakes (add a dollop of crème fraîche), or tossed into a salad of wild and brown rice, sliced mango, and green beans.

Serves 4

3 tablespoons sea salt flakes
3 tablespoons packed light brown sugar
4 fillets of salmon, skin on (thickish
   fillets are best; about 5½–6oz each)

FOR THE MARINADE/GLAZE

½ cup bourbon
½ cup dark maple syrup
1 teaspoon Dijon mustard
2 tablespoons light brown sugar
good grinding of black pepper

1 Prepare the salmon in salt and sugar as on page 119, then put in the refrigerator for two hours.

2 Put all the marinade ingredients in a small saucepan and heat until the sugar dissolves. Simmer until you have about ¾ cup left. Let cool. Make four small cuts in the sides of each fillet, then put them into a nonreactive dish and pour three-quarters of the marinade over the fish. Turn the fillets until they are completely coated in the marinade and refrigerate for another couple of hours.

3 Prepare a wok or stove-top smoker (*see* page 114 or 119) and put the fish on the rack. Smoke for 20 minutes; glaze halfway through and repeat three minutes before the end of cooking.

4 Check that the salmon is cooking, using a food thermometer, and transfer to an oven, at 160°F, if necessary, then cool, wrap in aluminum foil, and refrigerate for up to two days. (I prefer it cold.) Remove from the refrigerator before you serve it so it's not too cold.

also try

HONEY, SOY, AND FIVE-SPICE HOT SMOKED SALMON

The kind of sweet-savory dish I love, the smoke just makes it even better. Cold, this salmon makes a wonderful salad (try it instead of chicken in the salad on page 124).

Lay 4 thickish salmon fillets on a plate and prepare with salt and sugar as on page 119. Rinse the fish and put back on a plate. Refrigerate for two hours. To make the marinade, put ¼ cup soy sauce, ⅓ cup honey, 3 tablespoons packed light brown sugar, 1 garlic clove, minced, a ¾ inch square of fresh ginger root, sliced, ¼ teaspoon five spice seasoning, and a good grinding of black pepper in a saucepan and bring to a boil. Reduce the heat and simmer until reduced by about one-third, then let cool. Strain to remove the ginger. Cut and marinate the fish as above. Prepare the smoker as on page 114 or 119, and smoke the fish for 20 minutes. After 10 minutes, brush on more marinade. After 20 minutes, check to see if the salmon is cooked through (see above). Serve warm (brushed with some reserved marinade, if you prefer) with rice and stir-fried bok choy. Serves 4.

hot-smoked scallops

I used to have smoked scallops sent to me every Christmas by the Hebridean Smokehouse in Scotland. Theirs are cold smoked, so have a stronger smoky flavor than these, but hot smoked are a delicious alternative and you have the advantage of eating them warm. You can smoke fat shrimp in exactly the same way.

Serves 6
18 fat, very fresh, scallops

2 tablespoons sea salt flakes
1½ tablespoons oak sawdust

1 Remove the corals—they seem to shrivel and don't taste that great when hot smoked—and feel around the side of each scallop for the muscle. Remove it, because it toughens during cooking.

2 Sprinkle salt over the scallops on both sides and let them sit for 30 minutes. Rinse, pat dry, put onto a clean plate, and refrigerate. Let dry for one hour.

3 Get your wok or stove-top smoker ready (*see* page 114 or 119). Lay the scallops on the rack. Cook for 12 minutes on low heat, then check; some will be cooked, others might need another two minutes, but you don't want them to go too far. The scallops should be *just* cooked through. Serve immediately with black pepper and a squeeze of lemon.

how to use

Apart from eating just with lemon juice, you can make a great salad of smoked scallops and crisp, warm bacon pieces, tossing them with vinaigrette and lentils or mâche. Also try putting them on lightly dressed salad greens and sliced new potatoes, pouring hot melted butter over them and scattering with fresh grated horseradish. They're good, too, warm with sautéed wild mushrooms and a puree of Jerusalem artichokes, or with the same puree and chunks of fried chorizo.

and also

HOT-SMOKED SAUSAGES

Sausages require no preparation—you shouldn't even prick them—you just need to prepare your grill as a smoker. They make the best barbecue food: remove from the smoker, put in warm rolls, and add condiments.

Buy good-quality, interesting link sausages. Those with smoked paprika make a Spanish treat with sweet roasted tomatoes, while thin Middle Eastern lamb sausages are good in flatbread with lettuce and hot sauce.

Put your sausages on the rack, leaving room for smoke to circulate around. Smoke for 20 minutes (thin sausages take only 15), then see if they are cooked. If not, smoke for another four minutes. Slice them warm and toss with new potatoes, baby spinach leaves, and a mustard dressing, or serve with lentils and Dijon.

wok-smoked trout with dill

Trout is not my favorite fish—I always think it tastes muddy—but smoking really transforms it. The skin develops a wonderful golden-bronze hue.

Serves 2

FOR THE BRINE

½ cup sea salt

½ cup firmly packed light brown sugar

1 tablespoon caraway seeds, lightly crushed

handful of dill, coarsely chopped

FOR THE TROUT

2 small whole trout, cleaned and gutted

about 6 sprigs of dill

1 tablespoon oak sawdust

1 Put all the brine ingredients into a saucepan with 4 cups of boiling water and stir to help the salt and sugar dissolve. Let cool completely.

2 Wash the trout really well, getting rid of any signs of blood inside. You can make three slashes in the flesh on each side if you want the brine to penetrate more. Put into a nonreactive container and pour the brine over them; the fish must be completely covered. Refrigerate for one hour.

3 Rinse the fish, then put onto a clean, dry plate and refrigerate to dry out for about three hours. If you have somewhere cold you can hang the fish to dry (a garage, safe from cats, is good in colder months), then thread string through the fish and hang them there instead.

4 Put sprigs of dill inside each fish. Prepare a wok (*see* page 114) and put the sawdust in the bottom.

5 Set a rack into the wok, big enough to take the trout. If you don't have a rack, improvise with metal skewers. Arrange the fish on it, leaving room for smoke to circulate around and put the lid on. It should fit tightly, if it doesn't, make a seal using aluminum foil. Set over moderate heat. Once the first wisps of smoke appear, reduce the heat and smoke for 15 minutes. Check the fish is cooked through and transfer to an oven, at 160°F, if it isn't. Eat within 24 hours.

how to use

Eat hot or cold with warm new potatoes tossed with buttermilk, scallions, and fried bacon pieces, or new potatoes and fava beans in a sweet dill dressing. It's also great in a risotto with leeks.

also try

SUGAR-GLAZED SMOKED TROUT

This adds a wonderful deep bronze color and a sweet smoky flavor. Mix ¼ cup firmly packed light brown sugar with ¼ cup of cider vinegar and stir until the sugar dissolves. Prepare the trout as above (omit the dill) then brush the marinade over the fish after brining, just before you smoke it. Serves 2.

oak-smoked chicken, mango, and cilantro salad with ginger dressing

For years, this was one of my favorite salads, but I wasn't happy with the sliced smoked chicken available, and buying a half or whole smoked chicken was expensive. Smoking your own chicken breasts means you can have it whenever you want.

Serves 4

FOR THE BRINE

3 tablespoons sea salt

¼–⅓ cup honey

½ tablespoon bruised black peppercorns

FOR THE CHICKEN

3 chicken breasts (with or without skin)

1 tablespoon oak sawdust or chips

FOR THE DRESSING

1½ tablespoons rice vinegar

juice of 1 lime, plus more if needed

¼ cup peanut oil

1 globe of preserved ginger, finely chopped

3 tablespoons ginger syrup (from the preserved ginger jar)

2 garlic cloves, very finely chopped

2 red chiles, halved, seeded, and shredded

about ¾ teaspoon Thai fish sauce, or to taste

FOR THE SALAD

1 large just-ripe mango

5½ cups salad greens (I like watercress and baby spinach)

1 cup cilantro leaves

1 To make the brine, simply put all the ingredients into a saucepan with 4 cups of boiling water and stir to help the salt dissolve. Let cool completely.

2 Put the chicken breasts in a shallow nonreactive dish and pierce each a few times with a sharp knife. Pour the cool brine over them and let sit for three hours in the refrigerator.

3 Remove the chicken from the brine and rinse briefly. Return it to the refrigerator for four to eight hours so the salt can permeate better. (Don't leave it any longer or the breasts will be too salty.)

4 Prepare a wok or stove-top smoker (*see* page 114 or 119). Put the sawdust in the bottom. Set a rack in it, big enough to take the chicken. Arrange the chicken on it, making sure there is room for smoke to circulate. Set over medium heat. Once the first wisps appear, reduce the heat and smoke for 30 minutes. Check to see if the chicken is cooked by using a food thermometer. If it isn't, transfer to a 375°F oven until cooked through. Let cool, or serve it warm. Cut each breast into slices. (If preparing this in advance, eat it within two days.)

5 Whisk together everything for the dressing and taste for a balance of hot, sour, sweet, and slightly salty. Peel the mango and cut the cheeks from the pit. Cut each half in slices, horizontally, about the thickness of a penny. If you can do it neatly, cut the remaining mango (still clinging to the pit) into neat slices. If not—sometimes they are too ripe—use the remaining flesh in a smoothie.

6 Toss together the salad greens, cilantro, mango, chicken, and dressing very lightly (you don't want to break up the mango), or plate the various ingredients then drizzle the dressing over them.

hot-smoked duck breasts

The first smoked duck I tasted was in a salad with mâche, green beans, hazelnuts, and a nut oil dressing. I loved it. After that, I spent a fortune over the years, buying smoked duck whenever I saw it. Once I even purchased an entire smoked duck in Harrods (a British store that can be expensive) for a birthday treat. I wish I had known then about the joys of home smoking. This is easy and tastes absolutley sublime. You can serve it hot, or let it get cold and use it in that salad.

Makes 2 breasts

FOR THE CURE
½ cup sea salt flakes
⅔ cup firmly packed light brown sugar
2 teaspoons black peppercorns
4 bay leaves, crushed

FOR THE DUCK
2 large duck breasts
2 tablespoons oak sawdust or chips

1 Mix together all the ingredients for the cure. Lay half of it in a shallow, nonreactive dish and put the duck on top, skin side down. Cover with the rest of the cure mix and refrigerate for two hours.

2 Rinse the duck breasts briefly and pat them dry with paper towels. Set them on a plate and refrigerate for eight hours to dry out. You'll find the flesh feels slightly firmer and a bit tacky.

3 Prepare the wok or stove-top smoker (*see* page 114 or 119) with the oak sawdust, lay the duck on the rack, and smoke over low heat for 20 minutes. The breasts should be golden outside but tenderly pink—not raw—in the middle. Check with a food thermometer in the meaty part, but not near the bone. If they're not ready, transfer to a 375°F oven until cooked through.

4 Let the duck rest for about 10 minutes before eating (see the slightly different version below if you want to serve them hot with a crispy skin), or wrap them in aluminum foil once they are cool and refrigerate for up to two days, returning to room temperature before you serve them.

if you want to serve them hot …

… it looks better if you color the skin. Salt and dry as above, then make three slashes in the fat. Heat a skillet until hot. Put the duck in, fat side down. Cook for two minutes, until golden. Hot smoke as above.

also try

Hot-smoke duck with the flavorings used for Smoked Maple and Bourbon Chicken (*see* right). Apply the glaze 10 minutes into cooking, then five minutes before the end. Brush more on when it is cooked.

how to use

Make one of my favorite salads: slice the duck and toss with watercress or spinach, walnuts, and nut oil vinaigrette. You can add grilled figs (in which case use Sweet Fig Vinegar, *see* page 90, in the vinaigrette).

smoked maple and bourbon chicken

Maple and bourbon is a great combination. This is excellent food for a Halloween dinner, and also for sultry late-summer nights. You can, if you want a glossy, crispy skin and a golden color, finish this off in the oven instead of cooking it completely in the smoker.

Serves 6

FOR THE BRINE

1¼ cups maple syrup
⅔ cup sea salt
½ cup firmly packed light brown sugar
1 cup bourbon
4 sprigs of thyme
1 tablespoon allspice berries

FOR THE CHICKEN

1 chicken, about 4lb

FOR THE GLAZE

⅔ cup maple syrup
⅔ cup bourbon
¼ cup firmly packed dark brown sugar
½ teaspoon dried red chili flakes or cayenne pepper, or to taste (optional)

1 To make the brine, put 8½ cups of boiling water into a large saucepan and add all the ingredients. Heat gently, stirring to help the salt and sugar dissolve, then let sit until cold. Pierce the chicken all over with a sharp knife. Add 8½ cups of cold water to the brine. If there is room to immerse the chicken in the saucepan, do that, or transfer the brine to a scrupulously clean bucket or large plastic container and immerse the chicken in it. Weigh it down with a plate so it is completely covered. Refrigerate (I take the vegetable bins out and put the chicken there) and let sit for 24 hours.

2 Lift the chicken out of the brine and shake off the excess liquid. Carefully dry with paper towels, put it on a plate, and refrigerate to dry for 12 hours.

3 To make the glaze, just mix together the ingredients in a saucepan. Bring to a boil, stirring to help the sugar dissolve. Reduce the heat and simmer until you have a syrup. You should end up with about 1 cup. Let cool; this is important because it will thicken. If you try to apply the glaze when it's hot, it will run off the top of the chicken.

4 Prepare a wok or a stove-top smoker (*see* page 114 or 119). With either, you won't have a lid that will cover the chicken, so put the chicken on the rack and use a double layer of aluminum foil to cover, leaving room for air to circulate. Make a seal all the way around the edges so smoke doesn't escape. Alternatively, use a grill (*see* page 113).

5 Set over medium heat and wait until it starts to smoke. Reduce the heat to low and cook for about 2¼–2½ hours, brushing with the glaze about three times during this time.

6 You can either cook the chicken completely over smoke, or finish it off in the oven to give it a crispy skin. To do this, once the bird has smoked for two hours, cook in a preheated oven at 375°F for 15–30 minutes, or until the glaze is glossy and dark and the chicken cooked. It is cooked when the juices that run from between the thigh and the body are clear, with no trace of pink, but it is best to use a food thermometer to check. If the glaze is getting too dark, cover the bird with foil. Serve hot (it's wonderful with baked potatoes or rice and salad), or let cool and eat cold, within two days.

syrups, alcohols, fruits, and spoon sweets

This chapter is a veritable treasure trove of sinful pleasures. There is nothing here that is remotely necessary. Some of these preserves even cost money (on top of your cheap or free bumper crop of fruit), in the form of booze. But when you produce Greek sour cherry syrup for pouring over ice cream, ice-cold rhubarb schnapps to finish an eastern European supper, or homemade lemonade for your children, you'll glow with the pleasure that offering something truly special bestows.

And once you have put a ripe pear into a big glass jar with half a nutmeg, a furl of citrus zest, and a rush of crystal-clear vodka, you will want to do it again. To watch that pear turn the clear liquor a deep gold, and to see the way the liquid magnifies and contorts the shape of the fruit, is quietly thrilling. You have captured a true thing of beauty. And what colors you get when making liqueurs: red currants produce the kind of bright clear red a child likes, plums a crimson that makes you think of archbishops, oranges—if you can get a good batch—a warm amber that's like the end of a hot day.

As I was growing up, I would hear snippets about alcohols that were made in people's homes: dandelion wine, haw liqueur, and, as I'm from Ireland, moonshine or hooch. I thought they sounded magical. As an adult, I can say "no" to homemade wine and I've never been interested in home brewing, but I love homemade liqueurs. In France, some of them are called *vins de fenêtre*, because bottles and jars sit on windowsills, developing in the heat. And they're not just made with fruit, but with green walnuts, apricot kernels, peach leaves, lavender, herbs, and spices. Some aren't sweetened at all but are simply—as with the thyme liqueur *riquiqui*—herb-infused booze.

Similar drinks are made in Russia, eastern Europe, and Scandinavia. It's part of the tradition—even more important in places that are cold—of capturing the flavor of summer to enjoy later in the year. The names and flavorings vary. Scandinavians add ingredients to vodka—dill, horseradish, mint, ginger, coriander, cinnamon—to make what they call snapps. These, generally, aren't sweetened, although fruit may be used to make snapps that are delicately fruity. (Blueberries are a favorite.)

Scandinavians also have acquavit (often made with a potato-based liquor) that is heavily flavored with spices (even wormwood) and can be aged in oak casks. You can make a very good mock acquavit at home (commercial ones are expensive) by adding a mixture of caraway, dill, fennel, and coriander seeds (2 tablespoons all together) plus 1 star anise and a piece of cinnamon stick to a 1 liter bottle (4 cups) of vodka. Let sit for three weeks. Taste to check if it's as flavored as you would like, strain, and rebottle.

In Russia, sweet flavored vodkas are made with peach and apricot pits, raspberries, plums, cherries, rose petals, and spices (Elena Molokhovets in her *Classic Russian Cooking* distinguishes between "sweet vodkas or ratafias" and "very sweet vodkas, like liqueurs"). But unsweetened vodkas flavored with lemon, caraway, anise, pepper, tea, juniper, and saffron (very similar to the snapps of Scandinavia) are more popular. These vodkas are an important feature of the zakuski table (a spread of Russian "mezze" type dishes, read about it on page 229), so it's worth making some if you are planning this kind of feast. In Ivan Bunin's short story, *Ida*, the narrator writes about lunching at Christmas in the deserted restaurant of the Grand Moscow Hotel. It's a gray day, but the tables are spread with "stiff, snow-white tablecloths," which are soon covered with an array of different colored liquors, salmon, sturgeon, shellfish on shaved ice, and a block of black caviar, a very luxurious zakuski spread. "We began," he writes, with a certain anticipation, "with pepper vodka …"

In Poland and parts of the former Soviet Union, sweet, spicy vodkas are more popular (there's a wonderful recipe for Gdansk Vodka in this chapter, *see* page 155). Some of these are meant to be drunk hot instead of cold. Ukrainian honey and spice vodka is flavored with dried fruits—which are actually baked in the vodka—before the liquor is strained off and served warm.

In Britain, we have sloe and damson gin, drinks of which we should be very proud, and we've had ratafias (there's a recipe for Quince Ratafia on page 144) since they came from France in the 17th century. A ratafia is simply a fruit liqueur based on brandy, and they're a great thing to make at home—very rich tasting—but because brandy is now more expensive than when they first became fashionable, cost seems to make them prohibitive. Or perhaps people just don't know about them.

We're better at fruit syrups than boozy tipples (and seem to love them, about 38 million bottles of a popular brand of black currant syrup are sold every year). There is real satisfaction in making these, too—watching brightly colored liquids flow down the insides of bottles is something children love—and they're economical. However, if you don't want the hassle of dealing with a water bath (*see* pages 268–269 for complete instructions), they're a seasonal treat.

Canning fruits in alcohol—vodka, eau de vie, brandy, bourbon—is simple, because the alcohol acts as a preservative. With this little effort, you can line your cupboards with jars of indulgence. Cherries, peaches, apricots, plums, and prunes (you can use both fresh and dried fruits) are all easy to plump up with either brandy, vodka, eau de vie, or rum and keep as a secret stash.

The only warning I give is that I have tended to hoard my stash of liqueurs and fruits in alcohol. They do last a long time (a jar of prunes in brandy sat for so many years that the syrup surrounding them was as thick and dark as molasses), but you are supposed to consume them, or give them away. There is no point in capturing flavor by suspending it in alcohol and then thinking there is no occasion special enough to warrant digging in. These foods are for treats on rainy nights in March or wintry Sunday lunches with friends. That's when you want apricots in muscat and cherries in eau de vie. So open the jars and enjoy.

crème de cassis

Crème de cassis is the liqueur I use the most. It is very satisfying—and easy—to make your own. I think brandy is better than gin, but use what you have (or can afford). You can make crème de mûre (with blackberries) and crème de framboise (with raspberries) in the same way.

Fills 1 (1½ pint) bottle
4½ cups black currants,
   stems removed

2½ cups brandy or gin
about 1⅓ cups superfine or granulated sugar

1 Put the black currants into a large jar with a lid. Crush the berries (I use a flat-ended rolling pin to do this, as if muddling ingredients for a cocktail). Pour the alcohol over them and cover tightly. Let sit in a cool, dark place for two months.

2 Strain the liquor through a nylon strainer into a liquid measuring cup. For every 2½ cups of liquid, add scant 1 cup of sugar. Mix well, cover, and let sit for two days, stirring occasionally to dissolve the sugar.

3 Line a nylon strainer with cheesecloth and strain into a bottle. Seal and let sit for six months before using. This keeps for a year.

plum and almond hooch

I used to luxuriate in *The Elusive Truffle,* a book by Mirabel Osler about her journey eating around France. The chapter on Alsace was called "Ice-cold Mirabelle." She is referring to the eau de vie you get there, but the boozy liquor from this recipe (when I make it with mirabelles) is *my* mirabelle. And it is wonderful ice cold. You can use vodka instead of rum.

Fills 1 (1 quart) jar
8 small firm-but-ripe plums, greengages,
   or mirabelles (1lb)

1 cup granulated sugar
¼ cup blanched almonds
1 cup rum

1 Wash the plums, prick each four times with a sharp knife, and put into a sterilized jar (*see* page 11), sprinkling generously with sugar and almonds as you work. Pack tightly and cover with a thick layer of sugar, then pour in the rum. Weigh the fruit down with a small saucer, so it stays under the alcohol.

2 Cover with a tight-fitting lid and let sit in a cool, dark place for six months (or longer) before using, shaking every so often. Check to make sure the alcohol is completely covering the fruit and add more if you need. The hooch will be good for more than a year.

how to use

You get delicious plums to eat—heat them with more sugar—and a few glasses of liqueur. The fruit is wonderful with almond ice cream.

confiture de vieux garçon

This is also known as *rumtopf* in Germany, and both France and Germany lay claim to it. I love the French name. A middle-age man without a partner is called a *vieux garçon* in France and presumably, as he has no wife, this is the best thing he can make to provide himself with dessert over the winter. It's a great lazy way to preserve fruit, because it's simply layered up with sugar and alcohol (you can use rum, brandy, or kirsch). Traditionally, you add fruits to the jar as they come into season over the summer, but you can make it all at once, if you prefer. It's heaven eaten on a cold November day, or at Christmas.

You need to use fruit that is just ripe and in perfect condition. The only fruits that aren't suitable are rhubarb (it gets bitter), normal gooseberries (although you can use the less-tart eating types), and melon (melon is a "wet" fruit, so it dilutes the alcohol, thereby increasing the possibility of fermentation or mold). Citrus fruits don't work well either. Berries turn soft but I don't mind that (although I think it's better without strawberries).

You are supposed to layer the fruit in a glazed stone or earthenware jar, but I prefer to use a glass jar so I can see the fruit. Just make sure to keep it somewhere cool and dark.

Fills 1 (2½ quart) jar
1lb prepared fruit

1¼ cups superfine or granulated sugar
rum, brandy, or kirsch, to cover

1 Wash the fruit and gently dry it. Strawberries should be hulled; raspberries and all currants and grapes need to be removed from their stems. Halve, pit, and slice (or quarter) fruits with pits.

2 Spread a layer of fruit on a large tray and sprinkle with the sugar, turning it over so that every part of it is covered. Let sit for about an hour.

3 Transfer the sugary fruit to a wide-necked jar and cover completely with alcohol. Put a saucer on top to help keep the fruit submerged, then cover the neck of the jar with plastic wrap and, finally, a lid. Store in a cool, dry place until you are ready to add the next layer of fruit and never stir the mixture until the very end, when you want to serve it.

4 As more fruit becomes available, mix it with half its weight in sugar and go through the whole process again, replacing the saucer with a clean one and using fresh plastic wrap. When you have added the last batch of fruit (you can add halved figs and peeled pear slices in early fall), fill up with more alcohol, cover, and label. Let sit for at least a month. Fill up again with more alcohol if you notice that it needs it (the fruit must be completely covered). Old boy's jam will keep for a year.

how to use

Don't do anything fancy—just serve in bowls or glasses or, as the French do, coffee cups, after a meal. I like crème fraîche with it, too. The liquor makes a wonderful drink, chilled, or add it to sparkling wine.

home-steeped southern succour

Americans are very good at making simple luxuries that are deeply comforting. This does, indeed, provide succour. It's as good on a stormy winter's night as at the height of summer.

Fills 1 (1 quart) bottle
4 peaches, halved
juice and finely grated zest of 1 orange

3 cups bourbon
¾ cup granulated sugar

1 Put the peaches—with pits—into a sterilized jar (*see* page 11) and add the orange juice and zest. Pour in the bourbon, using a saucer to keep the peaches under the alcohol. Let sit for six weeks.

2 Gently heat the sugar with ⅓ cup of water, stirring to help the sugar dissolve. Let cool. Strain off the liquor and add the sugar syrup. Shake well, then put into a clean bottle and seal. Let sit for at least two weeks before drinking. At room temperature, it lasts almost indefinitely.

how to use

Drink at room temperature, undiluted, with ice, or club water. It's great over ice cream, or add to whipped cream to serve with poached peaches.

peaches in brandy

You can halve the peaches for this (they take up less room in the jar), but whole fruits look lovely. It's important they are small, however, so it's easy to poach them through to the middle.

Fills 2 (1 quart) jars
9 small, just-ripe peaches (3¼lb)
3 cups granulated sugar

1 cinnamon stick (optional)
about 2½ cups brandy, plus more if needed

1 Skin the peaches by plunging them in boiling water for a minute, then gently peeling off the skins.

2 Put half the sugar in a saucepan with 3 cups of water and the cinnamon, if using. Heat, stirring to help the sugar dissolve, then bring to a simmer. Add the peaches and gently poach, turning, until tender. Remove the fruit to a bowl and reserve the syrup.

3 Add the remaining sugar to the reserved syrup and slowly bring to a boil, stirring to help the sugar dissolve. Boil the liquid until it reaches 221°F, then remove it from the heat. Let cool.

4 Measure the syrup and add an equal amount of brandy. Put the fruit in sterilized jars (*see* page 11), pour the syrup over them, and seal. (The syrup must cover the fruit; add more brandy if it doesn't.) Keep for a month before eating. These last for ages.

greek spoon sweets

I first read about the custom of offering jam and preserved fruits to guests who come calling in Claudia Roden's *Book of Middle Eastern Food*. She describes the practice, followed in the Middle East, Greece, Turkey, and the Balkans, of serving jams and fruits by the spoonful, set on a pretty saucer, with small glasses of water. Greece reigns supreme in this area and they make a whole range of "spoon sweets." Their allure is that they are small and pretty, and many are perfumed with flower waters or scented leaves. They show care for your guests and offer a little taste of the good life. I like them with strong coffee as well, to counteract the sweetness, and you can serve them with yogurt at breakfast and with cheeses.

In making spoon sweets, the key thing is to create a very thick syrup, so the fruits are held in a high density of sugar. Make sure that you boil the sugar syrup until it reaches the right temperature on a candy thermometer and don't feel bad about the amount of sugar, that is what preserves the fruit and you are going to eat a only couple of pieces at a time. Citrus fruits, nuts, even flower blossoms are preserved this way, too, but the following are an easy place to start.

melon and fig spoon sweet with rose water

I have a range of scented geraniums that I bought specifically to cook with (the leaves can be used to scent cream, ice cream, and fruit compotes) for their scent. However, I've adapted the recipe to use 1 tablespoon or so (to taste) of rose water or orange flower water instead.

Fills 1 (1 pint) jar
2¼ cups granulated sugar
1 tablespoon rose water

1½ cups, peeled, seeded, and cubed melon
5 figs, halved
juice of 1 lemon

1 Put the sugar and ½ cup of water into a saucepan and bring slowly to a boil, stirring to help the sugar dissolve. Add the rose water. Reduce the heat and simmer for five minutes. Add the fruit and simmer for three minutes. Remove from the heat, cover, and let sit for 24 hours.

2 The next day, remove the fruit with a slotted spoon, add the lemon juice, and cook the liquid until it reaches 230°F on a candy thermometer. Remove from the heat and skim any scum from the surface. Add the fruit and stir together. The fruit should become thickly covered in the sugar syrup.

3 Ladle into a warm, sterilized jar (*see* page 11) and seal. Store in the refrigerator for up to four months.

apricot spoon sweet

This is my favorite spoon sweet because the apricots retain a lovely tartness and the syrup is absolutely ambrosial.

Fills 1 (1 quart) jar
2½ cups granulated sugar

2¼lb apricots , halved and pitted
juice of 2 lemons

1 Put the sugar and 1¼ cups of water into a saucepan and bring slowly to a boil, stirring to help the sugar dissolve. Simmer, uncovered, for 10 minutes. Add the apricots and simmer for five minutes (until only *just* tender). Remove from the heat, cover, and let sit at room temperature for 24 hours. If any of your apricots have fallen apart, remove them, but they should be fine (if wrinkled).

2 The next day, lift the apricots from the syrup using a slotted spoon. Heat the liquid until it reaches 230°F on a candy thermometer. Remove from the heat. Add the lemon juice and skim off any scum. Add the apricots and stir gently; the syrup should bind with the fruit, thickly coating it. Ladle into a warm, sterilized jar (*see* page 11) and seal. Store in the refrigerator for four months.

sour cherry spoon sweet

It's hard to find sour cherries, but check pick-your-own farms—that's how I hit gold. You get two recipes in one here, *vissino* and *vissinada*, spoon sweets and Greek sour cherry syrup.

Fills 1 (1 pint) jar with cherries and
1 (1 quart) bottle with sour cherry syrup
6½ cups sour cherries (2lb)

4 cups granulated sugar
juice of ½ lemon

1 Stem and pit the cherries, keeping them intact. Put the sugar and 1¾ cups of water into a saucepan and bring slowly to a boil, stirring to help the sugar dissolve. Reduce the heat and simmer for five minutes. Add the fruit and simmer for four minutes. Cover and let sit for 24 hours.

2 The next day, remove the fruit with a slotted spoon and boil the liquid until it reaches 230°F on a candy thermometer. Remove from the heat and skim off any scum. Return the fruit, add the lemon juice, and gently stir. Ladle into a warm, sterilized jar (*see* page 11) and seal. Put the remaining syrup into a warm, sterilized bottle and seal. Refrigerate both for up to four months.

how to use
Offer the spoon sweet with Greek myzithra cheese, pecorino, or with ricotta. To use the syrup, pour some into a glass of cold water, add ice, and stir. It is a lovely dusky pink. You can also pour it over ice cream.

prunes from paradise

These recipes constitute the real treat at the end of making preserves. They are expensive, luxurious and—luckily—easy to make. The first packs a punch; the second, despite appearances, is more mellow. A big jar of each is a great thing to have stashed away, either to drink or to eat. Make sure you read the paragraph on what you can do with them. Heavenly mouthfuls lie ahead.

pruneaux à l'armagnac

Fills 1 (1 quart) jar
2½ cups prunes (dried plums; 1lb)
1 vanilla bean

1 cup granulated sugar
1 cup armagnac

1 Put the prunes in a saucepan and cover with 1¼ cups of water. Split the vanilla bean and scrape out the seeds with the tip of your knife. Add the seeds and the bean to the pan. Bring the water to a boil, then immediately remove from offthe heat and let the prunes sit overnight.

2 The next day, drain the prunes and put the soaking liquid back into the pan with the sugar. Bring to a boil, stirring occasionally to help the sugar dissolve. Add the armagnac.

3 Put the prunes in a sterilized jar (*see* page 11) with the vanilla bean and pour in the syrup. Seal. Let sit for a month before using. They will keep for at least a year.

pruneaux au monbazillac

Fills 1 (1 quart) jar
2½ cups prunes (1lb)
⅔ cup eau de vie de prune
⅔ cup rum

⅓ cup granulated sugar
1¼ cup monbazillac or other rich,
    sweet white wine

1 Put the prunes into a saucepan. Pour in the eau de vie and rum and gently bring to just under a boil. Immediately remove the pan from the heat and let the prunes soak in the liquid overnight.

2 The next day, drain the prunes and return the liquid to the pan. Add the sugar and heat, stirring to help the sugar dissolve. Put the prunes in a sterilized jar (*see* page 11) and pour in the boozy syrup. Fill up with monbazillac to cover well. Seal. Let sit for at least a month before trying. These keep for a year.

how to use

Of course, you can eat these as a dessert. And Australian food writer Stephanie Alexander gives a wonderful recipe for apéritif Agenais. Put 1 prune in a champagne flute. Cover with its liquor and fill up with champagne. Provide long spoons so your guests can eat their prunes.

cherries in somerset eau de vie

I started making these after tasting chef Mark Hix's version. He uses the liquid for his cocktail, the "Hix Fix," and serves the cherries with buttermilk pannacotta. The cider maker Julian· Temperley produces an apple-base eau de vie from his apple trees in Somerset, England, which is wonderful in this.

Fills 1 (1 quart) jar
7 cups cherries (2¼lb)

¾ cup superfine or granulated sugar
4 cups eau de vie (clear, colorless fruit brandy)

1 Wash the cherries and pack them into a wide-neck, sterilized jar (*see* page 11), sprinkling in the sugar as you work. Pour in the eau de vie, making sure the fruit is completely covered.

2 Seal and let sit for at least six weeks before eating, giving the jars a shake every so often to help dissolve the sugar. Serve the cherries with ice cream or pannacotta. Mark Hix slightly thickens the boozy juices with arrowroot, but I prefer them just as they are. These will keep for a year.

apricots in muscat

The first recipe I ever read for this—basically dried apricots plumped up in sweet wine—suggested sauternes. A delicious idea, but not one I have ever splashed out on (if I am in the happy position of being able to afford a bottle of sauternes, I prefer to drink it). But you can use muscat de rivesaltes, muscat de beaumes de venise, or any of the gorgeous Australian "stickies," which are less expensive than sauternes. I use Brown Brothers orange muscat and flora. It still doesn't make it a bargain preserve, but this is food for the gods. A preserving jar full of apricots fat with sweet, fragrant wine not only looks lovely, but it also makes a great impromptu dessert (a real treat) and keeps for ages.

Fills 1 (1 quart) jar
4 cups dried apricots

3 cups muscat

1 Put the apricots into a sterilized jar (*see* page 11); it needs to be large enough for apricots after they have plumped up with liquid. Pour the muscat over the fruit and seal.

2 Fill up with more alcohol if the apricots plump up so much that they are no longer covered in liquid. Let sit for at least a month before eating. They will keep for more than a year.

shaken red currants

Rysteribs are a fantastic idea from Scandinavia. You can use black currants or white currants, too, but I think a single fruit on its own looks best. The sight of a jar of glowing currants will cheer you up every time you open the refrigerator.

Fills 1 (1 quart) jar

4 cups red currants (stems removed)

2 cups granulated sugar

1 Layer the red currants up in a sterilized jar (*see* page 11), sprinkling with the sugar and shaking the jar as you work.

2 Put into the refrigerator and shake every so often; the sugar will eventually dissolve. Keep them in the refrigerator. The red currants will last for one week.

how to use

In Scandinavia, they serve shaken currants with savory dishes, such as fried fish, *frikadeller* (meatballs), and roasted pork. They are sweet-tart, so work very well, but they're just as good spooned over ice cream or used to fill a cake or top a meringue, and they're sensational with oatmeal. Serve them, too, with ripe, musky melons: the tartness of the berries is wonderful against the scented sweetness of the melon flesh.

sweet pear barlett (and other luscious treats)

To be honest, I'd make this even if I didn't drink. Putting a golden pear in a glass jar, covering it with clear liquid, then looking at it, magnified by the glass, seems such a magical thing to do.

Fills 1 (1 quart) jar
1 ripe Barlett pear
1 cinnamon stick
½ whole nutmeg

1 piece organic orange zest (without any white pith)
3½ cups vodka or eau de vie
1 cup superfine or granulated sugar

1 Put the pear into a large jar with the cinnamon, nutmeg, and orange zest. Pour in the alcohol. Let sit on a windowsill for about a month.

2 Now add the sugar, shake, and reseal. Let sit for four months before you try it, shaking from time to time. You can leave it for more than a year; it just gets more mature and delicious.

also try

QUINCE RATAFIA

You can make a version of the above recipe with quinces, and brandy instead of vodka. Chop 3 quinces (that you've wiped clean) and put into a 1½ quart jar. Cover with 5 cups of brandy (you only need cheap stuff) and add 1⅓ cups of superfine or granulated sugar. You can add more sugar, but I prefer it not too sweet. I don't add anything else (I like the pure flavor of quinces), but you can put spices (star anise, cinnamon … whatever you like) into the jar, too. Seal and shake. Let sit for 3 months and as much as a year before drinking. You can then strain the liquid off and put it into a bottle, or leave the fruit and just pour out whatever amount you want. Fills 1 (1 quart) jar.

how to use

You can obviously just drink these undiluted, but they have other delicious uses. Make a very British kir with the quince ratafia and English sparkling wine, or a Breton-type kir, filling up quince ratafia with hard dry cider. Both pear and quince liqueur are delicious added to whipped cream to eat with pear or apple tarts, or baked fruit.

vin de pêches

You can make a peach apéritif with peach leaves but, because you're not likely to come across them in some parts of the country, I have settled for a different approach and one which, in any case, looks lovelier in the making. You can use nectarines in just the same way.

Fills 1 (1 ½ quart) bottle
6 peaches, plus the pits from 6 more
1 vanilla bean

2 cups dry white wine
1 cup granulated sugar
about 3¾ cups eau de vie or vodka

1 Put the peaches into boiling water for two minutes, then scoop them out with a slotted spoon and, when cool enough to handle, slip the skins off. Put the fruits into a sterilized, wide-neck, 2 quart jar (halve or quarter the peaches if you have to so they fit in the jar), add the extra pits, the vanilla bean and the wine. Let sit for six days.

2 Now strain off the juice (you can eat the peaches with sugar and cream, or cook them and puree them to make a dessert). Pour the peach-infused wine into a pitcher, add the sugar, and stir really well. Pour into a 1½ quart bottle and add enough eau de vie or vodka to fill it right to the top. Seal and let sit for three weeks before drinking (shake the jar every so often). Serve, chilled, as an apéritif. This will keep for a year.

russian plum liqueur

Russians make a myriad of fruit liqueurs and brandies and take great pride in their recipes. Their love of them can be seen in Chekhov's *The Siren*, in which a character says, "I can tell you truthfully … that homemade brandy is better than any champagne. After the first glass, your sense of smell enlarges, envelops your whole being. It's a great illusion. It seems to you that you're no longer sitting at home in your easy chair, but are somewhere in Australia, astride the softest imaginable ostrich …" What more inducement could you need to make this?

Fills 1 (2 quart) jar
12 ripe plums (1¾lb)
2¼ cups superfine or granulated sugar

3 cups vodka
1 cup brandy

1 Halve the plums and pit them. Layer them up in a 2 quart jar with the sugar. Pour in the alcohol, seal, and shake the jar.

2 Let sit for a couple of months, shaking every so often. Scoop servings out of the jar, leaving the plums, or strain through a cheesecloth-lined nylon strainer and bottle. This keeps for two years.

a little something french:
the art of the apéritif

The words "Tu veux un apéritif?" can be as heart warming as "Je t'aime," and as uplifting as the sound of a cork being pulled from a bottle. They make you feel simultaneously cherished and excited. An apéritif signals relaxation and, often, a luxurious preamble to a good meal, although the "apéro" can be an occasion in itself, just half an hour's drinking with friends. The habit of the apéritif is one of the most civilizing customs the French have given us, a simple pleasure that makes a small but significant difference to everyday life. And it crosses all classes. While madame is serving kirs on her vine-covered terrace, the local builders, sweat-smeared and dusty, will be knocking back glasses of milky pastis. The custom exists in other countries, too, of course, but we got it from the French; that's why we use their word for it.

The first apéritif I tasted (in France when I was totally unaccustomed to alcohol) was pineau des charentes, a fortified wine made from cognac. It's commercially produced but, at subsequent meals, glasses of homemade vin d'orange or kirs with homemade vin de pêches were served. These *vins maisons*, or *boissons de ménage*, were lovingly made by tante (aunt) so-and-so or "mammi" (granny) in their kitchens. The food that accompanied them was always simple: slices of saussicon, olives or almonds, croûtes spread with goat cheese, radishes with butter and salt, hard-boiled eggs with tapenade, or a small spread of crudités. The apéritif broke the ice and oiled conversation about the important things in life (wine, politics, and infidelities), and could, if they were served with enough little morsels, act as an easy appetizer.

The apéritif was originally seen as something therapeutic, even medicinal, in fact. As far back as the Middle Ages, alcoholic drinks flavored with herbs or spices were thought to be health giving, and in the 19th century they started to be produced commercially.

If you want to buy your apéritif, there are plenty of them, but this chapter contains recipes for *vins maisons*. Some, such as vin d'orange, can be drunk straight, but others are used as mixers to produce drinks that are less well known outside France. Mix your homemade crème de cassis with hard dry cider to make a kir Breton, or add champagne to Breton sloe liqueur. A Parisian martini is made with gin, dry vermouth, and crème de cassis. If you make crème de cassis with raspberries instead of black currants and mix it with white wine, you have a *communard*. In some areas, crème de cassis is mixed with red wine—producing a wintry kind of kir, a *cardinal*—and in Provence, fragrant vin de pêches is mixed with rosé.

Most *vins maisons* are the result of steeping fruit (sometimes leaves, herbs, spices, or nuts) in eau de vie, but there are also ratafias. These are made in the same way, but use brandy. Once you've made a batch of either type, you'll get the bug, and can make a host of different drinks from summer and fall fruits. And you don't have to stick to French drinks at "apéro" time. There are other tipples in this chapter to open your evening, such as rhubarb schnapps or damson gin. And some drinks that can go at the other end of the meal, too, drunk as a digestif. But that's a whole other delicious story ...

colette's vin d'orange

I'm a sucker for recipes from favorite writers. And who knows more about the sensual pleasures of food than Colette? I found this in Paula Wolfert's excellent book, *Mediterranean Cooking*. The color of the drink varies from a deep gold to a pale yellow (reminiscent of a powdered orange drink with too much water). You just have to hope you get a good golden batch. Whatever the color, the drink is delicious; however, if you use rosé wine, you can be sure of a lovely hue.

Fills 1 (1 quart) bottle
3 organic oranges (1lb),
   coarsely chopped

1 bottle dry white wine
1 cup granulated sugar
1/3 cup brandy

1 Put the orange pieces in a sterilized jar (*see* page 11) and pour in the wine. Cover and set in a cool, dark place for two weeks.

2 Strain the juice into a saucepan and add the sugar. Heat gently, stirring to help the sugar dissolve. Cool, then add the brandy. You can also add 1 cup of eau de vie, if you like.

3 Pour into a sterilized bottle and put a cork in. Let it sit for a week in a cool, dark place before using. Serve well chilled, with a twist of orange zest. This keeps for at least a year.

apricot liqueur

I never want to give any of this away, I love it so much. Booze-soaked apricots are a wonderful by-product. Make this at the height of the season, when apricots are available cheaply. Even woolly, hard apricots yield flavor when heated.

Fills 2 (1½ pint) bottles
2¼ cups granulated sugar
1 bottle dry white wine

1lb apricots, halved and pitted
1¼ cups vodka

1 Put the sugar and wine in a saucepan and heat gently, stirring to help the sugar dissolve. Add the apricots. Bring to a boil, then reduce the heat and poach gently until tender. Remove from the heat. Stir in the vodka. Pour into a large container that has a tight-fitting lid. Let sit for about a week.

2 Strain through a cheesecloth-lined nylon strainer into sterilized bottles (*see* page 11) and keep for a month before use. This keeps for at least a year.

how to use

Drink undiluted (chilled), or with dry or sparkling white wine. Add it to syrups for poaching fruits with pits, or stir into whipped cream.

damson gin

A measure of this, served in a plain glass at the end of a meal, is one of the great pleasures of an fall or winter spread. And the sight of a big jar of purple damsons soaking in sugar and gin on the kitchen windowsill warms the heart. I marginally prefer damson gin to sloe gin, but both are delicious as well as being easy and relatively cheap to make.

Fills 1 (1 quart) bottle
8 damsons (1lb)

1¼ cups superfine or granulated sugar
2½ cups gin

1 Prick each damson with a sharp knife and put into a large jar or bottle with the sugar and gin. Seal the top and give the jar a really good shake.

2 Now let it somewhere so the damsons can infuse the gin with their flavor, and shake it every day for a week, then every week for 10 weeks or so. Taste and see whether you want to leave it for longer.

3 If you are happy with the flavor, pour through a nylon strainer and bottle. You are supposed to let it sit for about 18 months before drinking. That's a good reason to make loads, so you can have the odd tipple when you want to and still have enough to matur e... It'll keep for two years.

and also ...

SLOE GIN

Put 8 sloes (1lb) in the freezer. As they defrost, they will burst and the juices will start to run. Sloe skin is pretty robust and freezing is an easier way of getting through it than sitting pricking every one with a sharp knife. Proceed as above, using 2½ cups granulated sugar and 2½ gin. It keeps for a year. The sloes left behind can be mixed with cream and used as a filling for cake, made into a fruit dessert (mix it with applesauce) or served with ice cream. A company in Yorkshire, SLOEmotion, uses them to make dark chocolate truffles. A delicious idea ...

how to use

Drink undiluted or use to make a British kir, either plain (with dry white wine) or royale (with champagne). Both drinks also make a great sorbet when paired with plums, and can be added to fruity jellies (try blackberry and sloe gin). A drop of either is good in the red wine syrup in which you've poached pears. Or use them to add a rich booziness to your damson or plum jam.

rhubarb schnapps

This is wonderful to make and the sight of it glowing in your kitchen will make everyone gasp. Vodka takes on the color of whatever it is mixed with, so it draws out the pink of the rhubarb. In Germany and Eastern Europe, schnapps are distilled from fruit (so kirsch is cherry schnapps, for example) and aren't sweet. In Scandinavia, snapps are flavored vodkas, not usually sweetened, although some are made with fruits (there are suggestions for a few different snapps below). In the United States, schnapps are drinks made with clear liquor and fruit and sweetened (they are called schnapps although they are technically liqueurs). Russians make the same thing, sweet vodkas and vodka liqueurs (containing different quantities of sugar), based on fruit. The terminology is a minefield, I know, but sweet or not, all these vodka-base drinks taste delicious. You can add much less sugar to this, if you prefer.

Fills 1 (1½ quart) jar
18 young pink rhubarb stalks

1¾ cups granulated sugar
3¾ cups vodka

1 Trim the rhubarb and cut it into ¾ inch lengths. Put it into the jar. Add the sugar and shake everything together. Cover and let sit overnight (the juice will be drawn out).

2 The next day, pour the vodka into the jar, shake, and seal. Let sit for four weeks, shaking every so often, before drinking. You can scoop the schnapps out into glasses from the jar, or strain everything through a cheesecloth-lined nylon strainer into a bottle. This keeps for a year, but the color fades.

and also

PEACH OR APRICOT SCHNAPPS

Make as for rhubarb schnapps, using ripe fruit that you have pitted and sliced.

SNAPPS WITH LEMON

Peel the zest from 1 unwaxed lemon (remove the bitter white pith), and add it to 4 cups of vodka in a large jar. Let sit for two to four days, depending on how strong you want the flavor to be. Strain the snapps into a bottle.

SNAPPS WITH DILL

Make as for Snapps with Lemon, but put sprigs of dill instead of lemon zest into the vodka.

SNAPPS WITH CINNAMON AND CARDAMOM

Good for winter drinking. Put 1 cinnamon stick and 2 cardamom pods into the vodka (you can just add these straight to the bottle), and leave them. You don't need to strain the vodka to remove the spices, just leave them there indefinitely.

vodka: dear little water

You can tell just how precious vodka is to Russians by its name. Vodka is the diminutive of "voda," the Russian word for water. Translated literally, it means "dear little water." The way it hits your tongue and the inside of your stomach, spreading liquid warmth, helps you understand why it is loved. It soothes both in cold weather and hard times, however, it has to be said, it is as much a scourge in Russian life as a comfort.

There, vodka is served straight from the freezer—or a bottle is retrieved from a mound of snow on the windowsill outside—poured into small shot glasses, and drunk in a single gulp. The finest is distilled primarily from rye, although other grains can be used, and flavored vodkas are not considered a travesty. In Russia, they use romantic and elusive ingredients, such as nuts from Siberian cedars, as well as more regular flavors, such as dill, horseradish, juniper, tea, and ginger. Vodkas are a favorite fixture of the zakuski table (*see* page 229), because chilled vodka goes wonderfully with the strong salty flavors—pickled mushrooms, caviar, smoked fish—of little zakuski dishes.

Most flavored vodkas are savory, but there are more perfumed ones, too (those that are flavored with vanilla, for example), and vodka is also used to make sweet drinks, such as the Krupnik below and the Russian plum liqueur on page 146. It's hard to think of a better cold cure than Polish honey vodka, drunk hot, with a little pat of butter melting on top.

krupnik polish honey vodka

Oh, I love this. Served hot—as it should be—it's basically a mulled vodka. But because you can make it in advance and reheat it, it has advantages over mulled wine. You can get it ready in November, well in time for Christmas.

Fills 1 (1 quart) bottle

1¼ cup honey	2 blades of mace
2 cinnamon sticks	1½ inch piece of vanilla bean
small chunk of nutmeg	pared zest of 2 organic oranges
	2½ cups vodka

1 Put the honey and 1¼ cups of water into a saucepan and bring to a boil, skimming any scum. Add the spices and orange zest, cover, and simmer over gentle heat for about 15 minutes.

2 Remove from the heat, add the vodka, and let sit—covered—for 48 hours. Strain through a double layer of cheesecloth. Pour into a bottle, seal, and keep in a cool, dark place. After a week, you'll see sediment on the bottom. Strain off the clear liquid (leave the sediment) and put it into a clean bottle.

3 *Krupnik* should be heated before drinking and is often served with a pat of butter melting in it. It keeps for a year.

gdansk vodka

This is adapted from a recipe in *The Polish Kitchen* by Mary Pininska. It's warming and has just the right amount of sweetness. It also mellows and changes over time. You can keep it for as long as three years.

Fills 1 (1½ quart) bottle

2 cinnamon sticks
4 blades of mace
8 cloves
10 cardamom pods
1 star anise
10 juniper berries
thinly pared zest of 2 organic oranges
thinly pared zest of 6 unwaxed lemons
1½ cup granulated sugar
4 cups vodka

1 Coarsely crush all the spices in a mortar. Put these into a big lidded container with the citrus zests.

2 Put 4 cups of water into a saucepan with the sugar and bring slowly to a boil, stirring to help the sugar dissolve. Simmer for 20 minutes (don't cover the pan). Skim the froth from the surface, then pour onto the spices and citrus rind and let sit for 30 minutes. Add the vodka. Put a lid on and let sit for two weeks in a cool, dark place.

3 Taste to see whether you are happy with the flavor (it will develop further even when you have removed the spices). You might want to leave it a little longer at this stage.

4 Strain the liquid through a double layer of cheesecloth, pour into a bottle, seal, and label. It's best to keep for two months before trying it. It will actually be good for several years (a friend who makes a similar spice and citrus-infused vodka says it is best on the fourth Christmas after making it).

and also

CARAWAY VODKA

Lightly crush 2 teaspoons of caraway seeds, put them into a piece of folded paper (which acts as a little chute) and pour them into a bottle containing 2 cups of vodka. Let sit until the seeds have flavored the vodka to a degree that you like, then strain and pour into a clean bottle. Fills 1 (1 pint) bottle. This keeps for three years.

CHILE VODKA

Pertsovka, or chile vodka, is the Russian cure-all. Prick an unblemished red chile several times with a toothpick or needle and put it inside a bottle containing 2 cups of vodka. You can add some black peppercorns as well if you want another layer of heat. Let sit until the vodka is as hot as you would like it to be, then strain and pour into a clean bottle. Fills 1 l (1 pint) bottle. This keeps for three years.

liqueur de blosses

Can you think of a more mellifluous name than this? The British "sloe and apple brandy liqueur" sounds boring in comparison. *Blosses* sounds like something you would lie on a bed of … for months. In fact, it's the Breton word for sloes, and evokes their soft bloomy skin.

Fills 1 (1 quart) jar
2¼lb sloes

1½ cups superfine or granulated sugar
4 cups apple brandy

1 Pick over the sloes, removing any leaves, twigs, or blemished berries. Either pierce each sloe with a needle, or put them into a freezer bag and freeze; they will burst as they defrost.

2 Layer the sloes in a large jar, sprinkling with sugar as you work, then pour in the brandy. It should completely cover the berries. Seal, shake vigorously, and then let sit for three to four months, shaking every so often. Strain and pour the liqueur into a clean bottle. This keeps for two years.

how to use

Use in just the way you would use sloe gin or vodka. This has a softer, richer, deeper flavour, though. A real treat to drink neat.

black currant syrup

Your children will love you and your mommy friends will feel inadequate … You can make this syrup with berries (blackberries a are nice). Serve as a drink diluted with plain water.

Fills 1 (1½ pint) bottle
9 cups black currants (2¼lb),
    stems removed

juice of about 3 lemons
about 3 cups granulated sugar

1 Put the fruit into a saucepan with 2½ cups of water. Bring to a boil, then reduce the heat to a simmer and cook for 10 minutes, until the berries are completely soft and pulpy.

2 Pour into a jelly bag suspended over a bowl to catch the juice, and let sit overnight.

3 The next day, measure the liquid. Add the juice of 2 lemons and 2 cups of sugar (more if you like) for every 2 cups of liquid. Heat gently until the sugar has dissolved, then pour into a warm sterilized bottle (*see* page 11) and seal. It will keep in the refrigerator for a couple of months.

elderflower syrup

Ten years ago few people made this—called elderflower cordial in Britain—but nowadays it is all the rage (resulting in my local pharmacist running out of citric acid this year). Here's how. Get a carrier bag (or a roomy basket, if you want the full bucolic experience) and a pair of scissors. Work out where your nearest elderflowers are. You will be surprised how many there are and—very likely—how close to your home. You may have passed them without noticing many times. I have lived in London for 25 years and in all my homes in the city I have been within a walk or a short train ride from a good source of elderflowers. You'll find them in many parts of the United States, too. The first time I went to collect elderflowers I actually took a picture with me printed from the Internet. The scent is a real giveaway (elderflowers smell of muscat), but I was still nervous and wanted to be sure I was picking the right thing (a lot of other plants look like elderflowers, but if you have a picture, you will be sure to get it right). Go with a pal and you will spend a thoroughly enjoyable couple of hours pulling on branches, snipping off the twigs with the freshest looking blooms, and getting grass stains on your clothes. Be sure to choose bushes that are away from busy roads, and pick only those blooms that are newly opened and are a pure creamy white color (brown blossoms are past their best). When you sniff them, they should have a gentle fragrance. Once home, cook them the same day, if possible. After 24 hours, they will start to smell of cat's pee (not good) and even after a night sitting in the kitchen they will be giving off a slightly sickly smell, so use them when they are at their freshest.

Fills 2 (1 quart) bottles
25 heads very fresh elderflowers
7½ cups granulated sugar

3 large unwaxed lemons, plus more if needed
⅓ cup citric acid (buy this in the pharmacy)

1 Gently shake the elderflower heads to dislodge any bugs.

2 Put the sugar and 6½ cups of water into a saucepan and bring to a boil, stirring from time to time to help the sugar dissolve. Remove the zest from the lemons in broad strips with a sharp knife and put in a bowl with the elderflowers. Slice the lemon flesh thinly and add to the bowl. When the sugar syrup has come to a boil, pour it over the flowers and lemons. Stir in the citric acid. Cover with a clean, dry cloth and let sit in a cool, dark place for 24 hours.

3 The next day, taste the liquid and judge whether you want it to be any tarter (I sometimes add the juice of one more lemon; it depends on how tart you want the syrup to be). Strain the syrup through a cheesecloth-lined nylon strainer into a large pitcher. Pour this into warm, sterilized bottles (*see* page 11) and seal.

4 Let cool and keep in the refrigerator. It will be okay for about five weeks. Keeping it for longer involves heating the bottles of syrup in a water bath. I can never be bothered to do this, but you can freeze it, or just drink it when it's fresh—you need to dilute it with water.

raspberry and rose syrup

Fragrant. Summery. And with a little Middle Eastern magic. Mix in pitchers and float fresh berries and rose petals on top for a romantic summer drink.

Fills 1 (1½ pint) bottle
3 pints raspberries
juice of 2 lemons

about 2½ cups granulated sugar, or to taste
about 3 tablespoons rose water (add gradually,
   tasting as you work; they vary in intensity)

1 Put the raspberries into a saucepan with ⅔ cup of water and heat gradually to boiling point, crushing the fruit with a wooden spoon from time to time. Reduce the heat and simmer for about five minutes. (If you simmer them too much, they end up tasting "cooked" and much less fresh.)

2 Suspend a jelly bag from a frame over a bowl and pour the juice into it. Let sit overnight.

3 The next day, measure the collected juice, stir in the juice of the lemons, and add 1¾ cups of sugar for every 2 cups of juice (add more sugar if you prefer it less tart). Put the mixture in a saucepan and heat slowly, stirring to help the sugar dissolve. Add the rose water to taste. Pour through a plastic funnel into a warm sterilized bottle (*see* page 11). Seal and let cool. If you put t into the bottle while warm, it will last for a couple of months in the refrigerator.

mrs. leyel's syrup of rhubarb

Hilda Leyel, who wrote under the name Mrs. CF Leyel, was an excellent cook and herbalist who penned some charming books (often featuring recipes using flowers and herbs). This is from *Summer Drinks and Winter Syrups*, published in the 1930s. I've adapted it only slightly. It is thinner than Middle Eastern sharbat (*see* page 162), and more zingy due to the citric acid.

Fills 3 (1½ pint) bottles
5lb rhubarb, trimmed and chopped into
   ¾ inch chunks

3 tablespoons citric acid
about 6 cups granulated sugar
juice of 2 lemons

1 Put the rhubarb into a large bowl and add enough water just to cover. Add the citric acid and stir. Let sit for 24 hours (and I mean 24 hours, not just overnight).

2 The next day, strain the rhubarb through a nylon strainer into a large bowl. Measure the liquid, put it in a large saucepan, and add 1¾ cups of sugar for every 2½ cups of juice. Heat gently, stirring to help the sugar dissolve. Add the lemon juice, bring to a boil, and boil for five minutes.

3 Cool and pour into sterilized bottles (*see* page 11). This will keep in the refrigerator for a month, or freeze it if you want to keep it for longer.

my mum's lemonade

My mum used to make this every summer—in really big batches—and it would keep us going for ages. It's really a lemon syrup that you dilute, and is much nicer than anything similar you could buy. It's also unbelievably economical. Citric acid is available in pharmacies.

Fills 3 x (1 quart) bottles
2 organic oranges
12 unwaxed lemons

6½ cups granulated sugar
¼ cup citric acid

1 Finely grate the zest of the oranges and lemons and put into a bowl with the sugar. Add 7½ cups of boiling water and let sit overnight.

2 The next day, squeeze the juice from the citrus fruits and add that with the citric acid. Mix well. Strain and pour into sterilized bottles (*see* page 11). Serve it well diluted by adding water (plain or sparkling) to taste. It will keep for two months in the refrigerator.

rose hip syrup

A real taste of childhood; this has a special exotic-floral, slightly musky flavor. However, it's a labor of love—I won't pretend. You need a lot of rose hips (which translates into a lot of picking) to make a couple of bottles. But it's worth it for that unusual flavor. It is wonderful on warm rice pudding, weekend brunch pancakes, and on ice cream. Diluted, you can drink it. too.

Fills 3 (½ pint) bottles
2¼lb rose hips, removed from stems

3¾ cups granulated sugar, plus more if needed
juice of 1 lemon

1 Pick over the rose hips, discarding any that are squishy or bruised. Wash them, then chop by hand or put through the coarse blade of a food processor. Have ready a saucepan containing 8 cups of boiling water—you mustn't let the rose hips stand once you've chopped them or you'll lose some of their vitamin C content—and add the rose hips. Return to a boil, then let sit for 15 minutes.

2 Get a jelly bag set up with a large bowl underneath. Pour the infused water and rose hips into the bag and let the liquid drip through. Return the pulp to the saucepan and add 4 cups of water. Reboil the pulp, then let sit for 15 minutes again. Strain through the jelly bag as before. Mix both lots of juice in a clean saucepan and boil it until you have 4 cups of liquid. Add the sugar, stir to help it dissolve, then bring to a boil and boil for five minutes. Add the lemon juice. Taste. If you want it sweeter, add more sugar and stir to dissolve. The liquid will become more syrupy as it cools, of course, but you should see that you have a light syrup at this stage.

3 While hot, pour into hot sterilized bottles (*see* page 11) and seal. (Use small bottles, because once the syrup is open, it only keeps for a week.) Once cool, store in the refrigerator for up to six weeks.

quince sharbat

Sharbats are Middle Eastern syrups and have enchanted travelers over the years. There are accounts of seeing violet sharbats being made by pounding the flowers and mixing them with sugar and boiling water. Mulberry sharbat was also popular, and even sorrel. My recipes are adapted from Middle Eastern versions, but use half the amount of sugar. I prefer them when they are more fruity and less sweet. If you want a sharbat as sweet as it would be in the Middle East, then double the amount of sugar (yes, that's what I said: double it).

Fills 1 (1 ½ pint) bottle
2 quinces

juice of 2 lemons
2½ cups granulated sugar

1 Peel and core the quinces and chop into chunks. Put in a saucepan with 2 cups of water and the juice of 1 lemon. Bring to a boil, reduce the heat and cook gently until completely soft (about 45 minutes). They will become a beautiful rosy pink, which makes a wonderful-looking syrup.

2 Line a large nylon strainer with cheesecloth and put it over a large saucepan. Pour the quince and its cooking liquid through it. (You can use the pulp to make Quince Paste, *see* page 64). Add the sugar and bring to a boil, stirring to help the sugar dissolve. Add the rest of the lemon juice, then remove from the heat. Most sharbats need to be boiled to a syrup but, because quinces are so high in pectin, you may find you actually have to add boiled water so that it doesn't set to a jelly.

3 Pour into a warm sterilized bottle (*see* page 11) and seal. Keep in the refrigerator. It will be okay for a couple of months, but you can freeze it if you want to keep it for longer.

and also

RHUBARB SHARBAT

Use 10 rhubarb stalks and 2½ cups granulated sugar. What a color! Make as above (the cooking time is shorter because rhubarb softens quickly). Bring to a boil, simmer to reduce to a syrup, and put up in a bottle.

SOUR CHERRY SHARBAT

Make as above, with 3½ cups sour cherries, 2½ cups granulated sugar, and the juice of 1 lemon. Stone the cherries, then cook with their pits until completely soft. Proceed as above. Add lemon juice to taste once the syrup has boiled.

how to use

Dilute with water and serve with ice. All of these make great syrups to pour on ice cream, yogurt, or crepes. Or mix with fruit juices: cherry and rhubarb sharbat are both great with apple juice and sparkling water. Add a drop of rose water to the rhubarb and cherry sharbats, or orange flower water to the quince, if you like your syrups slightly scented.

rose syrup

Add a drop to whipped cream to serve with berries, or drizzle over meringue with berries. In the Middle East, it is diluted and taken as a drink, but this is too much even for me ...

Fills 1 (1 pint) bottle
2½ cups granulated sugar
juice of 1 lemon (you may want less or more)

¼ rose water, or to taste (add gradually, tasting as you work; they vary in intensity)
splash of red food coloring (optional)

1 Put 1¼ cups of water and the sugar into a saucepan and heat gently until the sugar has dissolved. Boil for two minutes, then strain in the lemon juice through a nylon strainer and add rose water to taste. You can add a tiny dash of food coloring if you want, from the end of a toothpick, for a pale pink. Pour through a funnel into a sterilized bottle (*see* page 11) and refrigerate for up to a month.

2 If you find an abundance of dark, fragrant roses (about 2½ cups), boil the water and let the petals to steep for three hours. Strain, add the sugar, and do as above (you may want to omit the lemon and you should get color from the fresh petals if they are dark enough).

sekanjabin

This Persian sweet-sour syrup is used as a cooling drink in hot weather. The balance of sweetness to acidity varies according to the cook, so make it to your own taste. *Sekanjabin* is the name of the syrup. When used to make a drink, the drink itself is called *sharbat-e sekanjabin*.

Fills 1 (1½ pint) bottle
5 cups granulated sugar

1¼ cups white wine vinegar
leaves from 16 sprigs of mint

1 Put 2½ cups of water into a saucepan with the sugar and bring gently to a boil, stirring a little to help the sugar dissolve. Add the vinegar, reduce the heat, and simmer for 15 minutes.

2 Remove from the heat and add the mint; it perfumes the syrup as it cools. Remove the mint and pour into a sterilized bottle (*see* page 11). Serve with ice-cold plain or sparkling water with ice. Refrigerate and drink within two months.

how to use

This makes a wonderful drink mixed with apple juice filled up with water. Add mint, sliced lemons, and chopped apples. In Iran, this is used as a kind of dip for lettuce leaves. Odd although it sounds, this lettuce and mint syrup combination is wonderful with rice (mixed with herbs and fava beans) and roasted lamb or white fish.

sharbats and mint tea:
middle eastern pleasures

Middle Eastern food was the first kind I really fell in love with. And it all happened in my head. Growing up in Northern Ireland, I was a million miles away from the heat and color of the Middle East, but I thought I had a clear picture of it, formed by reading *The Arabian Nights* and poring over its illustrations. The foods—figs, pomegranates, dates, and flower waters—enchanted me. This didn't change when I became an adult. I bought Claudia Roden's *Book of Middle Eastern Food* as soon as I came to live in London and marveled at the exoticism. Syrups and jams seemed the most romantic branch of this great culinary culture. I read about the sharbat sellers of Roden's childhood in Cairo, as they carried drinks around the streets in gigantic glass flasks of color. Their shouts and the tinkling of the little metal cups they carried drew people out of their houses to quench their thirst. Sharbats—the name for syrups in the Middle East, from the Arabic for "sweet drink"—were made from roses, barberries, mint, quinces, limes, and sour cherries. They became popular as Islam took hold and wine was phased out. Served over shards of crushed ice, they seemed just as good as wine and were probably the forerunner to the water ices—sorbets and granitas—that later developed in Italy and France.

The jams of the Middle East are just as exquisite as the sharbats, but are not what we recognize as "jam." They are much runnier, almost thick fruity syrups. As well as being eaten with bread, they are spooned over yogurt, served as a dessert, and used to sweeten tea. Carrots and even eggplants are used as well as quinces and cherries. Greek spoon sweets are like Middle Eastern jams. They are fruits in a thick syrup, served in small quantities to visitors who call in for coffee (usually with a little glass of cold water, too). As a guest, you may be given just two halves of a purple fig in a pool of syrup, but that one fig is a special offering—a sweet gift from your hostess—and is all the more lovely for coming in a small portion. Jams in the Middle East are usually served the same way, on saucers with little spoons.

Appreciation of beauty, flavor, color, and scent is a significant part of Middle Eastern culture. It fits in with their love of gardens and the Islamic idea of paradise. Just a glance at the intricate patterns on their tiles will show you their love of the decorative. Embellishing and embracing the ordinary things in life—houses, gardens, and food—is central. Jams, preserved fruits, and sharbats are just another facet of this approach.

The other thing that is special about Middle Eastern preserves is that they seem to embody the uncapturable. In the same way that poetry sometimes says the unsayable, bottles of quince sharbat and jars of rose jelly or orange blossom preserve seem to capture something that is almost impossible to pin down. Floral smells and flavors are evanescent; the seasons for quinces or sour cherries are short, so unless you capture their essence in sugar and put it behind glass, it is hard to recall how they taste and smell when they are no longer around. But sharbats and jams mean you don't need to; open a bottle or a jar and taste again what you thought was lost. And you can get it in just one spoonful of fruit or cold sip from a diluted syrup.

salted, cured, and potted

This is a serious chapter. Pork terrine, duck confit, Italian cured beef. These dishes take time and attention. In an age when you can have sushi delivered to your door, or down a freshly blended wheat grass energy drink in the office, why should we bother? Partly because they have a history. Of course, just because a recipe has history doesn't mean it's good—I wouldn't suggest you roast a swan—but often when dishes survive, there's a good reason. They're well lodged in a country's culture; they're not faddy. The process of making them is rewarding and they're delicious.

A lot of what happens to food when we cook it is hidden. We put a chicken in the oven and it ends up golden and delicious. We haven't had that much of a hand in it. But with curing, we preside over the kind of cooking that takes days, sometimes weeks. Not all that time is hands on, but if you rub a salt cure into pork to make bacon, you'll feel the flesh. After a couple of days, when you rub more in, you'll feel it again, and, by the end of the curing time, you will notice that the texture has changed: it's firmer. You witness the process of transformation. This is not the kind of cooking that can be fitted in between picking the kids up from school and going out for the evening. You have to be aware of it and take care of it. Having said that, it is not difficult to pull off duck confit or salmon gravlax. However, it is the kind of cooking that makes you feel like more than just a cook. You're not exactly becoming an artisan—a food producer who has practiced his craft every day for years—but you are making food, not just preparing a meal. And that's a thrill.

The fat content in some of the dishes in this chapter may set alarm bells ringing, but you won't be eating duck confit or pork terrine every day. And just think how much fat there is in that doughnut you grab on the way to work.

SALT AND SALT CURES

Salt seems to play a minor role in our eating. We season dishes with it as we are cooking. We might sprinkle more on before eating, but basically it sits there quietly, plain and white. However, it has shaped what we eat and is partly responsible for why we have survived at all. That is because it isn't time that spoils food, but bacteria and other microbes that feed on it. If we prepare food with salt—either with brines (salt solutions) or dry cures—we disable or kill those microbes, so stop or at least delay the destruction of our food. It is salt that enabled us to put food away for long-term keeping, or to take it with us on journeys of exploration. Salt has been fundamental to human survival and expansion. Luckily, it also does great things to the taste of food by concentrating its flavors. Why is duck confit so much more delicious than duck? It's partly because of those little white crystals you rubbed it with.

Salt is an important component of nearly every dish in this chapter (it's only in the few potted dishes that it acts more as a seasoning than as a preservative). This is how it works: Cells that are enclosed by semipermeable membranes feel compelled to get themselves in balance with whatever lies outside them. Heightened salt concentration outside a cell results in an exchange of fluid out of that cell. Water moves across the membrane to reduce the sodium concentration outside the cell and raise the potassium concentration inside it. If salt is rubbed on any piece of meat, the cells inside it leach their water as they try to get in sync with what surrounds them. They are desperate to dilute the salt. This process also changes the shape of the proteins in the meat, loosening them and allowing them to contain more moisture, which is good news for the eater.

If you salt a piece of meat, you pull moisture out of it, dehydrating it. When salt enters the cells of the meat it also dehydrates the microbes in it, either killing them or inhibiting their ability to multiply. With preserved meats that you will be eating fairly quickly, such as the two bacon recipes in this chapter, preserving with salt is enough. (I suggest using the bacon within two weeks.)

Any kind of slow-cured meat (salami, for example) whose life you really want to extend, needs to have chemical preservatives added. These are generally nitrates and nitrites. They change the flavor of meat, preserve its pink color, prevent the fat from developing rancid flavors, and stop bacteria from growing—most notably those responsible for botulism. However, nitrates and nitrates can be toxic. You do have to be careful about how much you use and you need to store them safely. Because you need to use them in such small quantities that it can be difficult to measure them safely, the safest way to use them is to use a commercially prepared premix cure. The chemicals have been diluted by mixing them with salt; you can use it to replace the salt and nitrite (and nitrate) in a cure recipe. There are several premixes available; Morton® Tender Quick® is one of several brands that is often stocked in local grocery stores.

The recipes in this chapter are designed to provide a taster to the world of curing. If you find they have whetted your appetite, do some research—the National Center for Home Food Preservation has a Web site that is a good place to start—and look for books specifically on meat curing for expert advice before getting more involved with nitrates and nitrites—and always follow the instructions precisely.

I have suggested using "pink salt," or sodium nitrite, in the corned beef recipe because it makes a difference to the appearance (producing a lovely rosy pink), but it tastes every bit as good without it and isn't necessary if you prefer to omit it or use a premix cure. I tried many different amounts in the brining process, building it up gradually so I would get optimum color. Pink salt is sold as Prague powder number 1, Insta-Cure, Modern Cure, and DQ Curing Salt—these are all the same thing, which is sodium nitrite at 6.25%. A number 2 version is used in one of the bresaola recipes in this chapter.

These preservatives have been getting a bad press as we worry more about any chemical additives in our food. However, sausage and salami makers have been using them for centuries. And when the alternative to using them is to risk creating a food product that could kill someone (the risk of botulism is very real), I am happy to cure with these preservatives.

Sugar is also an important part of a cure, because it softens the effect of the salt. In fact, the cure for Scandinavian gravlax—their classic cured salmon dish—has almost as much sugar as salt. The sugar produces a sweeter, moister cure, known as a "soft cure."

PRESERVING UNDER FAT

Food is dried or salted to kill—or suppress—potentially harmful organisms within it. However, there are other processes that can come after salting, or after cooking, that stop microbes from getting through to the food. The simplest way of stopping airborne organisms getting through to meat or fish is to create a barrier of fat (the fact that it's edible and delicious just makes eating the preserve all the better). This is why there is layer of clarified butter on top of chicken liver pâté, and why duck confit comes enrobed in a layer of creamy duck fat. Pâté, confit, and rillettes (rillettes are cooked and pounded pork, rabbit, or poultry flesh) are French dishes, but "potted" meats were all the rage in Britain in the 17th century and are still loved, although we don't make them much nowadays. Potting is a wonderful way to use up leftovers. In the summer, it's a perfect way to deal with leftover poached salmon and, after Christmas, when you're sick of looking at it, it's a good solution for what to do with the leftover ham.

CAUTIONARY NOTES

I don't like sounding alarm bells when it comes to cooking, because it usually is such a downer. But preserving meat and fish isn't something to approach in a casual fashion. I've never had a disaster—although I've chucked out a few jars of fermented jam in my time—but you have to be careful. You will be spending a considerable time making something.
To make it worth it, use the best meat and fish you can, because pork belly from a free-range beast (even better if you are prepared to shell out on a particular breed) will give you a great result. And freshness is paramount. Herring, salmon, meat, all need to be absolutely fresh, otherwise you risk them spoiling. This is dangerous, but also a waste of time and ingredients.

Use the exact amount of salt, the right density of brine, and the correct amount of curing salts as suggested in the recipes. And measure them out instead of guessing.

Hygiene. It might seem obvious but, in your zeal, you may forget about it. All the equipment you use—cutting boards, spoons, forks, and knives—should be sterilized (wash really well in hot soapy water, then immerse them in boiling water). Clean your work surface thoroughly with an antibacterial. Keep washing your hands and dry them on paper towels instead of using and reusing the same kitchen towel. Work in a reasonably cool kitchen: Neither the meat nor the fish you are curing should ever be in a warm environment.

You're curing, it's a living process. The foods you are working with will change as they cure. Keep an eye on the meat or fish and if, at any time during the process, or once it is stored, you smell or see that it is off, throw it out. Rely on your senses and don't take risks.

cured duck breasts

This is one of the easiest of home-curing recipes you can do (and a good place to start). I first read about home-cured duck breasts in Franco Taruschio's book, *Leaves from the Walnut Tree*. He adapted it from an old Welsh recipe, "Lady Llanover's duck" and it was constantly on his menu at the Walnut Tree Inn in Abergavenny, Wales. The following recipe is a little easier than that version and was given to me by another Wales-based chef, Matt Tebbutt.

Make sure you get large duck breasts—if they're smaller, they just turn gray in the cooking time—and be very careful and exact about the time you cook them and the temperature of your oven (I now keep a thermometer in my oven to make sure it's at the temperature it says it is). You want lovely pink slices of duck.

Serves 8 as an appetizer

3 tablespoons kosher sea salt
¼ cup superfine sugar
1 teaspoon black peppercorns
1 teaspoon coriander seeds
1 teaspoon thyme leaves
2 bay leaves
4 large duck breasts, each 9–9¾oz

1 Put everything except the duck breasts into a mortar and crush with the pestle. Spread half of this—the cure—in the bottom of a ceramic or plastic dish. Lay the duck breasts on it, skin side down, and sprinkle the rest of the cure on top. Cover and refrigerate for 24 hours.

2 Preheat the oven to 325°F. Rinse the cure from the duck breasts and put them into an ovenproof dish. Add 1 cup of water, or enough to come about halfway up the side of the breasts. Cook in the oven for 20 minutes.

3 Take the dish out of the oven, remove the breasts, and put them onto a plate. Cover and let sit until they are firm and completely cool (they need to be firm enough to slice). They will keep for three days in the refrigerator. Slice and serve half a duck breast per person for an appetizer.

how to use

These make a great salad. Matt Tebbutt serves the duck with slices of melon or ripe mango, pickled ginger and mizuna leaves, a dab of wasabi paste, and a little dipping bowl of soy sauce.

You can make a less formal (and slightly spicier) salad by tossing slices of the duck with mango, salad greens, cooked green beans, sliced red chiles, and a dressing made from peanut oil, rice vinegar, grated fresh ginger root, Thai fish sauce, and lime juice seasoned with granulated sugar. (Have a look at the one used with smoked chicken, *see* page 124.)

corned beef

I love corned beef (oh, those sandwiches you get in New York delis!) but was scared of making it. Once I tried it, however, I found it simple (and exciting, my kids were intrigued at the big chunk of meat brining in the house). It's also unbelievably economical, providing a huge piece of beef for a crowd (with leftovers for those delicious sandwiches …) Ask your butcher for a lovely fatty piece of brisket. Tell him what it's for. The more fat, the better the flavor. Pink salt isn't mandatory, but it produces a lovely pink color.

Serves 8, with leftovers to use in other dishes or sandwiches

FOR THE BRINE

1¼ cups firmly packed light brown sugar
1½ cups kosher sea salt
2 teaspoons black peppercorns
½ tablespoon juniper berries
4 cloves
4 bay leaves
4 sprigs of thyme
4 teaspoons pink salt (optional)

FOR THE BEEF

5½lb piece of beef brisket
1 large carrot, coarsely chopped
1 onion, coarsely chopped
1 celery stick, coarsely chopped
1 leek, cut into large chunks
1 bouquet garni (such as sprigs of parsley, thyme, and bay leaf tied together)
½ head of garlic

1 Put all the ingredients for the brine into a large saucepan, pour in 10½ cups of water, and gradually bring to a boil, stirring to help the sugar and salt dissolve. Once it comes to a boil, let it simmer for two minutes. Remove from the heat and let cool completely.

2 Pierce the meat all over with a sharp knife. Put it in a large, sterilized plastic container or bucket (something nonreactive) and cover the meat with the brine; it must be completely immersed. I have to say the best thing I've found with which to weigh the meat down is two massive bottles of vodka. Just put them in on top of the meat and it will stay below the level of the brine. Refrigerate for seven days.

3 Take the beef out of the brine and rinse it. Roll and tie the beef and put it in a Dutch oven with the vegetables, bouquet garni, and garlic, adding enough cold water to cover. Bring the water to simmering point, then let poach gently—I mean *gently*—on the stove top for 2½–3 hours. Cook until the meat is completely tender (you can check with the tip of a sharp knife—it is very easy to gauge the texture with one).

4 Serve in slices with pickles (Bread and Butter Pickles, *see* page 218, are excellent), Horseradish Cream or Chrain (*see* page 196), or English mustard or piccalilli. You can serve it hot (reheat it in the broth in which it has cooked) or cold. Corned beef will keep for a week in the refrigerator; wrap it well so it stays moist.

bacon

This is unbelievably easy to make. If you see "streaky" bacon mentioned in a British recipe, this is it. Your BLT sandwiches will be heavenly, and use it in recipes calling for bacon pieces. You need a sharp knife to cut this and it's hard to slice the bacon into thin slices (but what's wrong with thick ones?). If you find you love making your own bacon, invest in a bacon slicer.

Makes 4¼lb
4½lb thick piece of boned pork belly, with the rind

FOR THE CURE
2¼ cups kosher salt
3 bay leaves, chopped
15 juniper berries, crushed
¾ cup firmly packed light brown sugar

1 Crush together all the ingredients for the cure in a food processor or a mortar and pestle. Lay the pork on a (very clean) kitchen surface or cutting board and rub about two-thirds of the cure all over it (you won't need it all at this stage). Put into a nonreactive container (I use a big plastic container) and cover. Refrigerate (it needs to be kept at about 41°F) and store the leftover cure mix.

2 After 24 hours, you'll see liquid around the pork. Take the pork out of the container, pour off the liquid, and rub the pork with more of the cure. Do this again on day three, using up all the remaining cure. Leave for a fourth and fifth day, then your bacon will be ready. It should feel firm.

3 Rinse off the excess salt and dry the belly. Wrap it in cheesecloth and put it on a tray in the refrigerator. It will dry out a little and mature over the next few days. Cut pieces off as you need them. It will keep well for about two weeks, and you can also freeze it (sliced). If you find that the bacon too salty when you first cook it, soak the whole belly overnight in water, dry, and keep as before.

stephen harris's maple-cured bacon

Stephen Harris is one of the best chefs in the country and owner of The Sportsman in Seasalter, Kent (an outstanding dining pub). He showed me how to make bacon. Stephen is a self-taught cook and loves to learn a new skill, an attitude which is very infectious.

Makes 4¼lb
2 cups dark maple syrup

4½lb boneless pork loin
2 cups sea salt flakes

1 Rub the maple syrup all over the pork and put in a nonreactive container. Let sit for three days in the refrigerator, rubbing the maple syrup in a couple of times during this period. Take the meat out and rub the salt all over it. Put back into the container and let sit in the refrigerator for three-and-a-half to four days, then wash the salt off and treat the bacon just as in the previous recipe.

2 Stephen suggests using dark brown sugar if you want to make a less expensive sweet-cured bacon. If you find this bacon is too salty, then keep it in the salt for one day less next time around.

duck confit

Making confit is an ancient practice developed in France as a way of preserving fatty meats such as duck, goose, and pork. And the process doesn't just preserve, it intensifies the flavor. Homemade stuff is a special treat and it's very easy to serve, because all you have to do at the last minute is sauté the legs. I use lard to seal the confit, because it is denser than duck or goose fat.

Serves 4

3 tablespoons sea salt flakes
8 peppercorns, crushed
8 juniper berries, crushed
leaves from 4 sprigs of thyme, chopped

3 bay leaves, broken up
4 large duck legs, about 7oz each
4½lb duck or goose fat (you can buy this
  in cans or jars)
lard, to seal

1 Mix together the salt, pepper, juniper, thyme, and bay. Sprinkle half of the mixture into a nonreactive wide, shallow dish and set the duck legs, skin side down, into it. Sprinkle the rest of the mixture over the top. Put in the refrigerator (I cover it loosely with plastic wrap) and let sit for 24 hours. Brush the salt mixture off with a pastry brush and preheat the oven to 225°F.

2 Heat the duck or goose fat in a heavy Dutch oven in which the legs will fit snugly. Bring the fat to a gentle simmer—it should just be quivering—and add the legs. There should be enough fat to completely cover the duck. Cook in the oven for two-and-a-half to three hours. The duck should be completely soft and tender and the juices that run out when pierced with a knife should be clear. A meat thermometer inserted into the thickest part of the meat, away from bones, should read 165°F.

3 Remove from the oven and lift the legs onto a wire rack (put something underneath for the dripping fat). Put a strainer over a bowl and ladle the fat through it, being careful to leave behind the cooking juices. Put about ¾ inch of this fat into the sterilized Mason-style jar or earthenware pot you are going to keep the confit in. Let cool and set. Lift the legs with tongs and put them into the jar (they shouldn't touch the edges). Ladle in the rest of the fat to cover completely. Tap firmly on your counter to remove air bubbles. Refrigerate for an hour to firm up, then melt enough lard to provide a ½–¾ inch seal, pour it on top, and return to the refrigerator. When the lard has hardened, put a piece of wax paper over the top. Cover, if using an earthenware pot, or seal, if using a jar. Left like this, the duck should keep for about two months in the refrigerator.

how to use

To serve, remove the duck and scrape off most of the fat. Add 2 tablespoons of the duck fat to a skillet. Over medium heat, let the fat get hot, then add the legs, skin side down. Cook for four to five minutes, browning the skin well. Turn to sauté the other side briefly, another three to four minutes. The duck should be hot and the skin crispy.

Serve with sautéed potatoes (with garlic and parsley) and a watercress salad. It's also great in spring with stewed peas and scallions.

The fat from the confit can be reheated and strained through a strainer (as in the recipe) and can be reused three times for making more confit.

country pork terrine

This is the terrine I make most often. The most taxing thing about it is getting the ingredients out of the cupboard and the refrigerator. The one danger—and it can produce a disappointing terrine—is underseasoning or underspicing. Be aggressive! Other than that, just roll your sleeves up and get going. It's messy but rewarding cooking and feeds a lot of people at one time (wonderful for a big lunch, or when you have friends to stay for the weekend).

Serves 10

FOR THE PÂTÉ

7oz chicken livers

¼ cup brandy

2 tablespoons unsalted butter,
  plus more to grease

1 onion, finely chopped

9oz ground pork

9oz ground veal

9oz diced pork fat

6oz pork liver, finely chopped

4 garlic cloves, crushed

¾ teaspoon ground allspice

good pinch of ground cloves

½ teaspoon grated nutmeg

2 eggs, lightly beaten

sea salt

freshly ground black pepper

FOR LINING AND SEALING

13oz streaky bacon slices,

lard, or duck fat, to seal (optional)

1 Put the chicken livers into a dish and pour the brandy over. Melt the butter and sauté the onion until soft but not coloured. Leave to cool. Mix this with all the other ingredients, except the chicken livers in brandy. Combine with your hands and season really well. Fry a little of the mixture to check the seasoning. (This seems a hassle but it's worth it.) Preheat the oven to 180°C/350°F/gas mark 4.

2 Line a 1.5 litre (2½ pint) terrine mould or loaf tin with a double layer of cling film (if you want to unmould it to serve). Cut the rind off the bacon, then stretch each rasher with the back of a knife and use to cover the base and sides of the terrine; keep some back for the top. Spoon in half the meat, lay the livers on top and season. Put the other half of the meat on the livers. Lay the remaining bacon on top. Cover with buttered greaseproof paper. Put the terrine in a roasting tin and pour in boiling water to come halfway up the sides. Cook for 1¼ hours, until the juices run clear and it feels firm.

3 Let the pâté cool to lukewarm, then put a board (or a piece of cardboard, cut to fit and covered in foil) on top. Weigh down with weights or heavy cans. When completely cool, put it in the refrigerator. You should keep this for 48 hours before eating (it tastes better as it matures).

4 If you want to keep the terrine for longer, pour a layer of melted lard or duck fat over the top. It will keep in the refrigerator like this (uncut) for a week. Return to room temperature before serving.

how to use

Cut into slices (not too thick) and serve with a few salad greens, pickles (I especially like Cerises au Vinaigre, *see* page 239), pickled cucumber or cornichons, and good bread. Remove from the refrigerator about 45 minutes before serving—it is better not too cold.

potted shrimp

If you find a fish dealer who sells peeled brown shrimp, these are a cinch (and so much cheaper than buying them prepared from the store).

Serves 6
2½ sticks unsalted butter
2 blades of mace
good pinch of white pepper

good pinch of cayenne pepper
freshly grated nutmeg
2½ cups peeled, cooked brown shrimp

1 Melt the butter, remove it from the heat, and let sit for a few minutes to let the sediment settle at the bottom. Carefully pour the golden clarified butter into a dish, leaving behind the sediment.

2 Reserve one-quarter of the clarified butter. Put the rest into a skillet with the spices and shrimp and heat through, but don't let the mixture boil. Remove the mace and divide the shrimp among six ramekins. Let these cool, then put into the refrigerator to set.

3 Pour the rest of the clarified butter over the top (gently melt it if it has become solid), completely covering the shrimp, and refrigerate to set once more. These keep in the refrigerator for one week.

potted salmon

A more useful recipe since it's easier to find salmon. It's also a good way to use leftover poached fish (add it to the saucepan with the butter and cook briefly). This is great picnic food. Season it well—it's the seasoning that makes the difference between good and great potted salmon.

Serves 8–10
2 sticks unsalted butter
½ tablespoon olive oil
1½lb salmon fillets
slug of dry vermouth

sea salt
freshly ground black pepper
juice of ½ lemon
½ teaspoon ground cayenne
½ teaspoon freshly grated nutmeg

1 Heat 1½ tablespoons of the butter and all the oil in a skillet and add the fish. Cook over medium heat for two minutes, then add the vermouth. Cover and cook for three minutes, until just cooked.

2 Remove from the skillet, skin, then break up the flesh with a fork until smooth in some parts and coarse in others. Mix with the cooking juices, salt and pepper, lemon juice, cayenne, nutmeg ,and another 1½ tablespoons of butter. Pack tightly into a terrine dish (or a 1 pint Mason-style jar).

3 Melt the rest of the butter and let the sediment settle. Carefully pour the clarified butter over the salmon, leaving the sediment behind, to cover. Cool, then chill to set. This keeps in the refrigerator for one week. Bring out of the refrigerator 20 minutes before serving.

pork rillettes

Rillettes, which are similar to pâtés, are cheap to make. It's good to have a stash if you have a crowd for the weekend. To render pork fat, cut it into cubes, melt them in a heavy saucepan over low heat, then strain.

Makes about 2¼lb rillettes
1lb 2oz pork shoulder
1lb 2oz pork belly (bones and
  rind removed)
12oz pork fat, rendered, plus more
  to grease or store
4 sprigs of thyme

3 bay leaves
4 cloves
very generous pinch of ground allspice
very generous grating of nutmeg
sea salt
freshly ground black pepper

1 Cut the pork shoulder into strips about ¾ inch across, along the grain of the meat. Cut the belly into slices about ½ inch thick. Put the fat and ½ cup of water into a wide, heavy saucepan and set it over very low heat. Add all the meat. Tie the thyme, bay, and cloves in a little square piece of cheesecloth and put it in the pan, too.

2 Cook over very low heat so the liquid just quivers, not bubbles, for three to four hours. It must always be covered in a layer of fat. It's easier to cook this on the stove where you can keep an eye on it. The meat shouldn't brown; it just poaches. Make sure it doesn't stick to the bottom and turn it from time to time. It is ready when completely tender and feels as though you can pull it gently apart.

3 Once the meat has cooled a little, remove the spices and herbs and shred it in the pan, pulling it apart with two forks. Strain the meat through a colander—it should break down into soft strands— and collect the fat. Put the meat in a bowl and add the allspice, nutmeg, and salt and pepper; you need to season well to make good rillettes. Add enough of the fat to make a creamy mixture.

4 Put the mixture into bowls and cover with wax paper that you've greased with pork fat. When they've become firm, melt some more pork fat and pour it over the rillettes. Cover once again with the paper and, once cool, refrigerate. The rillettes taste better after a couple of days in the refrigerator, but eat them within two weeks. Once you've started eating it (and have, therefore, broken the layer of fat), you should consume it within five days. You *must* take the rillettes from the refrigerator two hours before serving, or they will be horribly cold and fatty.

how to use

Rillettes make great snack food (in fact, they are a little too tempting) to spread on toasted sourdough. They are also good lunch food and are wonderful for a crowd: serve with salami, cornichons, radishes, and lentil salad and you have a meal that will make you feel like a *traiteur*.

a dream of bresaola …

I used to fantasize about curing beef and, when I tried it, I found that it gives you a curious thrill, different to that you get from cooking. It feels as though you're nurturing or growing something … You are using the elements instead of hard work and just have to keep an eye on it.

The two versions below and on the next pages taste different, so I'm giving both. I marginally prefer the wet-cured. If you worry about it going wrong—and you shouldn't try this with a gung-ho attitude—depend on your nose. You can smell when it's off; it should smell herby and beefy. Of course, you should only make this when it is very cold, in the fall and winter months.

Slicing is a problem. Bresaola should be paper thin, although the wet-cured version can be cut thicker than the dry-cured. I managed to persuade a deli owner to slice mine, but you may find it difficult to do the same. You can, of course, buy a slicing machine, but they ain't cheap …

bresaola (dry-cured)

This version is both more beefy and sweeter than the wet-brined version. Make sure you read the introduction to this chapter before you start making this. You might prefer to replace the salt and Prague powder with a premix cure.

Makes 2¼lb
⅓ cup flaked sea salt
½ cup firmly packed light brown sugar
2 teaspoons black peppercorns
⅛oz Prague powder number 2
leaves from 2 sprigs of rosemary

1 tablespoon juniper berries
the main muscle from the top round of beef
(that is exactly what you should ask your
butcher for; it will weigh about 3¼lb)

1 Put everything but the beef into your food processor and process. Put into a bowl (make sure you wash the food processor well afterward, because of the curing salt).

2 Trim the surface fat and silverskin from the meat. Rub half the cure into the meat and put it in a sealable freezer bag. Label the bag with the weight and the date. You might think you'll remember when you put it in but you probably won't (I know whereof I speak …). Put the rest of the cure into an airtight container. Put the bag in the refrigerator and let sit for a week, turning it twice a day.

3 Remove the meat, mop it dry with paper towels, and rub the rest of the cure all over it. Put the beef into a clean freezer bag, label, and let sit in the refrigerator for another week, again turning it daily.

4 Rinse the meat and pat dry. Wrap it in a double layer of cheesecloth, tie it up with kitchen string to keep the cloth in place, label, and put it in refrigerator for three weeks. It should be firm to the touch and have lost about 30 percent of its weight (weigh it to check). It will now keep for two weeks in the refrigerator. Slice and serve with extra virgin olive oil, lemon wedges, salad greens, and shavings of parmesan (don't go over the top with embellishments). It can also be served as plain, as you like.

bresaola (wet-cured)

This version, based on the recipe Franco Taruschio used at The Walnut Tree Inn in Wales, tastes really winey and herby. Franco writes that this isn't worth doing unless you cure a really big piece (around 6½lb–11lb), but I never have that many people to feed bresaola to, and I've always found this works really well.

Makes about 2lb

3¼lb bottom round roast
1⅓ cups salt
6 sprigs of rosemary
5 bay leaves
10 cloves

3 garlic cloves, crushed
½ tablespoon crushed black peppercorns
3 strips of organic orange zest
2 bottles red wine (Chilean merlot or similar, nothing too expensive)

1 Trim the meat of any fatty or sinewy parts and remove the string if it has been tied.

2 Mix together all the other ingredients and put in a plastic container in which the beef can fit snugly. Put the meat into the cure and turn it over so it is well coated. Cover and let sit in the refrigerator for five days, turning twice a day.

3 Take the meat out and pat it dry. Tie it up and let cure in the refrigerator as on page 183.

4 Once you've unwrapped it, you'll find that the meat looks unappetizing on the outside, but it should be fine on the inside. You may find a little mold on it; white mold is fine, others are not. (If the meat smells bad or has any mold other than white, get rid of it.) If it has a white mold, just wash the beef with some brine or vinegar, then pat it dry.

5 Slice the beef very, very thinly across the grain. The meat is browner at the edges and pinker in the middle; this is the way it's supposed to be. Wrap it in clean cheesecloth and put it in the refrigerator. (Don't wrap it in plastic wrap or it will sweat). I only recommend keeping it for 10 days from this stage (although I have eaten it afterward with no ill effects). Serve the slices as on page 183.

petit salé aux lentilles

Petit salé is the name the French give to cured pork belly that is boiled instead of fried, and that is lightly salted (hence "petit salé," or "a little salted"). Serve it with white beans, peas, or lentils or, in summer, pureed fresh peas or fava beans. It's a classic of French bourgeois cooking, old-fashioned food of the best kind. There are different approaches. Some people like to cook the lentils in the pot with the cured pork, but I find they often overcook like that.

Serves 6

FOR THE CURE

¾ cup plus 1 tablespoon kosher sea salt

1 tablespoons packed light brown sugar

2 bay leaves

1 teaspoon cloves

1 teaspoon allspice berries

2 teaspoons juniper berries

FOR THE PORK

2¼lb pork belly (a piece with plenty of fat), rind on

2 large carrots, coarsely chopped

1 large onion, coarsely chopped

4 celery sticks, coarsely chopped

2 bay leaves

handful of parsley stalks

8 peppercorns

FOR THE LENTILS

1 tablespoon unsalted butter

½ onion, finely chopped

1 celery stick, diced

1 garlic clove, finely chopped

1 carrot, peeled and diced

1 bay leaf

1 sprig of thyme

1¼ cups green lentils, well rinsed

1 tablespoon finely chopped flat-leaf parsley

freshly ground black pepper

1 To make the cure, just put the ingredients into a food processor and process, or pound in a mortar. You need to salt the pork for about four hours (you can leave it for longer but I prefer a light salting). Place it in a nonreactive dish and rub half the cure into it, then turn it over and massage the rest into the other side. Cover the container, and refrigerate for four to six hours, then rinse.

2 Put the pork in a saucepan with the vegetables, herbs, and peppercorns and cover with cold water. Bring slowly to the boil, skim the surface, then reduce the heat and simmer gently for 1½–2 hours, or until it is completely tender. Reserve the cooking liquid, but discard the vegetables and herbs.

3 For the lentils, melt the butter in a saucepan and sauté the onion and celery until soft but not browned. Add the garlic and cook gently for another minute, then add the carrot, bay, thyme, lentils, and 2½ cups of the pork cooking water. Bring to a boil, reduce the heat ,and cook until the lentils are just tender but still have a little bite (reckon on 15–20 minutes). Keep an eye on them because they can turn to mush suddenly. All the stock should have been absorbed. Remove the bay and thyme and stir in the parsley. Check for seasoning, you probably won't need any salt, but add some pepper.

4 Gently reheat the petit salé in its remaining cooking water, then carve it into slices and serve each person with a pile of lentils topped with a thick slice—or chunks—of petit salé.

bathing beauties

Curing foods in a brining solution is one of the most exciting methods for treating food I have discovered in the last few years. It was an American book (*In the Hands of a Chef* by Jody Adams) that got me hooked. Now the Christmas turkey, basic pork chops, and the occasional whole chicken are regularly submerged in sweet, salty water in my kitchen.

Although curing in brine is a way of preserving meat, it can be done simply to flavor food. And it does this wonderfully. The salt, sugar, herbs, and spices in the brine get through to the very core of the meat and increase its moistness, too.

The process works because of osmosis. If you cure a piece of meat in brine, there is a greater concentration of salt outside the meat than inside it. The salt will flow from where it is more concentrated (the brine) to where it is less concentrated (the cells in the meat). The brine dehydrates the meat. You might think that would mean you end up with dry meat. But no, because something else happens, too. The salt also changes the shape of the protein in the meat. It allows the protein molecules to get bigger and to hang together more loosely, so they end up retaining more water within each cell, not less. When the brined meat is exposed to heat, it retains this moisture—which is really locked in—as the meat is cooking. So brined meat is always moister than unbrined meat. That's the science. However, you'll only really be convinced when you discover the flavor.

The effect of curing on pork is profound, especially now that pigs are bred with less fat than they were in the past. It's also good for turkeys, which tend to dry out with cooking. It might seem like a hassle for a roasted chicken, but give it a try. You can also just salt your chicken a day ahead of cooking it. It will have a similar effect to curing with a brine solution, although you will not be able to get other flavorings to penetrate as effectively. (In Finland, there is an old-fashioned approach to preparing chickens by rubbing them with salt and pine needles and letting them sit for 24 hours before you cook them.)

Whether you use brine or dry salt, you also need sugar in the mixture. It helps to offset some of the harsher effects of salt; it softens it. It also enhances flavor in its own right.

You can play around with herbs and spices in brine solutions—curing in a brine is just another step in cooking, after all, much like marinating—but there are some rules. Use the brine indicated for each recipe and cure for the length of time suggested. More salt, or more time bathing in the brine, will produce saltier meat. Obviously, make sure your brine is cold when you add the meat. Keep the meat submerged (weigh it down with a plate to keep it below the level of the brine). After curing, put the meat in the refrigerator, uncovered, to dry. The brine continues to disperse in the meat, plus the surface of the meat dries.

The first time I did some curing in a brine, I did it on pork chops. They were good pork chops to start with, admittedly, but as my friends ate them (with nothing more exciting than fried potatoes and salad on the side), they kept saying "Are these really just pork chops?" Try it ... the proof of the pudding, etc.

sweet tea-cured chicken

I read about curing in sweet tea in an American magazine. It seemed like a great idea, and works for pork as well as chicken. Apart from seasoning the meat right through to the core, as all brines do, the tea gives it a fruity, herby flavor. My children actually prefer this to plain roasted chicken, because curing creates a very moist, tender bird. You can use this approach for chicken parts as well as for a whole chicken.

Serves 6

about 8 tea bags (I use Darjeeling)

heaping 1 cup firmly packed light brown sugar

1/3 cup sea salt

juice and zest of 1 organic orange, removed in broad
  strips (be sure it doesn't have white pith attached)

4lb oven-ready chicken

2 tablespoons unsalted butter

1 Make very strong tea (it's easiest with tea bags) in a large saucepan with 8½ cups of boiling water. While the tea is still hot, add the sugar, salt, and orange juice and zest. Stir to help the sugar and salt dissolve and let sit until completely cool.

2 Pierce the chicken all over with a sharp knife. Add 8½ cups of cold water to the cool brine. Transfer the brine to a suitable container (a bucket or a large plastic container) and immerse the chicken in it. Weigh it down with a plate so it is completely covered in the brine. Refrigerate (I take the vegetable bins out and put the chicken there) and let sit for six to eight hours, turning a couple of times.

3 Lift the chicken from the brine and shake off the excess liquid. Rinse. Carefully dry it with paper towels, and return to the refrigerator, uncovered, for three hours to dry completely. Return the bird to room temperature and put it in a roasting pan, and preheat the oven to 350°F. Calculate the cooking time for the chicken (20 minutes per 1lb, plus 10 minutes). Smear the butter over the skin and roast the chicken in the hot oven. You will need to cover the chicken with aluminum foil about halfway through cooking time, because the sugar in the brine makes the skin very dark. A food thermometer, inserted into the thickest part of the bird, away from any bones, should read 165°F.

how to use

As this is an American idea, I serve the bird with American trimmings: shoe string fries or potato wedges, a big green salad with ranch dressing (or another buttermilk-base dressing), and maybe corn cakes.

maple-cured pork chops with pear and juniper relish

This, based on a recipe by Jody Adams, is what first got me into curing. The chops are succulent, the meat seasoned right to its core, and the relish echoes the spicing in the meat.

Serves 4

FOR THE PEAR AND JUNIPER RELISH

4 slim pears (such as Bosc), peeled, halved, and cored

juice of ½ lemon

2 tablespoons gin

⅓ cup firmly packed light brown sugar

2 tablespoons maple syrup

½ teaspoon ground cloves

8 juniper berries, crushed

1 small red onion, finely chopped

2 garlic cloves, crushed

½ cup perry or cider vinegar

1 sprig of rosemary

FOR THE BRINE

½ cup salt

½ cup firmly packed light brown sugar

1 cup maple syrup

3 tablespoons Dijon mustard

2 tablespoons juniper berries

12 garlic cloves, crushed

needles from 4 sprigs of rosemary, chopped

small bunch of thyme

FOR THE PORK

4 large thick pork chops (about 1lb each)

sunflower oil or peanut oil

freshly ground black pepper

1 Preheat the oven to 350°F. To make the relish, mix the pears with the lemon juice, gin, and 2 tablespoons of the sugar. Put these in a roasting pan or dish where they can lie closely in a single layer. Bake in the oven for about 40 minutes, or until soft (it depends how ripe the pears are).

2 While the pears are cooking, mix all the rest of the ingredients for the relish in a saucepan. Bring gently to a boil, then reduce the heat and simmer for five minutes.

3 Chop the roasted pears and add them to the spicy vinegar. Bring to a boil and stir everything around so the flavors mix together. You can now just put this in a bowl and keep until you want to eat it, although I like it warm so keep it in the saucepan until I am serving the chops.

4 Mix together all the brine ingredients in a large saucepan with 6¾ cups of water and gently bring to a boil. Stir to help all the salt and sugar dissolve. Cool completely, then put into a nonreactive container with the pork chops. Cover and refrigerate for 12 hours, but no more.

5 Take the pork out of the brine, rinse, and pat dry with paper towels, then refrigerate, uncovered, for two hours to dry out. Return the pork to room temperature while you preheat the oven to 350°F. Heat a ridged grill pan until really hot, brush the chops on each side with oil, and sprinkle with pepper. Brown them really well on the grill pan on each side, then move them into the oven and cook for 30 minutes. They should be cooked through (do check that the flesh isn't pink by piercing to the center of one chop with a small sharp knife). A food thermometer should have a reading of 145°F. Serve with the relish.

honey and mustard-cured pork belly

Another big taste of America. You can use the brine for other cuts of pork, and for leg or shoulder of lamb, too. These large cuts can be left for 24 hours, longer than for chops.

Serves 8

FOR THE BRINE
⅓ cup sea salt
¾ cup honey
½ cup Dijon mustard
small bunch of thyme

FOR THE PORK
5lb thick end of pork belly (ask the butcher
    for the last six ribs, and get him to score
    the rind for crackling)
small bunch of thyme (14 or so sprigs)
1 tablespoon olive oil
fine-flaked sea salt
freshly ground black pepper

1 Put the brine ingredients in a large saucepan with 9½ cups of water. Bring to a boil, stirring to help the salt dissolve. Cool completely, then put the pork in a nonreactive container and pour the brine over it (you may have to weigh it to keep it under the surface). Refrigerate for 24 hours.

2 Rinse the pork, dry well, and return to the refrigerator for three to six hours. Preheat the oven to 425°F. Lay the meat in a roasting pan. Pull the leaves from the thyme and rub them into the skin with the oil, salt, and pepper. Roast for 30 minutes, then reduce the heat to 350°F and cook for an hour. Test; the juices should run clear when pierced and a food thermometer should read 145°F. If the crackling could be crispier, return the heat to 425°F and check after five minutes.

3 Remove the crackling. Serve each person with a good thick slice of the meat and some crackling.

home-salted cod

Don't be intimidated by the idea of salting your own cod. It is incredibly simple. You just need to remember to salt it two days before you need it.

Serves 8 as part of an aioli platter (see page 193)
3¼lb cod fillet with skin

kosher salt

1 Run your hand along the fish, feeling for any bones. If there are any there, pull them out (tweezers are good for this). Put a ½ inch layer of salt into a nonreactive container big enough to hold the cod. Set the fish on top, skin side down, then completely cover with another ½ inch layer of salt.

2 Cover and refrigerate for 24 hours. The next day remove the salt cod (the salt will have turned to brine), and rinse the fish in cold water.

3 Cover with fresh water and soak for 24 hours, changing the water three times. It is ready to cook.

winter aioli

The classic French use for your home-salted cod, adapted for the colder months.

Serves 8

FOR THE AUOLI

4 garlic cloves, peeled
sea salt
3 extra-large egg yolks
2 cups fruity extra virgin olive oil
juice of ½ lemon
freshly ground white pepper

FOR THE FISH

1¼ cups dry white wine
1 onion, roughly chopped
1 celery stick, coarsely chopped
1 small bunch of parsley

1 bay leaf
a few black peppercorns
1 recipe Home-Salted Cod (*see* page 191)

FOR THE VEGETABLES, AND TO SERVE

8 eggs
16 medium carrots (not too fat)
1 cauliflower
2–3 fennel bulbs
juice of 1 lemon (optional)
1lb baby broccoli
10–12 small new potatoes, unpeeled
1 generous bunch of watercress
extra virgin olive oil, to drizzle

1 To make the aioli, crush the garlic with a little salt and mix in the egg yolks until they are shiny. While beating—with a wooden spoon or an electric mixer—start adding olive oil in tiny drops. Make sure each drop has been incorporated before you add the next. Keep beating and adding the oil in a steadily increasing stream. If your mixture splits, start again with a new egg yolk and gradually add the curdled mixture, going slowly this time. Add the lemon juice a little at a time at the end, tasting before you've added it all to make sure you're happy with it, and season with salt and pepper. Don't worry if the aioli is thick—it's supposed to be. They don't call it "beurre de Provence" for nothing.

2 Make a court bouillon by putting enough water into a fish poacher or large saucepan to cover the fish. Add the wine and all the aromatics. Bring to a boil, reduce the heat, and simmer for an hour. Half an hour before serving, return it to a boil, then reduce the heat to a very gentle simmer. Lower in the cod, cover, and poach for 25 minutes. The flesh should be opaque, not translucent, and cooked through. (Check the fattest part.) Return to the fish poacher if it needs more time.

3 Meanwhile, boil the eggs for 10 minutes, and prepare the vegetables. The vegetables should be lukewarm, so count the cooking time backward to make sure they're all ready with the fish. Wash the carrots, snip off the fronds, leaving a little greenery behind, and scrape them. Remove the leaves from the cauliflower and break it into florets. Cut the coarse ends from the fennel, plus the fronds and tough outer leaves. (Keep these for soup.) Quarter each bulb lengthwise and cut out the core, leaving enough to hold the pieces together. If you have large bulbs, cut each quarter in half again. If you're doing this in advance, squeeze fresh lemon over the fennel so it doesn't discolor. Trim the broccoli.

4 Steam the vegetables: potatoes and carrots take 15 minutes; cauliflower, which should be al dente, takes eight; broccoli and fennel take four. Shell the eggs and halve them. Put them on a platter with the vegetables. Season with salt. Lift the fish from the poacher and remove the skin. Place on the platter with the watercress. Drizzle extra virgin olive oil over everything, and serve the aioli alongside.

japanese pickled mackerel

If you aren't going to eat this immediately, you must remove the dark flesh, as in the recipe.

Serves 2

2 especially fresh mackerel fillets
½ cup superfine sugar
4 teaspoons flaked sea salt
1 cup rice vinegar
⅔ cup mirin

TO SERVE

pickled ginger, or grated fresh ginger root
soy sauce
wasabi

1 Remove the dark flesh which was next to the spine, because it spoils quickly. Sprinkle with ¼ cup of the sugar and all the salt. Cover and refrigerate for 12 hours. Rinse and pat dry. If oily liquid has come to the surface, wipe, wash again, and pat dry.

2 Mix together the vinegar, mirin, and remaining sugar and stir to help the sugar dissolve. Put the fillets in a nonreactive dish and pour the marinade over them. Refrigerate for an hour. Remove the transparent membrane from the skin (this contains parasitic bacteria), then slice.

3 Eat immediately, with ginger, a soy sauce dip, and a dab of wasabi, or put the fish and vinegar into a sterilized jar (*see* page 11; the fish must be covered in vinegar), seal, and refrigerate for up to two weeks.

pickled lox

In 1920s New York—before there was smoked salmon—barrels of salmon in brine (shipped from Alaska) were desalted by deli owners and sold as "lox" (from the German for salmon, *lachs*). This will make your weekend brunches that bit more interesting.

Serves 4 as an appetizer

1 cup distilled white vinegar
½ firmly packed light brown sugar
1 tablespoon sea salt
6 bay leaves
2 teaspoons coriander seeds
2 teaspoons yellow mustard seeds

1 teaspoon black peppercorns
½ teaspoon allspice berries
¼ cup coarsely chopped dill
½ teaspoon celery seeds
1lb salmon fillet with skin
1 large onion, finely sliced

1 Put everything except the salmon and onion in a saucepan with 4 cups of water and simmer for five minutes. Cool. Put the salmon and onion in a nonreactive container and pour the brine over it.

2 Cover and refrigerate for four days, or up to two weeks, then skin, slice, and serve.

how to use

Mix the salmon with 1 cup sour cream, half the onion slices, and ¼ cup of pickling liquid. Add chopped sweet pickled cucumber, apple matchsticks, or chopped dill. Serve with boiled new potatoes.

beet-cured gravlax

I have been making straightforward gravlax—using just dill, salt, and sugar —for years, and always toyed with the idea of making a beet version. To be honest, the beet only flavors the fish flesh slightly, but makes its mark through the color it imparts. A platter of sliced beet-cured gravlax is just glorious looking: furls of coral edged with crimson. This is a splendid dish for feeding a lot of people (it's a boon at Christmas) and it doesn't take much effort. Go for organically farmed salmon from a good source, or wild Alaskan salmon.

Serves about 14

2¾lb tail piece of salmon in two halves, filleted, but skin left on

⅓ cup vodka

⅔ cup granulated sugar

⅓ cup sea salt flakes

2 tablespoons coarsely ground black pepper

large bunch of dill, roughly chopped

5 raw beets, grated

1 Check the salmon for any bones your fish dealer might have missed (rubbing your hand along the flesh is the best way to find them). Remove any you find with tweezers.

2 Line a dish big enough to hold the salmon with a double layer of aluminum foil (I usually use a roasting pan). Put one of the pieces of salmon, skin down, on top. Rub it with half the vodka. Mix together the sugar, salt, pepper, dill, and beet and spread it over the salmon. Pour the rest of the vodka over the fish and put the other piece of salmon (skin up) on top. Pull the foil up around the fish, then put some weights on top (such as cans, jars, or a heavy cutting board). Refrigerate and let cure for two to four days, turning every so often. Liquid will seep out of the salmon in this time; just pour it off.

3 Remove the foil and scrape the cure off both pieces of fish. To serve, slice as you would smoked salmon (leave the skin behind). Use as needed and keep, wrapped, in the refrigerator for a week.

how to use

Chrain, a Jewish relish, goes as well with Corned Beef (*see* page 173) as it does with gravlax. Horseradish Cream is also ideal with either.

CHRAIN

Put 4 cooked beets, peeled and cut into chunks, in a food processor with 2½ cups grated horseradish root, 1 tablespoon balsamic vinegar (preferably white), 2 tablespoons granulated sugar, and salt, to taste. Pulse-blend to a coarse mixture (not a puree). Serves 6; can be doubled.

HORSERADISH CREAM

Beat ⅔ cup heavy whipping cream, then add 2½ tablespoons grated horseradish root, ¾ tablespoon white wine vinegar, 1 teaspoon English mustard, sugar ,and salt to taste and a good squeeze of lemon. The vinegar and lemon will thicken the cream, so don't overbeat. Serves 6, but easily doubled.

whiskey and brown sugar-cured gravlax

Sweet and slightly peaty, I am very proud of having made gravlax into an almost Irish dish!
I actually prefer this to traditional gravlax with dill mustard sauce.

Serves about 14

2¾lb tail piece of salmon in two halves,
    filleted, but skin left on
½ cup whiskey
½ cup firmly packed light brown sugar

⅓ cup sea salt flakes
2 tablespoons coarsely ground black pepper
large bunch of dill, roughly chopped
1 large tart apple, peeled, cored, and coarsely grated

1 Check the salmon for any bones your fish dealer might have missed (rubbing your hand along the
flesh is the best way to find them). Remove any you find with tweezers.

2 Line a dish big enough to hold the salmon with a double layer of aluminum foil (I usually put the
salmon in a roasting pan). Put one of the pieces of salmon, skin down, on top. Rub it all over with
half the whiskey. Mix together the sugar, salt and pepper, dill, and apple in a bowl and spread it over
the salmon. Pour the rest of the whiskey over the fish and put the other piece of salmon (skin side
up) on top. Pull the foil up around the fish, then put some weights on top (cans or jars or a heavy
cutting board, for example). Put this into the refrigerator and let cure for two to four days, turning
every so often. Liquid will seep out of the salmon in this time; you can just pour it off.

3 Remove the foil and scrape the cure off both pieces of fish.

4 To serve, slice the salmon just as you would smoked salmon (leave the skin behind). Use as you
need it and keep, wrapped, in the refrigerator. It will keep for a week.

how to use

Unexpectedly good with this version of gravlax, a salad that is a great
balance of sweet and tart, and wonderfully refreshing with the fish.

SWEET AND SOUR APPLE SALAD

Halve and core 3 tart apples, then cut the flesh into little matchsticks.
Cut 1 red onion into wafer-thin slices (on a mandolin, if you have one).
Mix ⅓ cup rice wine vinegar with ¼ cup superfine or granulated sugar
and stir until dissolved. Toss the apple and onion immediately with this
and add 2 tablespoons chopped dill. Serves 6, but easily doubled.

in coolness, in silence and in shadow: scandinavian salt-cured fish

In the great North—the Scandinavian countries and beyond—preserving fish by drying, smoking, or (once it was economically viable) salting was, for centuries, necessary for survival. It meant you could still eat fish when frozen waters and storms made it impossible to catch them. The Scandinavians' mastery of this kind of curing, and their love of the food it produces, has ensured its survival, although we no longer need to treat food this way. The Scandinavian approach to fish is one of the easiest places for the home curer to start.

It's also one of the most calming things you can do in the kitchen. Perhaps it's because you are handling fish flesh, which always seems so pure. Or maybe it's the silvery skin. Salting meat is butch and no-nonsense. It makes you feel earthed. Showering fish with handfuls of salt— especially when it's flecked with dill—makes you feel light, uplifted. In fact, Scandinavians say you should make gravlax, their great classic dish of salt-cured salmon, "in coolness, in silence and in shadow." It's an activity that promotes contemplation. It also embodies what I think is a very Scandinavian attitude to food. They like to bring the outside into the kitchen. They want to put the forest and the sea onto their tables. Despite the fact that the Danish superchef René Redzepi, at his famous Noma restaurant in Copenhagen, cooks complicated fare, he still exhibits a desire to put wild things, such as pine needles, salmon, and berries, on the plate.

Gravlax is simple to make. You smother fish in salt, sugar, and dill, weigh it down, let it sit in the refrigerator for a few days, then brush off the cure and eat the flesh that has become firm, salty, and sweet. No heat is used. You have simply caught salmon in its tracks, temporarily stopping its deterioration. It's just as easy to cure herring, but a little more daunting because there are so many variations. When I was a child, my dad used to bring cured herrings back with him whenever he went abroad (he loves them). I was fascinated by jars in which you could see flashes of silver bathed in vinegar, peppered with spices, or sour cream and fronds of dill. It looked like food from a clean, pure world. I began making cured herring partly to regain a taste of childhood, and have developed a real love for them. (My partner jokes that he can't think of any other woman who can sigh wistfully and murmur, "God, I would really love a herring".)

Once you start looking at herring recipes—and even the cured herrings on the shelves of Scandinavian supermarket—you can get completely confused as to what's what. In the past, before refrigeration, all herrings were salted before further treatment. Now this isn't always the case, so here is a primer on what can be done to herrings.

First of all herrings can be soused; with this approach the herrings are cooked and then put into a pickling solution. Secondly, raw herrings—unsalted—can be put straight into a pickling solution (this can have many different flavors and be salty or salty-sweet). Finally, fresh herrings can be dry-salted or brined (you can do this yourself, following the instructions on the right, or buy them already prepared) and then put into flavored vinegar solutions or mixed into sour cream or sauces flavored with mustard, curry, sherry, or tomatoes. There are endless possibilities and hundreds of Scandinavian recipes using different flavors. As well as eating cured herrings cold, you can sauté them (dip them first in rye flour or rye bread crumbs) or you can layer them up in a potato gratin (try Jansson's Temptation made with cured herrings instead of anchovies: absolutely delicious).

QUICK-SALTED HERRING

I have always found it difficult to get hold of salt herring in Britain, so I follow a recipe from Jane Grigson and quick-salt my own. If you can get hold of salt herring then buy them, but making your own is easy and cheap.

Prepare a brine by dissolving 3 tablepoons of salt in 2 cups of water and immerse 12 herring fillets in this for three hours (the fish need to be completely covered in the brine). If you are using these in recipes, you don't have to soak them before use because they are salted to the right level (not too much, not too little), and can be used immediately.

FULLY SALTED HERRING

In Scandinavia, you can get fully salted herring, which are layered with salt (sometimes salt and spices) and left for three months (and longer) before being eaten. Most Scandinavians don't bother to make fully salted herrings at home, but it's worth doing if you get a generous haul of really fresh fish. (I've done it a few times with great success.)

If you want to make them, get your fish dealer to gut and scale the herrings, but leave the heads on. When you get home, wash them very well, removing all traces of blood, then drain them. You need either a earthernware pot or a plastic container. Sterilize the container. Mix together 2 cups of sea salt flakes, 1¼ cups of granulated sugar or 1 cup of frimly packedlight brown sugar, 1 tablespoon of crushed black peppercorns, 1 tablespoon of allspice berries, lightly crushed, and a handful of bay leaves. Put a ¾ inch thick layer of this in the bottom of your container. Place the fish side by side and head to tail and add enough of the salt mixture to cover. Add more fish and more salt, layering them, and finish with a thick layer of salt. Put a piece of aluminum foil on top and cover with a weight that has been sterilized (this will keep the fish under the brine that soon forms). Cover with a lid or plastic wrap and store in the refrigerator. It's important that all the equipment you use is sterilized and your hands are scrupulously clean when you are preparing fish in this way. The fish will be ready to eat in two to three months. These need to be soaked in water, or a mixture of milk and water, before you use them (the soaking time depends on the length of time they've been salted).

A NORTHERN FEAST

In Scandinavia, it's possible to eat salted or pickled fish at every meal. In fact, breakfast in an old-fashioned Scandinavian hotel, where cured herrings play a central role, is a glorious thing (and a healthy way to start the day). For a Scandinavian brunch, serve Cured Herrings with Dill and Juniper (*see* page 205) with hard-boiled eggs, sour cream, keta or caviar, cured ham, cheeses, rye bread, and Shaken Red Currants (*see* page 143), adding yogurt and rye bread crumbs fried with butter and sugar. A northern feast. And one within your reach.

eastern gravlax

You may be sighing … and yes, I admit, this is not a recipe for the purist. But gravlax is so good and so easy to make that I can never resist a spin on the original.

Serves about 14

2¾lb tail piece of salmon in two halves, filleted, but skin left on
½ cup sake or dry sherry
½ cup firmly packed light brown sugar
⅓ cup sea salt flakes
2 tablespoons coarsely ground black pepper
1½ inch fresh ginger root, finely grated
large bunch of cilantro, coarsely chopped
4 red chiles, halved, seeded, and shredded

1 Check the salmon for any bones your fish dealer might have missed (rubbing your hand along the flesh is the best way to find them). Remove any you find with tweezers.

2 Line a dish big enough to hold the salmon with a double layer of aluminum foil (I usually put the salmon in a roasting pan). Put one of the pieces of salmon, skin down, on top. Rub it all over with half the sake. Mix the sugar, salt and pepper, ginger, cilantro, and chiles in a bowl and spread over the salmon. Pour on the rest of the sake and put the other piece of salmon (skin side up) on top. Pull the foil up around the fish, then put some weights on top (cans or jars or a heavy cutting board, for example). Refrigerate and let cure for two to four days, turning every so often. Liquid will seep out of the salmon in this time, you can just pour it off.

3 Remove the foil and scrape the cure off the fish. To serve, slice just as you would smoked salmon (leave the skin behind). Use as you need and keep, wrapped, in the refrigerator, for a week.

how to use

Serve with the hot mango relish below, or a little jar of wasabi and some pickled ginger. Rice salad (or warm vinegared rice as used for sushi) makes this into a great lunch dish (and a fairly low-calorie one, too).

MANGO AND CUCUMBER RELISH

This is a like an Asian pickle and needs no cooking, it should be fresh. Make it no more than an hour ahead, or the mixture becomes flaccid.

Mix the juice of 2 limes with 2 teaspoon superfine sugar and stir to dissolve. Peel 2 only-just-ripe mangoes, and cut the flesh into ¼ inch cubes. Halve and seed 1 small cucumber and chop the flesh into cubes about the size of the mango. Mix the mango and cucumber with the lime solution, the finely grated zest of 1 lime, 2 red chiles, seeded and cut into slivers, 1 tablespoon peanut oil, 2 garlic cloves, finely chopped, 3 tablespoons chopped cilantro, 6 scallions, finely chopped, 5 teaspoons Thai fish sauce, and season to taste (you may not want any salt). Serves 8–10.

cider-cured herrings

This delicious recipe was given to me by chef Mark Hix, champion of all things British. It's a stunner (I've changed it only slightly) and will cheer any of you who would like to claim cured herring for the British. Kingston Black is an apple-based aperitif from Somerset cider and brandy maker Julian Temperley and well worth getting hold of for this (and to drink).

Serves 4

FOR THE MARINADE

1¼ cups cider vinegar

⅓ cup superfine or granulated sugar

2 teaspoons sea salt

25–30 fresh green peppercorns

1 teaspoon fennel seeds

4 juniper berries

2 bay leaves

6 shallots, cut into rings

FOR THE FISH

16 herring fillets, scaled, boned, and trimmed

FOR THE SAUCE

⅓ cup good mayonnaise (preferably homemade)

⅓ cup sour cream

1 teaspoon Tewkesbury mustard, Dijon mustard. or grainu mustard

2 tablespoons Kingston Black or apple brandy

2 tablespoons chopped dill or fennel

1 Bring all the ingredients for the marinade (except the shallots) to a boil with 1¼ cups of water, then let cool and add the shallots. Mix with the herring fillets, then lay the fish in a nonreactive container and pour the marinade over them. Refrigerate for at least four or five days.

2 To make the sauce, whisk together the mayonnaise, sour cream, and mustard, add the Kingston Black or brandy and enough marinade to make a sauce with the consistency of a heavy cream. Stir in the dill.

3 To serve, remove the fillets from the marinade and dry on paper towels. Fold them in half with the skin on the outside and arrange on a serving platter (or divide among plates), with a few of the shallots and green peppercorns sprinkled on top. You can either pour the sauce over the herring or serve it separately. Because of the cream, this should be refrigerated and eaten within 48 hours. Serve with rye bread or new potatoes.

cured herrings with dill and juniper

Our "rollmops" can be of questionable quality, often cured in harsh vinegar. The Scandinavians make much better versions and there are hundreds of variations on this theme. Using this recipe as a blueprint, you can try different flavorings—coriander, mustard seeds, a little star anise, horseradish, fresh ginger root—so experiment. You can also reduce the sugar, but I do love a sweet herring.

Serves 3—4

12 salted herring fillets
1 carrot, thinly sliced
sprigs from a small bunch of dill
1 red onion, finely sliced

FOR THE VINEGAR SOLUTION

1 cup white wine vinegar
1¼ cups granulated sugar
3 bay leaves
10 black peppercorns
¾ tablespoon juniper berries, lightly crushed
2 teaspoons caraway seeds, crushed

1 Soak the salted herrings in cold water for six hours, then drain and rinse in cold water. (If you have used the quick-salting method on page 201, there's no need to soak because they will be ready to use.)

2 Put all the ingredients for the vinegar solution, with 1 cup of water, into a saucepan and bring slowly to a boil, stirring to help the sugar dissolve, then reduce the heat and simmer for 15 minutes. Remove from the heat and let to cool completely.

3 Drain the herring fillets and either leave them whole or cut them into 2 inch lengths. Layer them up in a sterilized jar (*see* page 11) with the carrot, sprigs of dill, and onion. Pour the cold sweet vinegar over them, seal with a vinegar-proof lid, refrigerate, and let sit for four days before eating. Remove the fish as you want it (although make sure the fish remaining in the jar is always covered by the vinegar solution). Keep, refrigerated, for a month.

and also

HERRINGS IN SOUR CREAM

Soak 1lb salted herring fillets in cold water for six hours, then drain and rinse in cold water. (If you have quick-salted your herring as on page 201, they will be ready to use immediately.) Roll the herrings into spirals and arrange in a wide, shallow bowl. Mix together 4 shallots, finely sliced, 1¼ cups sour cream, 1 teaspoon Swedish mustard, 1 teaspoon cayenne pepper, ½ tablespoon superfine sugar, and 3 tablespoons chopped dill and beat well. Combine with the fish, then cover and refrigerate for about four hours or overnight. Don't serve straight from the refrigerator (the cream can become a bit "set"), but let it sit for about 20 minutes before you dish it up. Because there is cream in this dish, you need to eat it within 48 hours. Serves four as an appetizer.

chutneys, relishes, and pickles

When I was ten, I had a pickled onion addiction. I could get through half a jar of pickled onions during an evening's TV (I would have eaten more, but questions would have been asked). I'd sneak one little pearl from the refrigerator, then return over and over again. The sweet onions and the tart vinegar (and the coldness of both) was irresistible.

In the British tradition, pickles with meat or cheese provides the richness and variety that is part of good eating. Pickles and chutneys were designed to preserve food, but even when it was necessary they gave delight. Small salty or sour morsels are satisfying. The Romans were adept picklers and bathed a vast range of things (even lettuce) in vinegar. And the British, who love that sweet-sour tang, took to it with gusto. The great British food book of the 17th century, *Acetaria*, included recipes for pickling ash "keys" (the helicopter seeds from the European ash tree), sea asparagus, and elder shoots. Chutneys, which the British made their own, imitate the fresh chutneys of India but making them richer and sweeter.

There are good chutneys and pickles to buy nowadays, but the big sellers mostly taste either bland or harsh. I have sympathy with Eliza Acton. She favored domestically produced pickles and is wonderful in full sail (in *Modern Cookery for Private Families*, 1845), taking commercial picklers to task for the dangerous practice of cooking in brass pans to produce a green color (cookbooks of the time, amazingly, also recommended this method).

Homemade pickles and chutneys are economical, and there is a real thrill in creating your own combinations inspired by bumper crops, travels abroad, or your imagination. There's such wonderful stuff you can't buy: pickled rhubarb to eat with pork, or pickled gooseberries for goat cheese; Moldavian pepper and dill relish for fish; the kind of pickled cucumbers you get in Moscow's market on a hot day ... when did you see those in a supermarket near you?

Innovation and adventure are perfectly possible with pickles and chutneys. You don't have to worry too much about science, and it becomes a cinch once you've made a few jars. Pickles and chutneys look beautiful, coming in all shapes and hues. American-Iranian poet Arash Saedinia, remembering childhood preserves, wrote of jars of vegetables "gossiping in vinegar." Chutneys and pickles present a multicultural, lesser-known world. So here's the knowledge.

CHUTNEYS AND RELISHES

These are mixtures of chopped fruit or vegetables (or both), usually cooked with vinegar, sugar, and spices (I'll deal with "fresh" chutneys later). Chutneys need long, slow cooking, while relishes taste lighter and fresher and are cooked for shorter periods. Relishes are ready to eat immediately and should be refrigerated once opened. (Some should be kept in the refrigerator from the start. The recipe will direct you.)

The produce used for chutneys can be slightly overripe, but first remove any bruised flesh. Chutneys and relishes should be made in stainless steel saucepans—copper and brass react badly with vinegar—but apart from that, you only need a wooden spoon for stirring and sterilized jars (*see* page 11), plus any other equipment if canning.

When I first started making chutneys, I was worried about them not thickening enough and so I overcooked them, which meant they became dry once canned. A chutney is ready when you can draw a channel across the bottom of the pan with your spoon that stays open for a few seconds before closing up again. While cooking, stir often and well to mack sure the chutney doesn't catch on the bottom of pan.

Canning is important, as with all other preserves (*see* pages 268–269 for complete instructions). Fill warm, dry sterilized jars, leaving a headspace, or gap of ¼ inch or ½ inch from the top, depending on the recipe (chunkier ingredients require a larger gap), and ladle in the chutney while hot (don't can in really hot jars or the chutney will continue to cook). I like covering chutneys with wax paper disks because I think it helps keep them moist, but the most important thing is to screw the lids on tightly, so the chutneys don't dry out. Use vinegar-proof lids (most lids are vinegar-proof these days), and store in a cool, dark place. It's best to let them sit for a couple of months before eating (unless they are fresh chutneys). They can taste very brash before they've aged. Refrigerate after opening.

PICKLES

The most common type of pickles are clear pickles. Think pickled onions. With these pickles, ingredients can be salted, using either dry salt or brine (a salt solution), then rinsed and canned in hot or cold vinegar or brine (cold vinegar produces crisper results). Vinegar is often flavored with spices or herbs and can include sugar. Some pickles (fruits, for example) are not salted, but preserved only in vinegar (usually sweetened vinegar). Foods to be pickled can be either raw or lightly cooked.

Thick pickles are a smaller group, of which piccalilli is a British favorite. The fruit or vegetables are cooked in a sweet vinegar solution with spices, then flour or cornstarch is added to thicken the mixture.

To make good pickles, use vegetables in perfect condition, rinse and drain well after salting, and prepare them in stainless steel saucepans. With canning, follow the recipe and make sure the pickles are completely covered in liquid (*see* page 268–269 for complete canning instructions), and refrigerate after opening.

QUICK PICKLES, FRESH PICKLES, REFRIGERATOR PICKLES, UNUSUAL PICKLES

I have offered some recipes that are not true pickles—in our eyes—they need to be refrigerated and have a short shelf life. However, they form an important part of the pickling traditions in particular cultures, and are increasingly part of the way we eat today. Some Middle Eastern pickles are soaked in brine and kept in the refrigerator. It's the same with Russian dill pickles. Others from southeast Asia are nothing more than raw ingredients mixed in rice vinegar and sugar, and there are recipes here, too, for fresh Indian chutneys (where our British versions started off) and Indian "oil pickles." Pickles and chutneys form a broad category. Explore them all.

ESSENTIAL INGREDIENTS

The Roman writer Columella wrote that "vinegar and hard brine are essential for making preserves." He hit the nail on the head.

VINEGAR

Bacteria and molds grow best in an alkaline or neutral solution; increase the acidity and growth is reduced. Vinegar for preserving needs to have an acetic acid content of at least five percent (all the main types do). Different vinegars produce varied results and colors.

MALT VINEGAR is made from malted barley and has a harsh flavor. It dominated pickle-making in Great Britain for more than 100 years, but is rarely used now.

WHITE DISTILLED VINEGAR is the clear result of distilling malt vinegar. It is less pungent and really useful where you want to preserve the color of a particular vegetable.

WINE VINEGAR is expensive (in large quantities), but sometimes worth it for the mild flavor.

CIDER AND PERRY VINEGAR have wonderful fruity flavors. I use them a lot.

RICE VINEGAR comes from the Far East and is mild and mellow. It is used a lot for quick pickles, which are kept in the refrigerator and eaten soon after they are made.

SALT

Salt preserves as well as flavors and works in two key ways simultaneously: it draws out liquid and, at the same time, flows into the tissues of the food. The combination of salt and a lack of moisture inhibits the growth of microorganisms, and so preserves food.

There are several main types: rock salt, which can be bought as unrefined crystals (make sure it is food grade); pickling salt, an additive-free, fine-grind salt often used in brines for pickling; kosher salt, an additive-free salt with irregular, coarse grains that are ideal for drawing blood out of meat; sea salt, produced by the evaporation of sea water; and table salt, highly refined and usually mixed with chemicals. Avoid using table salt for pickling; it has a dull flavor and the chemicals slow the rate at which it penetrates food.

Salt's talent for drawing water makes vegetables firm, and means pickles won't be diluted.

TO DRY-SALT, layer the chosen vegetables in a colander, sprinkling with salt as you work. Use 1 tablespoon of salt for 1 pound of vegetables. Let sit for anywhere from 2 to 24 hours.

TO WET-SALT, OR BRINE, use 3 tablespoons of salt to 2½ cups of water. When brining, put a plate on top to weigh down the vegetables under the liquid.

SUGAR

The sugar you use has a big effect on flavor. I use pale sugars for clear pickles so they look vibrant, but in chutneys and relishes you can use white granulated or light brown sugar. Dark sugars produce richer flavors. Honey can also replace some sugar, but it's more expensive.

SPICES

If you are making clear pickles, spices should be left whole so the vinegar isn't cloudy. You can either add the spices to the jars, or cook them in the vinegar in a cheesecloth bag that is then removed. Spices for chutneys and relishes will taste better when freshly toasted and ground (the exception is ginger; I nearly always use ground ginger in chutney).

hot date and preserved lemon relish

This isn't really a relish, because it is darker and stickier than most, but it cooks quickly so I'm not sure it qualifies as a chutney either! The original idea came from an excellent Indian cook I met, but then I (always yearning for preserved lemons) added a Moroccan note. I have suggested four preserved lemons, but that's if you are using commercially made ones (much smaller, as a Moroccan variety is used). If you have your own homemade Preserved Lemons (*see* page 256), use just one, then taste to see whether you would like to add more.

Fills 3 (½ pint) jars
1 tablespoon olive oil
1 red onion, very finely sliced
4 red chiles, seeded and sliced
   into thin strips
2¼ teaspoons ground cumin
1½ inch piece fresh ginger root,
   minced

5 garlic cloves, crushed with 1 teaspoon sea salt
2⅔ cups pitted and chopped dates
2 tablespoons tamarind paste
½ cup cider vinegar
⅓ cup firmly packed dark brown sugar
small bunch of cilantro, coarsely chopped
4 preserved lemons, rind only, shredded
2 tablespoons juice from the jar of preserved lemons

1 Heat the olive oil in a saucepan and sauté the onion until just beginning to soften. Add the chiles, cumin, ginger, and garlic and sauté for another minute.

2 Add the dates, tamarind, vinegar, ⅓ cup of water, and the sugar. Bring to a boil, then immediately reduce the heat and simmer for 10–15 minutes (you can take it further if you prefer more of a puree, the dates just break down into a mass if you keep cooking).

3 Stir in the cilantro and preserved lemon rind and juice. Put into warm sterilized jars (*see* page 11), cover with wax paper disks, seal with vinegar-proof lids, and let cool, then store in the refrigerator. It will keep for about six weeks, and tastes better after you've let it sit for a week.

how to use

Great with grilled chicken or spicy roasted lamb and couscous, and good in a cold roasted lamb sandwich. A spoonful or two is also excellent in a Moroccan tajine (especially a version made with fruit), because it adds good depth of flavor to this stew. Like Eggplant, Cardamom, and Pomegranate "Jam" (*see* page 244), its sweetness goes well with tart Greek yogurt.

eastern pickled ginger

If you make this with young ginger (track this down in an Asian store), it eventually becomes the most beautiful, tender pink color. You can make it with older ginger as well, although not too old because it can be too fibrous.

Fills 1 (1 pint) jar
1lb fresh ginger root,
   preferably young roots

1 tablespoon sea salt flakes
1 cup rice vinegar
²∕₃ cup granulated sugar

1 If you are using older ginger you will have to peel it; if it's younger, you should be able to scrape off the peel with a blunt knife. If you've been lucky enough to find young ginger, it doesn't need peeling.

2 Cut into wafer-thin slices—using a mandolin is by far the best way—and toss in a bowl with the salt. Let sit for an hour, then rinse and pat dry really well with a clean dish towel.

3 Pack into a warm sterilized jar (*see* page 11). Quickly heat together the vinegar and sugar in a saucepan until it comes to a boil and the sugar has dissolved. Immediately pour it over the ginger in the jar, cover with a vinegar-proof lid, and let cool. Once it's at room temperature, store in the refrigerator and use within three months.

asian carrot and daikon pickle

One of the many quick Asian pickles with a short shelf life. It can be eaten as a salad, or a relish used in sandwiches, such as *banh mi*, the spicy Vietnamese barbecued pork in a baguette. Add slivers of chile if you want, although the cool simple freshness of this pickle makes it special.

Fills 1 (1 quart) container
4 carrots (8oz), cut into matchsticks
1 daikon (Asian radish; 8oz) cut into
   matchsticks

1½ tablespoons pickling salt
²∕₃ cup rice vinegar
⅓ cup superfine or granulated sugar
juice of 2 limes

1 Put the carrots and daikon in a colander, sprinkle with salt, and gently toss. Set aside for 30 minutes.

2 Put the vinegar, sugar, and ²∕₃ cup of water into a saucepan and heat to boiling, stirring a little to help the sugar dissolve. Add the lime juice. Set aside to cool completely.

3 Rinse the vegetables in water, then dry them well on a clean dish towel. Put into a bowl. Pour the cooled vinegar mixture over the vegetables and mix well. Let sit for an hour before serving.

4 Keep in the refrigerator, covered, for up to four days, in a covered plastic container or bowl; make sure the liquid covers the vegetables. When you serve it, lift the vegetables from the vinegar; they should only be lightly coated. Black sesame seeds look great sprinkled on top.

scandinavian pickled cucumber

Sweet-sour, crisp, and fragrant with dill, this is how Scandinavian pickled cucumber should be (very different to the sour Russian pickles below).

Fills 1 (1 quart) jar

juice of 1 lemon

2 cups white wine vinegar

1 cup granulated sugar

1 teaspoon salt

10 black peppercorns

4 pickling cucumbers, cut into ¼ inch thick slices, plus more to fill

leaves from 4 large sprigs of dill, pulled from the stems in large fronds

1 Put all the ingredients, except the cucumbers and dill, into a saucepan and bring to a boil, stirring a little to help the sugar dissolve. Let cool completely.

2 Pack the cucumbers into a sterilized jar (*see* page 11), adding dill as you work. Pour the vinegar solution in, making sure the cucumbers are submerged. Cover with a vinegar-proof lid. Keep somewhere dark and cool. The cucumbers will sink in the vinegar solution so, the next day, add more cucumbers to the vinegar and seal. Refrigerate and use within two months.

crunchy russian dill pickles

Americans call these half-sours. They are, for many, the quintessential pickle. If you can't get little cucumbers (3–5 inches), use regular pickling ones, cut into 5 inch spears.

Fills 1 (1 quart) jar

¼ cup pickling salt

1¼lb small pickling cucumbers, blossom end removed

8 sprigs of dill, chopped

1 tablespoon dill or caraway seeds

12 black peppercorns

2 pieces horseradish root (each 1 inch square), peeled and cut into matchsticks

6 garlic cloves, halved lengthwise

1 thick slice of rye bread

1 Heat 3 cups of water with the salt in a saucepan, until the salt dissolves. Let cool. Wash and dry the cucumbers. Arrange them in a large, wide-necked jar, adding the herbs, spices, horseradish, and garlic as you work, then pour in the brine. It should cover the cucumbers completely. Put the bread on the cucumbers and set a small saucer and a weight on top of that.

2 Cover with a double layer of damp cheesecloth, tied with string. Set somewhere dry and warm for two days, then skim off any scum. Remove the bread, weigh down again, cover with fresh damp cheesecloth, and let sit for three days, skimming daily. Bubbles will rise after three days. This eventually stops and the cucumbers turn pale green. When that happens, transfer the cucumbers to a sterilized jar (*see* page 11), boil the brine, cool, then pour it into the jar. Seal with a vinegar-proof lid and refrigerate. The pickles will be crunchy and good for four weeks.

soy and ginger pickled green mango

What a jarful of flavor this is. It's great to have a quick pickle (this takes just minutes) that can enhance plain food wonderfully, and I much prefer it as soon as it's ready. The fiery, fruity flavors are great with roasted pork or oily fish. I particularly like it with grilled mackerel.

Fills 1 (1 pint) jar

scant ½ cup light Japanese soy sauce
½ cup mirin
½ cup white wine vinegar
½ cup orange juice

¾ inch piece of fresh ginger root,
    peeled and finely chopped
1 dried chile, crushed
3 tablespoons superfine or granulated sugar
2 green mangoes, peeled

1 Put all the ingredients, except the mangoes, into a sterilized wide-mouthed jar (*see* page 11) and mix. Cut the cheeks from each mango and cut these into long, spear-shaped slices. Put the mango into the liquid and put a saucer on top with a weight on it to keep the mangoes submerged.

2 Seal with a vinegar-proof lid and refrigerate for 12–24 hours. You can eat them then—it depends how much you want the flavor to penetrate the mangoes—or let them sit for two to three days. These taste best eaten within a week. The mangoes must always be covered with the pickling liquid.

eastern-spiced rhubarb relish

Even relishes, chutney's more vibrant cousin, often taste "cooked" and not fresh enough. But this is vibrant, zingy, and, because of the color, utterly beautiful. It lasts in the refrigerator for ages, too. Serve it with pork and broiled mackerel—it's not only for Asian dishes.

Fills 1 (1 pint) jar

1 cup cider vinegar
1½ cups granulated sugar
2 star anise
1 globe crystallized ginger in syrup, shredded

1 small red chile, halved, seeded
    and shredded
1 red onion, very finely sliced
8 rhubarb stalks, trimmed and sliced into chunks

1 Put the vinegar and sugar in a saucepan and bring to a boil, stirring occasionally to help the sugar dissolve. Add the spices, reduce the heat, and simmer for 10 minutes. Add the onion and cook, simmering and uncovered, for 10 minutes. The onion will soften and the mixture will become thicker.

2 Now add the rhubarb and simmer gently for another four minutes, or until the rhubarb is just tender. Don't overcook it; you want the rhubarb to remain pink and the shape of the pieces to stay intact; you are not making a chutney. Let cool. The mixture will thicken.

3 Put in sterilized jars (*see* page 11), cover with wax paper disks, seal with vinegar-proof lids, and refrigerate. You can eat it immediately, but it will keep for about three months (but it gets thicker).

malaysian cucumber and carrot pickle

One of the great things about chutneys and pickles is that they can take you to another clime without having to cook an entire meal from another country. I serve this with plain roasted chicken and rice (sometimes with coconut rice, which is what you'd eat with it in Malaysia). In fact, I eat bowls of rice just with this pickle as a complete meal. It's addictive. Sorry that the recipe looks long, but it isn't as complicated as it seems.

Fills 1 (1½ pint) jar

5 carrots, peeled

1 cucumber

3 shallots, sliced thinly lengthwise

2 red chiles, stems removed, sliced
  on the diagonal

2 teaspoons sea salt flakes

⅓ cup peanut oil

½ teaspoon black mustard seeds

¼ cup rice vinegar

¼ cup superfine or granulated sugar

FOR THE PASTE

4 shallots, coarsely chopped

2 garlic cloves, finely chopped

3 unsalted macadamia nuts

2 inch piece of fresh ginger root,
  cut into very fine julienne

3 small dried red chiles

1½ teaspoons turmeric

1 Cut the carrots into matchsticks 2 inches long and ¼ inch wide. Halve the cucumber lengthwise and scoop out the seeds. Cut it into matchsticks the same size as the carrots. Put the carrots, cucumber, shallots, and chiles in a bowl and toss with the salt. Let sit for two hours.

2 Put all the ingredients for the paste into a food processor (a small one makes life easier) and blend to a completely smooth paste. If you are using a large food processor and need liquid to help form a paste, add 2 tablespoons water. Keep scraping down the sides until everything is properly pureed.

3 Heat the oil in a skillet over high heat until it is hot but not smoking. Add the mustard seeds and cook until they begin to pop (about 30 seconds). Remove from the heat and let cool down for about a minute. Reduce the heat to medium and put the skillet back over the heat. You want the paste to sizzle gently when it's added, so test the temperature by adding a little. When the heat is right, add all the paste and cook over medium heat for about five minutes, moving it around with a wooden spatula. The smell of cooked ginger and shallot should tell you when the paste is at the right stage (taste a little, too; you will know when it is no longer "raw"). Reduce the heat, add the vinegar and sugar, and mix together everything, stirring to help the sugar dissolve. Remove the skillet from the heat.

4 Rinse the vegetables in a colander with cold water. Taste them; they should be slightly salty, but, if they seem very salty, put them into a bowl of water to soak for 30 minutes. Drain, then gently press them in a clean dish towel. Spread out the vegetables on paper towels to dry for another 15 minutes.

5 Stir the paste into the vegetables, making sure they are covered. You can eat this in about an hour's time, or put it into a jar, cover with a vinegar-proof lid, and keep in the refrigerator. The pickle will last for five days and will become stronger in flavor over that time.

perfect partners: the surprising possibilities of the cheese board

Within the pages of this book are jars of sweet and savory accompaniments that do something special for cheese. They can make a wedge of cheese into a meal, or just take that cheese somewhere else, making you notice things about it that would otherwise be hard to perceive. I rarely put together a cheese "board," finding the prospect of several cheeses a little too much at the end of a meal. But I like just one cheese with something original. And two or three with unexpected accompaniments make a fine Saturday lunch. Think about the following platefuls …

Blue cheeses are excellent with sweet pickled fruits, so try pickled quinces and crab apples with them. Pickled prunes—even prunes in armagnac—are wonderful with roquefort, and pickled peaches are great with a mixture of gorgonzola and mascarpone. Quince paste and damson paste work wonderfully with blues, too (and with Spanish manchego, of course). Bloomy rind cheeses (camembert and brie) go well with pickled pears and apples (before they've been too long in the jar), and cider and apple jellies are good bedfellows as well.

Washed rind cheeses—the smelly, strong ones with supple, creamy interiors and slightly tacky rinds, such as epoisses, reblochon, and vacherin, and Irish milleens—are a revelation with fruit jellies made with white currants, plums, or quinces. Taleggio is good with them, too. I've also had a lovely plateful of fontina with nuts and rose hip jelly in northern Italy.

A French cheese connoisseur (and you have to listen to one of those) persuaded me to try chile jam with strong goat cheese. It works (and is good with strong Corsican cheeses, too), although it has to be eaten on it's own. The lighter pickled fruits—cherries, gooseberries, rhubarb, and red currants—work well, too, as does rhubarb jelly. Banon is good with pear and chestnut jam. Spoon sweets—the cherries, apricots, and figs on pages 137 and 138—can be served with Greek myzithra. (It's hard to find outside Greece, but you can use fresh ricotta instead). Aged myzithra (better with the cherries) is available in Greek delis, (and pecorino is a reasonable substitute). It's not traditional, but I like cherry spoon sweets with barrel-aged feta, too, as long as it's not too salty.

Labneh, Middle Eastern yogurt cheese (there's a recipe for it on page 98), is not served as a cheese course but makes a wonderful snack or mezze, or, if unseasoned, a sweet treat. Spread it on toasted bread, or serve it in a wedge on its own. Its clean, mild acidity works with a lot of foods. Try it with Moroccan and Persian olives, pickled persimmons, pickled chiles, Persian pickled cherries, date and preserved lemon relish, eggplant "jam," or a little Turkish pepper paste (ouch, watch the heat …) On the sweet side, rhubarb and rose, or fig and pomegranate jams are fine partners.

Our sweeter British chutneys, as opposed to the Indian versions, go well with cheddar and Lancashire, but also try the American pecan preserve on the right with them, too. You see? There's more to cheese and preserves than a cheese and pickle sandwich …

ozarks pecan conserve

This is unusual. I found the idea in Billy Joe Tatum's *Wild Foods Field Guide and Cookbook*. It's good with pancakes and bacon, or with cheese, sliced sautéed apples, and crackers.

Fills 3 (½ pint) jars

1 cup firmly packed dark brown sugar
½ cup honey
1 cup cider vinegar
finely grated zest of 1 organic orange
¾ teaspoon ground allspice
½ teaspoon ground ginger
½ teaspoon ground cinnamon
½ teaspoon yellow mustard seeds
¼ teaspoon ground cloves
½ teaspoon salt
2½ cups pecans, lightly toasted
⅓ cup bourbon

1 Prepare a boiling-water canner (*see* pages 368–369) and keep the cleaned jars and lids warm.

2 Put everything except the nuts and bourbon in a saucepan with 1 cup of water and bring to a boil. Reduce the heat to a simmer and cook for 10 minutes. Add the nuts and cook for 10 minutes. The syrup should become thicker. When it's cool, stir in the bourbon.

3 Fill each jar, leaving a headspace of ¼ inch from the top. Process the filled jars in a boiling-water canner for 10 minutes at sea level (*see* pages 369). Let cool, seal the jars, and label before storing for at least a week before serving. Once opened, keep it in the refrigerator and use within six months.

summer afternoon corn relish

Nobody does barbecues like Americans. All that pork and sauce and iced tea, a fantasy to be realized in your yard in summer. Serve this as the sun sinks. Summer, smoke, relish ... heaven.

Fills 3 (1 pint) jars

2 teaspoons turmeric
3 teaspoons mustard powder
3 tablespoons all-purpose flour
1 onion, very finely sliced
1 red bell pepper, halved, seeded and diced
1 green bell pepper, halved, seeded and diced
2 celery sticks, diced
1 green and 1 red chile, seeded and sliced
8 garlic cloves, finely chopped
1 cup firmly packed light brown sugar
2 cups cider vinegar
2 tablespoons yellow mustard seeds
1 teaspoon celery seeds
1½ teaspoons sea salt
2½ cups fresh corn kernels, cut from 4–5 cobs

1 Put the turmeric, mustard, and flour in a bowl and mix with 2 tablespoons of cold water to a smooth paste. Put all the other ingredients into a saucepan and stir in the mustard mixture. Slowly bring to a boil, stirring to help the sugar dissolve. Reduce the heat to a simmer and cook for 20 minutes. The mixture should hold together, but shouldn't be as thick as a chutney.

2 Put in hot sterilized jars (*see* page 11), cover with wax paper disks, and seal with vinegar-proof lids. This will keep for three months in the refrigerator.

pickled pumpkin

There is something gloriously American sounding about this. Perhaps that's why I serve it with fried chicken and corn cakes, although it's also great with roasted chicken or pork, or as part of a salad of goat cheese with lentils. Choose a nice sweet variety of pumpkin or squash.

Fills 2 (1 pint) jars

3lb pumpkin or butternut squash
(about 5⅓ cups of flesh after preparing)
2 cups cider vinegar
2 cups granulated sugar
1 tablespoon salt

10 allspice berries
1 cinnamon stick
12 black peppercorns
3 dried chiles
¾ inch fresh ginger root, chopped
2–4 tablespoons medium or sweet sherry (optional)

1 Prepare a boiling-water canner (*see* pages 368–369) and keep the cleaned jars and lids warm. Halve the pumpkin, remove the seeds, and peel. Cut the flesh into chunks about ¾ inch square.

2 Put everything else, except the sherry, into a saucepan with 2 cups of water and slowly bring to a boil, stirring to help the sugar dissolve. Add the pumpkin and mix everything around. Reduce the heat to a simmer and cook the pumpkin until it is completely tender.

3 Lift the pumpkin into hot sterilized jars (*see* page 11). Pour the syrup and spices over the pumpkin, add the sherry, if you want (it adds a nice kick), leaving a ½ inch headspace. Process the filled jars in a boiling-water canner for 20 minutes at sea level (*see* pages 369). Let cool, seal the jars, and label before storing. Refrigerate after opening.

bread and butter pickles

One of the quintessential American pickles, so good that it was once thought they were all you needed on your bread. I wouldn't go that far, but I do find them delicious.

Fills 2 (1 pint) jars

1½ cucumbers (1lb)
2 large onions
2 tablespoons pickling salt
2 cups cider vinegar

1 cup firmly packed light brown sugar
2 teaspoon turmeric
½ tablespoons yellow mustard seeds
2 teaspoons dill seeds

1 Slice the cucumber into ¼ inch thick circles. Cut the onions into slices half that thickness. Place both in a glass bowl with the salt, mix, cover with a clean dish towel, and let sit overnight.

2 The next day, rinse and drain. Taste the cucumber. If it's too salty, soak for 15 minutes. Rinse and drain again.

3 Put all the other ingredients into a large saucepan. Bring to a boil, stirring to help the sugar dissolve, and boil for 10 minutes. Add the cucumber and onions and return to a boil. Ladle into warm, sterilized jars (*see* page 11), leaving a ½ inch headspace, and seal with vinegar-proof lids. When cool, refrigerate for at least two weeks before eating and use within three months.

two kinds of pickled grapes

I started off making a sour version of these that I'd read about in Middle Eastern books, but with my sweet tooth (and that British love of the sweet with the savory), I ended up doing them like this. You can alter the spices (star anise, cinnamon, and ginger are all good). At first, the grapes just wrinkle slightly in the syrup, but the longer you keep them, the more they shrink. I actually like them best after about a week.

FRAGRANT WHITE PICKLED GRAPES
Fills (1 quart) jar
3⅔ cups grapes (1¼lb), muscat if you
   can get them
1½ cups granulated sugar
1 cup white wine vinegar
1½ cups riesling or other white wine
1 bay leaf
10 white peppercorns

SPICED BLACK PICKLED GRAPES
Fills 1 (1 quart) jar
3⅔ cups seedless black grapes (1¼lb)
2½ cups granulated sugar
2 cups white wine or cider vinegar
10 black peppercorns
10 juniper berries, bruised
1 small dried chile (optional)
½ cinnamon stick

1 In either case, pull sprigs of the grapes off the main stem. Put everything else into a saucepan and bring to a boil, stirring to help the sugar dissolve. Boil for about four minutes, then cool completely.

2 Wash and dry the grapes and put them into a warm sterilized jar (*see* page 11). Pour the liquid over the grapes and seal with a vinegar-proof lid. You can eat these immediately. The longer they are in the vinegar the more "pickled" the grapes will taste and the more wrinkled they become. They will keep refrigerated for up to three months.

how to use

These are made for roasted pork—belly or loin—and look fabulous in little branches served alongside slices of the sweet, fatty meat. However, they are also very deicious with pâtés (and a smooth chicken liver parfait), terrines, and most cheeses.

barrel of cucumbers: preserving in america

America seems to be two countries. Some Europeans have an image of the United States as some kind of low-rent, fast food outlet, the home of fatty hamburgers and supersized buckets of cola. However, this is snobbish and ignores the wider picture. Americans' concern for freshness, localness, and seasonality, as expounded by such chefs as Alice Waters, the mother of Californian cuisine, has had a bigger effect on how we eat (and how chefs cook) in Great Britain than people may know, and many Americans take home-preserving seriously. They love their burgers and their corned beef sandwiches, and pickles and relishes are vital for these. They will wax lyrical about the sour fermented cucumbers they stole from the cloudy brine of a pickle barrel as kids. I have spent days traveling in New England, seduced by roadside stalls and farm stores into buying jars of bread and butter pickles, beach plum jelly, and pickled dilly beans.

In Vermont, I've watched people boil apple juice to make cider syrup to bottle and put up, seen notices for church dinners with a menu of baked ham, baked potatoes, and pickled pumpkin and attended "sugar on snow" parties to celebrate the maple syrup season, where the sweetness of the syrup was cut with bites of sour pickles. Make no mistake, American preserving isn't a folksy romantic notion; it is alive and well and increasing in popularity.

Native American Indians did some forms of preserving, most notably drying, before the first European settlers brought all kinds of domestic skills with them, especially pickling in brine and vinegar. Since then, waves of immigrants from Italy, Germany, Poland, Greece, and Korea, plus Jews from all over Europe, have imported their traditions.

At school, I loved the stories of Laura Ingalls Wilder and her *Little House in the Big Woods*. I was surprised when I reread them as an adult that they had held my attention, because they are, in large part, accounts of the preparations undertaken to put up food for the winter. The food that you preserved was crucial for getting through the cold months. In areas where such heavy snow was the norm that you couldn't even leave the house, families would have starved without food that had been pickled, bottled, dried, salted, or smoked.

The southern states don't have snowy winters, but preserving is a huge tradition in the South, too, because of a different instinct: the desire not to squander bounty. Who could waste the peaches and corn, the tomatoes and melons? You can't even read books set in the South without wanting to cook; southern literature is splattered with hunger and its cures. Sitting on a porch during one of Carson McCuller's "green and crazy" summers, you would want to eat smiling wedges of watermelon and pickle the rind later.

Very few countries have ever had a leader capable of writing this: 'On a hot day in Virginia, I know nothing more comforting than a fine spiced pickle, brought up troutlike from the sparkling depths of the aromatic jar below the stairs of Aunt Sally's cellar." That's Thomas Jefferson. Doesn't it make you want to fill your coolest, airiest cupboards with jars? It does me. So find me that porch. And get me a pitcher of lemonade. I've a load of peaches to pit.

american melon and ginger pickles

This is delicious. You might think you can't cook melon for this long (it takes about an hour to get it to the right stage), but the flesh becomes translucent, almost candied, slightly like a ginger-steeped Italian mostarda. It's great with smoked duck or chicken and prosciutto or Serrano ham. I also like it with rich, milky burrata. In the USA, however, it's for summery meals of cold baked ham. Try adding slivered red chiles to it as well. You ice and salt the melon to keep it as firm as possible—remember, this was originally made in hot kitchens—but even in the British more temperate climate, this step seems to help keep the fruit in peak condition.

Fills 3 (1 pint) jars
2 cantaloupe melons (3¼lb each)
3 tablespoons sea salt flakes
5 cups granulated sugar

3¼ cups cider vinegar
3 pieces preserved ginger, finely chopped
1 cinnamon stick, broken into 2 pieces

1 Halve the melons, remove the seeds, slice into wedges, and peel each one. Cut the flesh into cubes. You should have about 10 cups.

2 Put the melon in a colander and completely cover the flesh with ice cubes. Sprinkle a layer of salt on top of the ice. Set aside at room temperature (put something underneath to catch the liquid). When half the ice has melted and the remaining stuff looks brittle, rinse and drain the melon.

3 Put the fruit in a bowl and add the sugar, vinegar, and ginger. Gently stir to dissolve the sugar, then weight the fruit down under the vinegar (use a plate), cover with a dish towel, and let sit for 12 hours.

4 Prepare a boiling-water canner (*see* pages 368–369) and keep the cleaned jars and lids warm.

5 Put the melon and the syrup around it into a saucepan and add ½ cup of water and the cinnamon stick. Bring to a boil, then reduce the heat to low and cook until the liquid has reduced and the melon chunks look transparent. It takes 45 minutes to an hour. Don't heat for too long; there should still be enough liquid to cover the chunks of melon once they're canned. Remove the pieces of cinnamon stick.

5 Ladle into the jars—make sure the fruit is covered with the vinegar syrup—leaving a headspace of ½ inch from the top. Use a sterilized plastic spatula to remove any air bubbles. Process the filled jars in a boiling-water canner for 20 minutes at sea level (*see* pages 369). Let cool, seal the jars, and label before storing. Once opened, store the pickles in the refrigerator.

zuni café's red onion pickles

This is an adaptation of Judy Rodger's recipe in *The Zuni Café Cookbook*. Her San Francisco café is one of my favorite places to eat, and her book is outstanding: serious, original, and delicious. Rodgers is simply wonderful at laid-back food. She doesn't instruct you to boil the vinegar solution—that is my amendment of her recipe.

Fills 2 (1 pint) jars
5 firm red onions (2¼lb)
5 cups distilled white vinegar
2½ cups granulated sugar
2 cinnamon sticks, halved
6 cloves

8 allspice berries
2 small dried chiles
2 star anise
4 bay leaves
8 black peppercorns

1 Trim the ends of the onions and cut into ½ inch slices. Separate the slices into rings.

2 Put the all the other ingredients into a saucepan and bring to a boil, stirring to help the sugar dissolve. Once this is boiling, add about one-third of the onion rings and stir them into the liquid. As soon as the liquid begins to simmer again, stir the onions around in it again, then remove the pan from the heat and remove the onions with a slotted spoon Lay them out on something flat where they can cool. Repeat this procedure with the rest of the onions.

3 Now this may seem laborious, but go through this process another two times, always immersing the onions in boiling liquid, then removing them as the liquid returns to a simmer. After you've done this for the third time, boil the liquid until it has reduced by half, then cool it completely. As Zuni's chef Judy Rodgers explains, although this is a tedious way to make the pickles, they taste briny and pickled but stay pretty crunchy. It also means the color stays a bright fuschia pink.

4 Meanwhile, prepare a boiling-water canner (*see* pages 368–369) and keep the cleaned jars and lids warm.

5 Put the onions in the warm jars and cover with the vinegar solution, leaving a headspace of ½ inch from the top. Use a sterilized plastic spatula to remove any air bubbles. Process the filled jars in a boiling-water canner for 10 minutes at sea level (*see* pages 369). Let cool, seal the jars, and label before storing. Once opened, store the pickles in the refrigerator.

how to use

Fabulous with hamburgers, of course, but I also really like these with smoked trout or salmon and boiled potatoes tossed in dill. They work very well with Scandinavian foods.

pickled quinces

Pickled fruits work perfectly with cold meats, pâtés, terrines, and cheeses. You can serve them with hot dishes, such as roasted pork, duck, or baked ham. They're mostly made using the same technique—the fruit is poached in a sweet vinegar solution, then put in jars—but the vinegar-to-sugar ratio changes, depending on the sweetness of the fruit, and the spices can be varied. You can make pickled pears in the same way, but cook them for a shorter time, just until tender.

Fills 2 (1 pint) jars

2½ cups perry or cider vinegar

2 cups granulated sugar

6 cloves

6 juniper berries

12 black peppercorns

1 cinnamon stick, broken in two

4 strips of unwaxed lemon zest

2¼lb quinces

1 Prepare a boiling-water canner (*see* pages 368–369) and keep the cleaned jars and lids warm. Put all the ingredients, except the quinces, in a large saucepan and bring to a boil. Reduce to a simmer and stir a little until all the sugar has dissolved. Set aside.

2 Peel and halve the quinces. Remove the cores with a small sharp knife. Cut each quince half in four lengthwise. Heat the vinegar solution again and add the fruit. Cover and simmer until tender, for 20 minutes or longer; quinces are hard. Transfer the quinces to the warm jars with a slotted spoon.

3 Boil the vinegar until reduced to about 2 cups. Strain it through a nylon strainer over the quinces while everything is hot, leaving a headspace of a generous ½ inch from the top. Add the spices from your strainer (discard the zest). Use a sterilized plastic spatula to remove any air bubbles. Process the filled jars in a boiling-water canner for 20 minutes at sea level (*see* pages 369). Let cool, seal the jars, and label before storing. Once opened, store the pickles in the refrigerator.

and also

PICKLED CRAB APPLES

Make as above using 2¼lb crab apples and change the spices: use 1 cinnamon stick, ¾ inch piece of fresh ginger root, sliced, and 2 teaspoons allspice berries, bruised, plus 3 cups cider vinegar and 4 cups granulated sugar (this has to be sweeter because the apples are tart). Wash the crab apples, prick each with a sharp knife, and simmer for three minutes, until tender. Transfer with a slotted spoon to warm jars, then finish as above. Fills 2 (1 pint) jars.

AMERICAN PICKLED PEACHES

Make as above, but use 3¾ cups granulated sugar and 2 cups vinegar, 1 teaspoon allspice berries, 6 cloves, ¾ inch piece of fresh ginger root, sliced, and 2 cinnamon sticks. Pit 10 underripe peaches (3¼lb) and cut into wedges. Add to the syrup and cook until tender. Put into warm, jars, then finish as above. These are better after a few weeks. Fills 3 (1pint) jars.

russian marinated mushrooms

The first time I ate these wasn't in Russia, but at the home of a friend in Northern Ireland when I was about 15. A well-traveled Australian visitor made them for a buffet of Russian food. I, already a fan of tarragon but only just getting into mushrooms, thought they were the height of sophistication. They're great to have in the refrigerator. Very healthy, too. If you don't have any tarragon vinegar, use white wine vinegar and the leaves of four sprigs of fresh tarragon.

Fills 2 (1 pint) jars

1½lb very fresh button mushrooms, the
    smallest you can find
juice of 3 lemons
1 tablespoon pickling salt
1¾ cups tarragon vinegar

8 black peppercorns
1 tablespoon superfine or granulated sugar
4 garlic cloves, very finely sliced
6 sprigs of dill, coarsely chopped
¼ cup olive oil

1 Wipe the mushrooms carefully with paper towels or brush with a soft mushroom brush. Trim the stem end of each one. Halve or quarter any mushrooms that are larger than the others. Mix them with the lemon juice and let sit for 15 minutes.

2 Put the mushrooms in a saucepan with 5 cups of water. The mushrooms should be covered, so add more water if you need it. Add the salt, bring to a boil, reduce the heat, and simmer, uncovered, for 10 minutes. Remove the mushrooms with a slotted spoon and rinse under cold water. Strain the salt water through a cheesecloth-lined strainer. You need 3¾ cups; discard any extra.

3 Return this liquid to the saucepan with the vinegar, peppercorns, and sugar. Bring to a boil, stirring a little to help the sugar dissolve, then reduce the heat, cover the pan, and simmer for five minutes. Let cool.

4 Pack the mushrooms into sterilized jars (*see* page 11), distributing the garlic and dill as you work, then pour the cooled liquid on top. Cover with a layer of olive oil, seal with vinegar-proof lids, and refrigerate. They'll be ready to eat in about six hours but will keep, chilled, for a month.

how to use

You can serve these as they are, straight from the jar, or you can stir some sour cream or crème fraîche into them. Eat them with black bread or rye bread or serve them as part of a zakuski spread (*see* right). Don't forget the vodka …

from russia with love: the joy of the zakuski table

Imagine a table laid with a linen cloth, covered with bowls and small plates of all the delicacies that Russia and Eastern Europe has to offer: cured herrings, smoked fish, pickled cucumbers and bell peppers, fiery crimson radishes, winter-cold sour cream, cheeses, brined mushrooms, caviar, rare beef with horseradish, beet puree, preserved plums, and rye bread. This is the zakuski table—the table of "little bites"—the Russian version of Middle Eastern mezze, Spanish tapas, and Italian antipasti. Indeed, it is such a feast that it often becomes the whole meal.

Most credit Peter the Great for bringing this style of eating to Russia. He had certainly seen enough Scandinavian smörgåsbords (which the zakuski table resembles), while traveling and waging war to have adopted the idea. This table of plenty says much about Russian hospitality. It is well known that, even in hard times (and they've had plenty of those), Russian hosts pull out all the stops to produce a feast. A spread of zakuski can include the most luxurious items (in Gogol's *Dead Souls*, the chief of police offers delights that include an amazing pie made with the head and cheeks of 325lb of sturgeon), or it can be limited to the most frugal—a few herrings, some radishes, black bread, and pickles.

Zakuski became particularly popular in the 19th century and were served according to strict guidelines. Elena Molokhovets' *Classic Russian Cooking* (the Russian bible of cooking and household management, published in 1861) contains illustrations showing how to arrange the various elements. The key thing was to serve zakuski on an oval or round table, either beside the main dining table or in an anteroom. The table had to be placed away from the wall, so that guests could walk around it. Carafes of vodka were in the center, surrounded by bread and mounds of unsalted butter, and the various zakuski were placed around the edges.

The reason I'm telling you about zakuski is that there is an abundance of dishes in this book that are just right for this kind of meal. Apart from the Russian and Eastern European foods, there are also some Middle Eastern dishes that are perfect—fuchsia pickled turnips, Persian cherries with tarragon, stuffed pickled eggplants—plus Italian cured beef and, a regular on zakuski tables as Russians adore Georgian food, kidney beans in Georgian plum sauce. These all work with no dissonant notes, although they come from different cultures. You'll also find recipes for the other great zakuski essential: flavored vodka (*see* pages 154 and 155).

To homemade dishes, add store-bought produce and simple foods—cured ham, spicy dried sausage, hard-boiled eggs, warm new potatoes—and you have a feast for both the depths of winter and the brightness of spring. Choose your dishes according to the season and, in the colder months, add some hot dishes, too, such as warm roasted pork belly and savory pies.

You don't have to lay out your zakuski according to tradition: just make your table as rich and varied as possible, choose your most beautiful cloth and glassware, and pack your freezer with vodka. Food is partly about fantasy and romance, and there's nothing wrong with being Anna Karenina for an evening …

moldavian pepper relish

This is adapted from a recipe in a wonderful American book on Russian cookery by Anya von Bremzen and John Welchman called *Please to the Table*. It is full of flavor combinations that are slightly unusual. I love this because our Mediterraneanized palates assume you match basil or oregano with bell peppers, but not dill. It's quickly made and it keeps for only a month, but you'll eat it well within that time.

Fills 1 (1 quart) jar

3 red bell peppers, halved and seeded (or a mixture of colors)

2 cups cider or white wine vinegar

4 bay leaves

¼ cup superfine or granulated sugar

20 black peppercorns

2 tablespoons salt

2 onions, halved and thinly sliced

6 garlic cloves, very finely sliced

8 sprigs of dill, chopped

3 tablespoons olive oil, plus more if needed

1 Blanch the bell peppers in boiling water for five minutes, then rinse under cold water. Slice thinly.

2 Pour 1¼ cups of water, the vinegar, bay leaves, sugar, peppercorns, and salt into a saucepan and bring to a boil. Boil for three minutes.

3 Put all the other ingredients except the olive oil into a warm, sterilized jar (*see* page 11) and pour the hot liquid over them. Let cool. Pour the oil on top (the pickle should be completely covered with a layer of oil, so add more, if necessary), and seal with a vinegar-proof lid. Put into the refrigerator and let sit for 12 hours before eating. The relish will keep, chilled, for a month.

how to use

Bell peppers appear in a multitude of guises on the Moldavian table, and this relish is often eaten with fish, but I particularly like it with chicken kebabs. You can also serve it as part of a spread of Russian-inspired appetizers—zakuski (*see* page 229)—with cured and smoked fish and meats, cucumbers with dill, sour cream, and rye or black bread.

spiced beet relish with ginger and horseradish

Made just with horseradish, this is good with cold roasted beef, but adding ginger makes a great partner for broiled mackerel. Use both flavors or just one. It's also good just with star anise.

Fills 1 (1 pint) jar

1¾ cups cider vinegar

3 cups granulated sugar

2 globes crystallized ginger in syrup, cut into shreds

1 teaspoon ground ginger

4 red onions, very finely sliced

14 cooked beets (1½lb), cut into chunks

2 small cooking apples, peeled, cored, and cut into small chunks

1½ tablespoons freshly grated horseradish

1 Put the vinegar and sugar in a saucepan and bring to a boil, stirring to help the sugar to dissolve. Add the two types of ginger, reduce the heat, and simmer for 10 minutes. Add the onions and cook, simmering and uncovered, for 10 minutes. The onions will soften and the mixture become thicker.

2 Now add the beet and apples and simmer for about another 15 minutes, or until the apples are soft and the mixture is thick, adding the horseradish for the last five minutes. Put in a warm sterilized jar (*see* page 11), cover with a waxed paper disk, and seal with a vinegar-proof lid. This keeps for up to three months in the refrigerator.

cranberry and horseradish relish

Looking into the sauces of Russia, the former Soviet states, and Eastern Europe, I became fascinated by how different their combinations of flavors are to those we use. Horseradish is used with pork and often mixed with fruits; fruit can be paired with beef, pork, or game. This kind of discovery opens your mind. In Russia, this is made with raw, crushed lingonberries.

Fills 1 (½ pint) jar

2½ cups fresh or frozen cranberries

3 tablespoons red wine vinegar

½ cup granulated sugar

3 tablespoons freshly grated horseradish

1 Put the cranberries and vinegar into a saucepan set over low heat. As the cranberries heat up and soften, they will produce their own juices to add to the vinegar. Increase the heat to medium and cook until they are soft and have started to pop (about 10 minutes).

2 Add the sugar and horseradish and stir. Simmer until the sugar has dissolved and all the flavors have amalgamated. Ladle into a warm sterilized jar (*see* page 11) and cover with a wax paper disk. Seal with a vinegar-proof lid. When the relish has cooled, refrigerate for up to a month.

summer garden pickles

This is gorgeous—there is so much color and such a variety of shapes. Vary the ingredients according to what you have, and make it sweeter if you want (adding honey is good).

Fills 2 (1 quart) jars

4 celery sticks (with leaves)
6 small carrots
1 small zucchini (or 10 small baby zucchini)
1 red onion, cut into wedges
1 cup halved green beans,
1 cup halved radishes
1 red bell pepper, sliced
½ cup pickling salt
12 firm cherry tomatoes, stems on

6 cups white wine vinegar
⅔ cup granulated sugar
1 bay leaf
8 allspice berries
10 black peppercorns
1 blade of mace
2 cloves
good pinch of saffron (optional)
2 tablespoons chopped dill
⅓ cup olive oil, to seal

1 Cut the celery on the diagonal into ¾ inch lengths. Halve the small carrots. Slice the zucchini into circles. Layer all the vegetables with the salt, pour 5 cups of water over them, put a plate on top, and let sit overnight.

2 The next day, rinse the vegetables in cold water and pat dry. Prick the tomatoes with a sharp knife.

3 Put the vinegar, sugar, and spices into a saucepan. Boil for five minutes. Put the vegetables in warm sterilized jars, adding the dill, then the vinegar over them. Add the oil and seal with vinegar-proof lids. Store in the refrigerate and use within three months.

italian pickled peppers

Antonio Carluccio told me about the bell peppers his mum made (this recipe is based on his, but it's hotter). She fried them with spicy sausages and garlic. I do, too, but add broccoli.

Fills 1 (1 quart) jar

3 large red bell peppers
3 large yellow bell peppers
2½ cups white wine vinegar
⅓ cup granulated sugar
4 teaspoons pickling salt

2 dried chiles
2 bay leaves
3 garlic cloves
4 cloves
10 black peppercorns
olive oil, to seal

1 Quarter and seed the bell peppers. Put everything else, except the oil, with 1¼ cups of water in a saucepan and bring to a boil, stirring. Reduce to a simmer and add the peppers. Cook until tender.

2 Pack the peppers into a sterilized jar (*see* page 11). Reduce the vinegar to 2 cups, remove the garlic, and pour into the jar. Cover with oil and a vinegar-proof lid; refrigerate and use in three months.

pickled onions agrodolce

Onions pickled with the sweet-sour flavors of Sicily. You can use pearl onions, shallots, or those little flat Italian onions—*cipolline*—if you can find them.

Fills 2 (1 pint) jar
1½lb pearl onions
2½ tablespoons pickling salt
2 cups balsamic vinegar
⅔ cup firmly packed light brown sugar

1 teaspoon black peppercorns
2 teaspoons allspice berries
1 cinnamon stick
2 dried chiles
⅓ cup raisins

1 Don't peel the onions yet; blanching them first will make it much easier. Just snip off the tufty part at the top and the root part at the bottom, put the onions into a large bowl, and completely cover with boiling water. Let sit for 40 seconds, then drain and run cold water all over them. The skins will now come off relatively easily.

2 Put the peeled onions into a wide, shallow dish and sprinkle with the salt. Let sit overnight.

3 Meanwhile, pour the vinegar into a saucepan with ½ cup of the sugar and all the spices and bring to a boil, stirring a little to help the sugar dissolve. Add the raisins, reduce the heat, and simmer for 10 minutes. Let sit overnight, too.

4 The next day, prepare a boiling-water canner (*see* pages 368–369) and keep the cleaned jars and lids warm. Rinse the onions in cold water and carefully pat dry.

5 Put the reserved sugar into a skillet and gently heat until it turns a shade or two darker. Just before it starts to bubble, put the onions in and stir them around to brown in the sugar. Remove the onions with a slotted spoon and place into the warm jars.

6 Remove the cinnamon stick from the vinegar and raisin mixture, then reheat the mixture and pour it over the onions in the jars, leaving a headspace of ½ inch from the top. Use a sterilized plastic spatula to remove any air bubbles. Process the filled jars in a boiling-water canner for 10 minutes at sea level (*see* pages 369). Let cool, seal the jars, and label before storing. Let sit for six weeks before using. Once opened, store the pickles in the refrigerator.

how to use

Serve these as part of an antipasti spread (they're particularly good with salami), or with cold meats, pâté, or cheese. You can also use them as the basis of a good salad: slice the onions and toss them with some of their vinegar plus extra virgin olive oil, arugula, and toasted pine nuts.

pickled fennel

This is actually very delicate in flavor, so even people who aren't keen on fennel like it. You can add chopped dill if you want to emphasize the anise flavor, particularly to serve it with fish.

Fills 2 (1 pint) jars
1 tablespoon pickling salt
4 small fennel bulbs (2¼lb)
3½ cups cider vinegar

1½ tablespoons peppercorns (mixed colors)
½ cup granulated sugar
finely grated zest of 1 unwaxed lemon
1 teaspoon fennel seeds

1 Prepare a boiling-water canner (*see* pages 368–369) and keep the cleaned jars and lids warm. Fill a large saucepan with water and add the salt. Bring to a boil. Meanwhile, cut any leafy fronds from the fennel (keep these), remove the tough outer leaves, and trim the tops. Slice lengthwise into slices about ⅛ inch thick. Blanch the slices for 30 seconds—no more, so you need to work fast—and remove with a slotted spoon. Put into a colander and run cold water over. Thoroughly pat dry.

2 Put all the rest of the ingredients into a saucepan and slowly bring to a boil, stirring to help the sugar dissolve. Boil for 10 minutes.

3 Pack the fennel into the warm jars, putting any fennel fronds among the slices. Pour the vinegar solution and spices over the fennel, leaving a ½ inch headspace. Use a sterilized plastic spatula to remove any air bubbles. Process the filled jars in a boiling-water canner for 10 minutes at sea level (*see* pages 369). Let cool, seal the jars, and label before storing. Refrigerate once opened.

how to use
Pickled fennel is wonderful with fish, both with oily types, such as mackerel and salmon, and with white fish. I even mix chopped pickled fennel with chervil or dill and mayonnaise to make a summery sauce for fish. It's also good with salami—particularly those that contain fennel seeds as a flavoring—and roasted pork or porchetta.

cerises au vinaigre

I tasted these on my first trip to France when I was 15, and loved them with rillettes and pâtés (I can't resist the combination of fruit and meat in any cuisine). They are very easy to make, last for ages, and are much less expensive than any you can buy.

Fills 3 (1 pint) jars
2½ cups white wine vinegar
4½ cups granulated sugar

1 small cinnamon stick
4 whole cloves
6 cups cherries (2lb)

1 Prepare a boiling-water canner (*see* pages 368–369) and keep the cleaned jars and lids warm. Heat the vinegar, sugar, and spices in a saucepan, stirring a little to help the sugar dissolve.

2 Prick each cherry with a sharp knife (to prevent them from bursting) but try to keep the stems attached (for looks). Add them to the sweet vinegar and simmer for about four minutes. Do this gently to avoid breaking up the fruit. Lift the cherries with a slotted spoon into warm, dry jars.

3 Remove the spices and boil the vinegar until it becomes syrupy (it will thicken as it cools). Once cool, pour this over the cherries, leaving a ½ inch headspace. Use a sterilized plastic spatula to remove any air bubbles. Process the filled jars in a boiling-water canner for 10 minutes at sea level (*see* pages 369). Let cool, seal the jars, and label before storing. Refrigerate once opened.

also try

PICKLED GOOSEBERRIES

Make as above, being careful to poach the gooseberries briefly, about one to two minutes. Use sliced fresh ginger root instead of cinnamon and cloves. Spoon the gooseberries into a sterilized jar (*see* page 11) with a slotted spoon and cover. Reduce the vinegar syrup, then, once it's cold, pour it over the fruit, seal with a lid, and refrigerate for up to three months. (The gooseberries could fall apart in hot liquid.) These are wonderful with goat cheese and broiled mackerel. Fills 1 (1 quart) jar.

PICKLED RHUBARB

Cut rhubarb into 2 inch lengths and make as above (but you need an extra 1 cup of sugar because rhubarb is so tart, and sliced fresh ginger root is better than cinnamon and cloves). Poach the rhubarb briefly and gently; I watch it the whole time because it becomes too soft very quickly. Now follow the recipe for Pickled Gooseberries (above) for putting up in a jar. This is great with pâté, pork, and mackerel. Fills 1 (1 quart) jar.

PICKLED RED CURRANTS

Make as in the first recipe, but cook gently for 40 seconds. Now follow the recipe for Pickled Gooseberries for putting up in a jar. Fills 1 (1 quart) jar.

persian pickled cherries with tarragon

It may seem strange to pickle a fruit without sugar, but the cherries themselves are sweet. They're also surprisingly good with tarragon.

Fills 2 (1 pint) jars
2 cups white wine vinegar
3 tablespoons pickling salt

12 bruised black peppercorns
3 cups sweet cherries (1lb)
4–6 sprigs of tarragon

1 Prepare a boiling-water canner (*see* pages 368–369) and keep the cleaned jars and lids warm. Heat the vinegar with the salt and peppercorns until boiling, then let cool.

2 Put the cherries into the warm jars with the tarragon and pour the vinegar over them to cover completely, leaving a ½ inch headspace.Use a sterilized plastic spatula to remove any air bubbles. Process the filled jars in a boiling-water canner for 10 minutes at sea level (*see* pages 369). Let cool, seal the jars, and label before storing. Let sit for two weeks before eating; refrigerate once opened.

how to use

Sticking to the Persian theme, these are excellent with *sabzhi khordan*. This is simply a selection of herbs—mint, cilantro, parsley, tarragon—served with a slab of feta cheese and flatbread.

pickled garlic

Use garlic in May, when in season, if you can; it is milder. Pickling mellows the flavor and you can eat it from the jar, as you would pickled onions. I serve it with drinks, alongside olives and salted almonds. Make it more sweet-sour by increasing the sugar, or add dried chile.

Makes 3 (½ pint) jars
1lb garlic
1 cup white wine vinegar
¼ cup granulated sugar

6 white peppercorns
6 black peppercorns
6 bay leaves

1 Prepare a boiling-water canner (*see* pages 368–369) and keep the cleaned jars and lids warm. Separate the garlic cloves and carefully peel each one. As you peel them, drop them into warm jars.

2 Put the vinegar, sugar, peppercorns, and bay into a saucepan and bring to a boil, stirring a little to help the sugar dissolve. Boil for two minutes, then pour over the garlic (it needs to be completely covered), leaving a ½ inch headspace.Use a sterilized plastic spatula to remove any air bubbles. Process the filled jars in a boiling-water canner for 10 minutes at sea level (*see* pages 369). Let cool, seal the jars, and label before storing. Refrigerate once opened.

danish pickled prunes

My first taste of Scandinavia was the food from room service when I arrived in Copenhagen in a snow storm. They brought roasted pork, dill-pickled cucumber, rye bread, and these prunes—I knew I was in for a good time. You can treat dried, pitted apricots in the same way.

Fills 1 (1 quart) jar
1lb prunes (good quality, unpitted)
hot Darjeeling tea
2 cups white wine or cider vinegar
1½ cups firmly packed light brown sugar

1 cinnamon stick
6 juniper berries, crushed
6 black peppercorns
strip of organic orange zest

1 Put the prunes in a saucepan with enough tea to cover them. Bring to a boil. then reduce to a simmer and cook gently for 10 minutes. Remove from the heat and let soak overnight.

2 Next day, drain the prunes, reserving the juice. Put the other ingredients into a saucepan and heat gently, stirring, until dissolved. Add 1 cup of the prune soaking liquid, bring to a boil, then reduce the heat and simmer for four minutes. Put the prunes into a hot sterilized jar and pour over the liquid. Seal with a vinegar-proof lid and store in the refrigerator for up to a month.

middle eastern pickled persimmons

In this Middle Eastern recipe, the fruit isn't cooked but is raw and kept in a jar with a vinegar solution. You can also pickle slices of persimmon by first briefly poaching them, using the recipe for pickled peaches (*see* page 226), then storing in the refrigerater as below..

Fills 1 (1½ quart) jar
2¼lb persimmons, not too ripe
   (firm is better than mushy)
2 dried limes
2 teaspoons cardamom pods
1 tablespoon white mustard seeds

2 teaspoons black peppercorns
1 tablespoon toasted coriander seeds
1 cinnamon stick, broken in half
3 cups white wine vinegar
1½ teaspoons pickling salt
1 cup granulated sugar

1 Halve the persimmons and cut each half—lengthwise—into slices about ½ inch thick at the thickest part. Break the dried limes into pieces. Remove the seeds from the cardamom pods (just crush the pods then split them with your fingernail, the seeds will come out easily). Put these into a mortar with all the other spices (except the cinnamon) and bruise them by pounding a little.

2 Layer up the persimmons in a warm sterilized jar (*see* page 11) with the spices. Put the vinegar, salt, and sugar in a saucepan and heat, stirring to dissolve the sugar. Pour the hot vinegar mixture over the persimmons to cover, seal with a vinegar-proof lid, and refrigerate. Let sit for a week before using, and use within three months.

middle eastern pickled turnips

Torshi left is one of the most popular Middle Eastern pickles and much more delicious than it sounds (I can hear you muttering "Pickled turnips? Yeah, right …"). They also look spectacular: the white turnips become pink with the beet juice, a process you can see happening; it's like watching watercolor paint create tinted skies.

Fills 1 (1½ quart) jar
2¼lb small white turnips
handful of celery leaves
4 garlic cloves

1 small wedge of raw beet, chopped
1¼ cups white wine vinegar
⅓ cup pickling salt

1 Peel the turnips and cut them in halves or quarters (or leave really small ones whole). Put these in a sterilized jar (*see* page 11) with the celery leaves, garlic, and the beet piece among them.

2 Stir together the vinegar and salt in a bowl until the salt has dissolved. Add 4 cups of water and pour it over the turnips. Seal with a vinegar-proof lid and store in a warm place (a windowsill is good). Leave for about ten days, then refrigerate. They'll keep for six weeks.

middle eastern mixed pickles

These, *torshi meshakel*, can be picked at before a meal, or eaten as part of a mezze spread. You can adapt the recipe, making it less spicy, or adding turmeric or harissa.

Fills 3 (1 quart) jars
½ cup pickling salt
2 cups white wine vinegar
1 small cauliflower, separated into florets
4 carrots (slim, small young ones)
1 red onion, cut into crescent wedges
1 cup sliced small pickling cucumbers
   (¾ inch thick slices)

6 garlic cloves, quartered lengthwise
2 red chiles, cut into rounds
2 green chiles, cut into rounds
1 small red bell pepper, halved, seeded, and sliced
½ cup green beans, trimmed at the stem end
1 tablespoon dill seeds
9 sprigs of dill
12 black peppercorns

1 Heat 5 cups of water with the salt to dissolve. Let cool. Add the vinegar.

2 Wash and prepare all the vegetables, then pack them into sterilized jars (*see* page 11) with the dill seeds, dill, and peppercorns. Pour the vinegar solution over them (make more if this isn't enough).

3 Cover with vinegar-proof lids and store in a warm place for a couple of weeks, after which the pickles are ready to eat. After that, refrigerate and eat within two months.

eggplant, cardamom, and pomegranate "jam"

You do get eggplant jam in the Middle East but it is a genuinely sweet jam, not a sweet-sour chutney (the eggplants actually taste like bananas) … but it got me thinking. I wanted an eggplant relish—light, not too thick—with Middle Eastern flavors. This is what I came up with. I make it in small amounts at a time (just a couple of jars) and dip into it when I want a quick fix of Middle Eastern spicing. It's good as part of a mezze spread, where it's mixed with all kinds of other flavors (and great against bland things, such as beans and lentils). You can stir cilantro or mint into it before serving, and sprinkle fresh pomegranate seeds over the top.

Fills 2 (½ pint) jars
2 large eggplants (1lb)
¼ cup olive oil
2 small tomatoes, coarsely chopped
2 red chiles, halved, seeded, and shredded
seeds from about 15 cardamom pods, crushed

1½ teaspoons ground ginger
1 teaspoon ground cinnamon
juice of 1 lemon
¼ cup sherry vinegar
2 tablespoons pomegranate molasses
1 cup firmly packed light brown sugar

1 Cut the top from the eggplants, then chop the flesh into chunks about ¾ inch square. Heat the oil in a skillet and cook the eggplants in batches until golden all over. Reduce the heat and add all the other ingredients. Cook over gentle heat, stirring a little to help the sugar dissolve. Continue to cook until the mixture is soft and thick, like a soft-set jam.

2 Put into warm sterilized jars (*see* page 11), cover with wax paper disks, and seal with vinegar-proof lids, and refrigerate. Use within a week.

how to use

As its inspiration is Middle Eastern, this is best used with dishes that have their roots there. Serve it with spiced roasted leg of lamb, or lamb skewers, with flatbread and yogurt (the sweetness of this relish is perfect with the stark sourness of plain yogurt), or with labneh (yogurt cheese, *see* page 98). It makes a great sandwich when paired with cold roasted lamb or hot merguez sausages.

middle eastern pickled eggplants

A dish of these—looking like miniature stuffed purple slippers—is a delight. You can find various versions throughout Greece and in parts of the Middle East (sometimes the eggplants are tied together with strips of celery to keep them intact), but this recipe isn't too complicated. It isn't easy to find baby eggplants, but they're available at certain times of the year in Middle Eastern, Indian, and Thai stores with a fresh produce section. To make these more sweet-sour, increase the amount of honey in the vinegar solution.

Fills 1 (1 quart) jar
1lb eggplants
1½ cups white wine vinegar
1 tablespoon sea salt
5 allspice berries
8 black peppercorns
½ cinnamon stick
2 tablespoons honey
3 fresh red chiles, halved lengthwise

FOR THE FILLING
3 garlic cloves, finely chopped
¼ cup coarsely chopped walnuts
1 red chile, halved, seeded, and shredded
1 carrot, shredded
1½ tablespoons finely chopped flat-leaf parsley
1½ tablespoons finely chopped mint leaves
salt
freshly ground black pepper
½ tablespoons olive oil, plus more to seal

1 Wash the eggplants and trim the stems if they are long. Cut a slit lengthwise in each eggplant to create a pocket. Steam for five minutes, until they are just tender. Carefully remove and dry gently with paper towels (dry the inside as well as the outside).

2 To make the spiced vinegar, put 1 cup of water, the vinegar, salt, allspice, peppercorns, cinnamon, and honey into a saucepan. Bring to a boil, then reduce the heat and simmer for five minutes. Let cool.

3 For the filling, crush the garlic and half the walnuts in a mortar with a pestle. Mix with the rest of the ingredients, binding with the olive oil. Stuff the eggplants with the mixture, then pack them into a warm sterilized jar (*see* page 11), arranging them with the halved red chiles.

4 Pour the spiced vinegar over them—it should nearly cover them—then fill the jar to the top with olive oil. Seal with a vinegar-proof lid. Store in the refrigerator. They'll be fine there for a week, although you can eat them after a few days.

how to use

Serve as part of a selection of mezze. This is such a stunner that you can offer more prosaic things—hummus, feta, and olives—alongside.

carrot and coriander relish

The result of a taste memory. I sampled a delicious relish at a village fête and meant to go back and beg for the recipe … but the stallholder had gone and I was left with one lovely jarful and no idea how to reproduce it. This comes closest. It's very fresh and nothing like a dark chutney.

Fills 2 (1 pint) jars

8 carrots, shredded
1¼ inch piece of fresh ginger root, minced
1 teaspoon mustard seeds
1 red chile, seeded and finely sliced
1 tablespoon coriander seeds,
    toasted and crushed

finely grated zest and juice of 1 lime
¼ cup apple juice
good pinch of salt
8 garlic cloves, chopped
⅔ cup cider vinegar
¾ cup firmly packed light brown sugar
¼ cup chopped cilantro leaves (optional)

1 Mix everything except the cilantro leaves in a saucepan. Slowly bring to a boil, stirring to help the sugar dissolve, then reduce the heat to a simmer and cook for 10 minutes, until the carrot is soft. Increase the heat a little and cook for 15 minutes, until you have a soft mixture in which the carrots look almost candied and the liquid has really reduced. Stir to make sure it doesn't stick to the pan.

2 Remove from the heat and stir in the cilantro, if using (if so, use within five days). Put in warm sterilized jars (*see* page 11), cover with wax paper disks, and seal with vinegar-proof lids. Store in the refrigerator for up to three months; once opened, use within five days. If you've put in the jars without cilantro, you can stir the herb in before serving.

coconut and cilantro chutney

This is so addictive— in fact, I eat it straight from the jar with a spoon (bad manners, I know). It just has all those flavors that the British so love in Indian food.

Fills 1 (½ pint) jar

½ teaspoon cumin seeds
3 cups cilantro leaves
1¼ cups grated fresh coconut
2 green chiles, halved, seeded,
    and coarsely chopped
3 garlic cloves, coarsely chopped

1 inch square piece of fresh ginger root,
    coarsely chopped
finely grated zest of 1 lime and juice of 2
salt
3 teaspoon superfine or granulated sugar,
    for a sweet version (or to taste)

1 Put the cumin seeds in a saucepan and toast until fragrant (about 40 seconds). Put everything except the sugar in a food processor and process to a paste. For a sweet version, process again with the added sugar.

2 Transfer to a sterilized jar (*see* page 11), or if using on the same day, put it in a bowl and cover with plastic wrap. This is delicious fresh, but it can be stored for four days in the refrigerator.

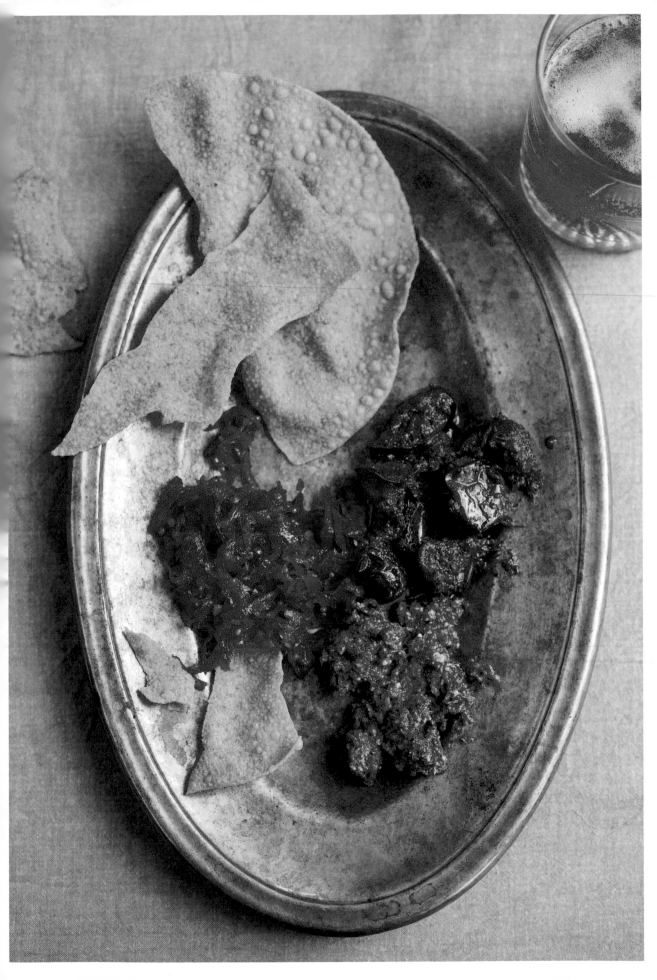

geeta's eggplant pickle

This is deep and almost meaty in flavor, not at all like the sweet commercial eggplant chutneys you can buy. It comes from Delhi-based Geeta Dhingra. Like Roopa's Lime Pickle opposite and the Pumpkin Achar (*see* page 253), it's an oil-base Indian pickle. Taste it over a couple of months and you'll be surprised how it changes and develops.

Fills 3 (½ pint) jars

2 eggplants, in ½ inch dice
2 tablespoons salt
1 teaspoon mustard seeds
1 teaspoon fennel seeds
1 teaspoon cumin seeds
pinch of fenugreek seeds
¾ teaspoon turmeric

1 teaspoon chili powder
⅔ cup vegetable oil, plus more to seal
6 garlic cloves, crushed
2 inch fresh ginger root, finely grated
½ cup cider or malt vinegar
2 tablespoons tamarind paste
2 tablespoons superfine or granulated sugar
small handful of fresh curry leaves

1 Put the eggplants in a big bowl and mix in the salt, tossing with your hands. Let sit overnight.

2 The next day, heat heavy skillet and toast the mustard, fennel, cumin, and fenugreek seeds for 30 seconds, or until you can smell their aromas. Using a mortar and pestle, grind to a powder and mix with the turmeric and chili powder.

3 Drain and discard any liquid that has come out of the eggplants. Squeeze together small handfuls of eggplant pieces to extract as much moisture as possible.

4 Heat the oil in a big skillet or wok. Sauté the eggplants over moderate heat for three to four minutes, until golden brown. Drain on paper towels.

5 Add the garlic, ginger, and vinegar to the oil in the same skillet and sauté for about five minutes, until most of the vinegar has evaporated. Reduce the heat to low and stir in the ground spices, followed by the tamarind, sugar, and curry leaves.

6 Return the eggplants to the skillet, stir well to mix everything together, and spoon the pickle into sterilized jars (*see* page 11). Let cool completely. Pour a ½ inch layer of oil over the eggplants, so the pickle is completely submerged, seal with vinegar-proof lids, and refrigerate. This tastes best if left to mature for three to four days before you eat it. It will keep for up to six months, covered, in the refrigerator.

roopa's lime pickle

This is from my friend Roopa Gulati, a wonderful Indian cook. It's made in the old-fashioned way, left to "cook" in warm sun (but in England, Roopa also uses the microwave to help her).

Fills 1 (1 pint) jar
7–8 limes (1lb)
10 fat garlic cloves,
1 teaspoon chili powder
½ cup sea salt flakes

FOR THE TEMPERING
1 teaspoon mustard seeds
¼ teaspoon fenugreek seeds
1 star anise
1 teaspoon paprika
⅓ cup vegetable oil, plus more if needed
2 inch fresh ginger root, minced
3 green chiles, seeded and finely chopped
¼ cup cider vinegar
3 tablespoons superfine or granulated sugar

1 Make a deep cross in each lime, cutting three-quarters of the way through. (You can chop the limes if you prefer a lime pickle that is broken up.) Crush the garlic to a paste and mix with the chili powder and salt. Using a teaspoon, spoon the spicy garlic mixture into the cuts made in the limes. Put the limes and any extra garlic mixture in a bowl and cook on "high" in the microwave for about four and a half minutes, or until the skins have softened.

2 Transfer these to a sterilized jar (*see* page 11) and let cool. Seal with a vinegar-proof lid and let sit in a warm place for about two weeks (the windowsill in summer is ideal). Give the jar a good shake every day.

3 By now, the salt will have drawn out some of the lime juice and the skins will have softened. Transfer the limes into a strainer, catching any juice in a bowl below. Set aside while you do some spice tempering.

4 Heat a heavy skillet over medium heat and toast the mustard seeds, fenugreek seeds, and star anise for about 40 seconds, stirring all the time. When they darken and release their aromas, transfer to a mortar and pound them to a powder. Stir in the paprika and set aside.

5 In a saucepan, heat the oil and sauté the ginger and green chiles for two to three minutes. Stir in the pounded spices, followed by the vinegar, sugar, and any juice from the limes. Simmer for two minutes before adding the limes to the pan. Stir well to mix everything together and let cool.

6 Put in a sterilized jar. Push the limes down the jar so they are completely immersed in the oil. Add a little more oil, if you need to, so the limes are covered. Seal with a vinegar-proof lid and let sit in the refrigerator for three to four days before eating. This will keep for up to six months, covered, in the refrigerator.

peanut and mint chutney

A recipe from the mother-in-law of my friend Roopa Gulati. It is customary, in India, for mothers-in-law to pass on their recipes for pickles and chutneys to their daughters-in-law (this ensures they will continue to be made), so Roopa has inherited more than a few.

This is a fresh chutney, hot and sweet and fragrant. You can also make a variation with freshly grated coconut. Or use cashew nuts or almonds instead of peanuts.

Fills 1 (½ pint) jar
⅔ cup skinned peanuts
2 green chiles, halved, seeded, and chopped
1½ inch square of fresh ginger root, chopped

juice of 2 limes
1½ teaspoons superfine or granulated sugar, or to taste
1 cup shredded mint leaves

1 Preheat the oven to 340°F. Put the peanuts into a roasting pan and roast them until they are pale gold, about 10–15 minutes. Set aside to cool.

2 Put the chiles, ginger, lime juice, and sugar in a food processor and pulse-blend. Add the peanuts and mint and process again, adding a couple of spoons of water, if needed, to get a coarse paste.

3 Transfer to a sterilized jar (*see* page 11) and seal with a vinegar-proof lid, or if you will be eating it on the same day, you can also put it in a bowl and cover with plastic wrap. This chutney is wonderful when it's fresh, but can be stored for five days in the refrigerator.

how to use

Perfect with poppadoms, obviously, but I especially like this with roasted lamb (British of me, I know). Marinate a leg of lamb in a mixture of yogurt, lemon juice, cayenne pepper, and plenty of crushed garlic for 24 hours. (Make incisions all over the meat so that the marinade can really penetrate.) Lift the lamb out of the marinade, shaking off the excess, then roast and serve with this chutney and boiled rice. What an alternative to the standard Sunday roast …

pumpkin achar

Achar is a kind of Indian pickle in which the preserving is done with spiced oil. It was completely unknown to me until I started work on this book, and has been one of the most delicious discoveries. This is adapted from a recipe I saw being made at River Cottage by Pam Corbin, the resident jam, chutney, and pickle expert. You need about ½ cup of lime juice; limes vary enormously in the amount of juice they hold.

Fills 2 (1½ pint) jars
1 small butternut squash
   or 1¾lb pumpking
1 large onion, coarsely chopped
¾ inch piece fresh ginger root
2 red chiles, halved, seeded, and sliced
6 garlic cloves
1 cup sunflower oil, plus more if needed
1 tablespoon turmeric

1 tablespoon mustard powder
1 tablespoon yellow mustard seeds
2 teaspoons black peppercorns, lightly crushed
finely grated zest of 4 limes and juice of 6–8
   (*see* recipe introduction)
1 cup cider vinegar
1½ cups granulated sugar
1 tablespoon salt

1 Peel the squash or pumpkin, remove the seeds, and cut the flesh into ½ inch chunks.

2 Put the onion, ginger, chiles, garlic, and ⅔ cup of the oil in a food processor and process. Heat the rest of the oil in a skillet and add the onion puree. Cook this gently for 10 minutes, then add the turmeric, mustard powder and seeds, and the peppercorns. Cook for another five minutes, keeping an eye on it and stirring from time to time to prevent the mixture from sticking and burning.

3 Add the lime zest and juice, vinegar, sugar, and salt. Continue to cook gently, stirring a little to help the sugar dissolve. Remove from the heat and let cool.

4 Get a saucepan of boiling water ready and drop the squash into it. Return to a boil and, when it has boiled for 90 seconds, drain the squash, rinse in cold water, and pat dry on a clean dish towel. Mix with the spicy sauce and bring to a boil.

5 Pack it into warm sterilized jars (*see* page 11), and shake each jar to make sure there are no air pockets. The sauce should come up over the squash. If it doesn't, add a thin layer of oil. Seal immediately with vinegar-proof lids. This keeps for a month in the refrigerator.

how to use

You can, of course, eat this with curries and whatever other Indian food you might have cooked, but I also like it just with lightly spiced roasted chicken thighs. Marinate thighs in a mixture of yogurt, crushed garlic, chopped chile or cayenne pepper, lime juice, and salt, then roast for 40 minutes. This is even good with plain roasted chicken and pork.

very hot mango chutney

Mango is probably the chutney we most often reach for when we have a curry. This version is hotter than regular mango chutney and spicier in taste (reduce the quantity of chiles if you prefer, but it is also the ginger that gives it kick). If I think it will be eaten quickly, I make a small batch and add chopped cilantro leaves at the end along with the lime. Delicious.

Fills 3 (½ pint) jars

3 onions, finely chopped
1¾ cups white malt vinegar
3 red chiles, seeded and shredded
3 green chiles, seeded and shredded
1½ teaspoons black mustard seeds
5 mangoes (3¼lb), peeled, pitted, and
    sliced into wedges

2 tart cooking apples, peeled, cored,
    and chopped
2¼ cups granulated sugar
2 teaspoons ground ginger
½ teaspoon ground allspice
¼ teaspoon ground cloves
grated zest and juice of 2 limes

1 Prepare a boiling-water canner (*see* pages 368–369) and keep the cleaned jars and lids warm. Put the onions into a large saucepan with the vinegar and chiles and simmer for 10 minutes, until the onions are nearly tender.

2 Toast the mustard seeds in a dry skillet until they begin to pop. Add the mangoes, apples, and mustard seeds to the onions in the pan and cook for about 15 minutes, until the fruit is soft.

3 Add the sugar, ginger, allspice, cloves, and lime zest and bring slowly to a boil, stirring to help the sugar dissolve. Reduce the heat and continue to cook until the mixture is thick and jamlike, stirring from time to time to make sure it isn't sticking on the bottom. Stir in the lime juice and mix well (this just gives a bit of freshness at the end).

4 While it is still hot, pot the chutney in warm, dry jars, leaving a ½ inch headspace. Use a sterilized plastic spatula to remove any air bubbles. Process the filled jars in a boiling-water canner for 10 minutes at sea level (*see* pages 369). Let cool, seal the jars, and label before storing. Refrigerate once opened.

sweet hot pickled limes

Use these alongside curries, or lay the slices on fish or chicken fillets, and roast.

Fills 2 (1 pint) jars
22 limes (3¼lb)
⅔ cup sea salt flakes
ground seeds from 1½ teaspoons
    cardamom pods
2 teaspoons cumin seeds

6 cloves
4 dried chiles
1 teaspoon turmeric
2½ inch fresh ginger root, finely chopped
3½ cups white granulated sugar or
    3¼ cups firmly packed light brown sugar

1 Put the limes in a bowl and cover with cold water. Let soak overnight, then drain. Cut slices off the top and bottom of each lime and discard these. Cut the limes into slices about ⅛ inch thick. Layer in a bowl, sprinkling with salt as you work. Cover with a dish towel and let sit overnight.

2 The next day, strain the limes. Put their liquid into a saucepan with the spices and sugar. Bring slowly to a boil, stirring to help the sugar dissolve, then cook for one minute. Let cool.

3 Add the limes, mix them with the spiced liquid, return to a boil, reduce the heat, and simmer for two minutes. Put in sterilized jars (*see* page 11) and seal with vinegar-proof lids. Leave in a sunny place for four to five days before storing in the refrigerator. The limes will be ready to eat in about four weeks, and will keep for six months in the refrigerator

preserved lemons

Reading about preserved lemons in *Palace Walk* by Egyptian writer Naguib Mafouz made my mouth water. They are soft and mellow, but salty, and work great with bland foods.

Fills 1 (1 quart) jar
6 unwaxed lemons (smaller lemons are
    better), plus another 3–4 for juicing
⅓ cup kosher sea salt

1 teaspoon coriander seeds
1 teaspoon black peppercorns
3 bay leaves
olive oil, to seal

1 Wash the lemons really well and quarter each lengthwise, but don't cut all the way through. You should end up with lemons that open like flowers.

2 Holding each lemon half open, put about 2 teaspoons of salt into it. Squeeze it closed then put into a sterilized jar (*see* page 11). Do this with all the lemons you want to preserve, then put a weight—such as a sterilized stone—on top and let sit in a warm place for a few days while the juices run out.

3 Remove the weight and add the coriander seeds, peppercorns, and bay leaves. Squeeze enough fresh lemon juice to cover completely, then pour a layer of oil on top. The fruit must be completely covered. Seal with a vinegar-proof lid and refrigerate. They will be ready to use in a month and will keep for six months.

mango and mustard seed pickle

A version of a particular style of Indian pickle known as an "oil pickle" (but this is my very British take on it). The oil is a preservative, but also a medium for carrying flavor. I like a little sweetness but, for an all-savory version, omit the sugar. This is fantastic with baked ham or spiced broiled mackerel. Nobody eats small spoonfuls, but big scoops, as if it were a salad.

Fills 3 (1 pint) jars
2 firm unripe mangoes
finely grated zest and juice of 2 limes
1/3 cup grated fresh ginger root
15 garlic cloves, finely chopped
2 1/2 tablespoons black mustard seeds
1 cup sunflower oil, plus more to seal

2 teaspoons hot mustard (I use grain mustard)
2 green chiles, halved, seeded, and finely sliced
2 red chiles, halved, seeded, and finely sliced
1 1/2 teaspoons pickling salt
freshly ground black pepper
1–2 tablespoons superfine or granulated sugar
  (optional)

1 Peel the mangoes and carefully remove the flesh from around the pit. Cut the flesh into wedges about 1/8 inch thick, put them in a bowl, and sprinkle with the lime zest and juice. Let sit for an hour, tossing the mango wedges in the lime juice every so often.

2 Put the ginger, garlic and 1/4 cup of water into a food processor and process to a paste. Set aside.

3 Pour the mustard seeds into a dry saucepan and toast them, shaking the pan frequently, until they begin to spit and jump. It will take about two minutes. Add the oil and the pureed mixture and cook for about five minutes over gentle heat. Remove from the heat and add the mustard. Mix it with the mangoes, chiles, salt, pepper, and sugar, if using.

4 Put the pickle into sterilized jars (*see* page 11) and pour a thin layer of oil over it. Seal with vinegar-proof lids. You can eat this as soon as it's made if you want, but the pickle softens and the flavor deepens with age … it's great to watch how it changes. Keep in the refrigerator and eat within a month. Stir it around every so often to mix it up again. I sometimes stir cilantro leaves through before serving a bowlful.

how to use

I always feel this is more than a pickle. Because it is made with long slices of mango it can feel like a really punchy salad instead of just a condiment, so don't be afraid to give it a starring role. Obviously it's good with curries, but more often I serve it at barbecues with chicken, pork, or salmon. In the winter, it is a lovely sunny jar to set on the table to eat with spicy roasted chicken and rice.

ash helicopters and mangoes on the roof: pickling in britain and india

"High tea," a very British kind of meal, was what I used to have at my great grandmother's house on a Sunday. It consisted of cold cuts, a white loaf of bread, tomatoes, a big cool pat of butter, hard-boiled eggs, soft-leafed lettuce, and a whole assortment of jars. Every jar had its own spoon and there was a special pickle fork, too. The British love their jars of pickles and chutneys. The basics of a meal—the meat or pie—may be solid and seemingly unexciting, but we are very good at "tracklements," the condiments and other morsels that are served on the side. The contents of these jars are also an illustration of our history, and our magpie tendencies to steal what we have fallen in love with from other cultures.

There has been an explosion in the range of "handcrafted" pickles and chutneys (although quite often the only thing handcrafted about them is that claim), and there are an increasing number of good artisan producers. We've come a long way since there was just commercial jars of mango chutney to go with our Vesta curry and pickled onions for cheese and pickle sandwiches. However, there was a whole world of chutneys and pickles before the commercial brands took off. The pantries of 16th- and 17th-century England would have been wondrous places to explore. We have pickled since the Roman invasion, but it became more popular in Elizabethan times, partly because a greater range of fruit and vegetables became available and partly because Elizabethans were concerned with how their food looked. They used delicate pickles, even pickled flowers—cowslips, violets, and gilly flowers—to decorate salads. In fact, almost anything was a potential pickle. Writers, such as Gervaise Markham, Robert May, and John Evelyn, described pickles made from ash helicopter seeds and broom buds as well as lettuce and cucumber.

Something approaching a mania for something on the side took hold when exotic pickles and chutneys from the East India Company began to arrive in the late 17th century (chutney comes from the Hindustani word *chatni*, meaning a strong, sweet relish). British cooks tried to imitate Chinese and Malayan "catsup," made from fermented fish, by making mushroom, anchovy, and walnut ketchups, and they used melons, cucumber, and peaches to make mock mango pickle. The first recipe for piccalilli (not as British as you think) actually appeared in 1694 with the title "To pickle lila, an Indian pickle."

Eliza Acton, in *Modern Cookery for Private Families*, published in 1845, has a short section on chutneys and pickles but writes very clear instructions, suggesting that she made them often. There are recipes for eastern "chatneys" meant to be eaten with curries and cold cuts, others that hark back to the Elizabethan age, (pickled nasturtiums), and plenty of pickled fruits (not surprising because they are excellent with traditional English strong cheeses and raised pies).

There was a plethora of commercially made pickles and chutneys in the Victorian era, all heavily flavored with the spices the English had come to love. Chutneys with glorious names like Major Grey and Bengal Club echoed the days of the Raj, days of tennis parties, pink gimlets, and blazing hot sun. Our British versions were good in their own right, but much sweeter, and nothing like as vibrant—in color or taste—as the Indian originals that had inspired them.

In India, pickles and chutneys have a more central role in the meal, and in life. "In India pickles are power," says Roopa Gulati. Roopa, brought up in India and Cumbria, was shocked when she began married life in Delhi to find just how much a woman's sense of self-worth is bound up with her pickle- and chutney-making skill. "Food is a weapon there as well as a nurturing tool. Women are so possessive of their pickling recipes and methods that they don't hand them to their daughters, that way the recipes would pass out of the family. They give them to their daughters-in-law so that they stay close to home." Roopa's former mother-in-law kept such a close eye on her pickles that she stored them in her bedroom. "Even the childrens' nanny wouldn't share her recipes!" Roopa whispers. "I used to say her mango chutney was the best I had ever tasted and ask what was in it. She would just smile and say 'Oh, this and that.' In all the years she lived with us, she got up early to prepare her chutneys so she could do it in private."

The relish tray is as important in an Indian household as the main meal. They're far more than just condiments. Some, especially fresh chutneys, can be eaten in large quantities, as if they were salads, and deciding which recipes to make fresh every day is a major preoccupation. That's small wonder, because the range of pickles and chutneys in India is vast. There are hot pickles, sour versions, oily recipes, even "water pickles," which are briny and can only be kept for a maximum of two weeks. Then there are chutneys. Chutneys are sweeter than pickles, and much less chunky. Many chutneys are made to be eaten fresh, others are designed to last, well stored, for years, aging and mellowing like wine. Sweetness is added to chutneys in the form of jaggery, and sourness comes from tamarind and limes as well as from vinegar.

Oil pickles—achar—are a particularly popular type of pickle that is relatively unknown in Britain outside Indian families. In India, mustard oil, untoasted sesame oil, and vegetable oil are used for these, and even meat and fish, as well as fruit and vegetables, can be pickled as achar. These pickles must always be protected under a good layer of oil and their success depends on a long marination time.

Chutneys and pickles are not used with rich or delicate foods, such as creamy kormas, but with plain rice pilafs, dals, and breads. Dharamjit Singh, in *Indian Cookery*, suggests eating plain rice and vegetables with raita and up to a dozen pickles and chutneys to experience them properly.

Chutney- and pickle-making is something that groups of women do together, especially family groups. "In rural areas in particular, you know when pickles are being made," says Roopa. "You can see ingredients drying outside. Mangoes on the rooftops." This is because many chutneys and pickles are "cooked" in the heat of the sun. "To make lime pickle, we would put a cross in the top of each fruit, then stuff them with chile, spices, and salt, put them in pots covered with cheesecloth, and leave them on the roof. Every day they had to be stirred with a wooden spoon. After two weeks in the sun the limes would be soft and salty. When I was growing up in Cumbria we did the same thing, but put them beside the fire [fireplace] to 'cook'."

The pickle recipes Roopa gave to me (*see* pages 250–252) are nothing like those you find in most Indian restaurants in Britain. They are vibrant and "living," their initial piquancy mellowing into something more rounded. And their flavors are very deep. The recipe she gave me for Eggplant Pickle (*see* page 250) is as multifaceted and meaty as a good beef braise. It helps you understand why Indians see pickles and chutneys as more than just accompaniments. And why this little scrap of Indian verse from the days of the Raj is so apt: "All things chickeney and mutton'y taste better far when served with chutney."

purple pickled eggs

Mad but wonderful … and it's so good to be able to ask, "Purple pickled egg, anyone?"

Fills 1 (1 quart) jar
14 eggs
4 cups white wine vinegar
1 beet, sliced

½ cup granulated sugar
2 tablespoons coriander seeds
½ cinnamon stick
3 dried chiles

1 Boil the eggs for 10 minutes, then drain, run cold water over them, and peel. Make a few punctures in each egg with a toothpick. Set aside.

2 Mix together all the rest of the ingredients in a saucepan and bring to a boil. Reduce the heat and let simmer for about 15 minutes. Put the eggs into a sterilized jar (*see* page 11) and pour the hot vinegar over them. Seal with a vinegar-proof lid and keep in the refrigerator once cold. The eggs will taste better after a couple of days. They'll keep—covered with the vinegar—for about a month.

pickled red cabbage

I'm not fond of vinegary pickled red cabbage. This is sweeter (and spicier). It's traditionally served with Lancashire lamb stew but is great with boiled ham (that's how we had it in Ireland). You'll be eating it straight out of the jar.

Fills 2 (1 pint) jars
1 red cabbage
¼ cup sea salt flakes
1⅓ cups cider vinegar
½ cup balsamic vinegar
2 cups red wine
1⅔ cups granulated sugar

2 star anise
1 teaspoon black peppercorns
2 whole dried red chiles
20 juniper berries
1 cinnamon stick, broken into three
6 cloves

1 Shred the cabbage finely, getting rid of the tough central core. Layer in a bowl, sprinkling with salt as you work, and let sit for four hours. Wash and drain the cabbage and pat dry with a clean dish towel.

2 Put the vinegars, wine, and sugar in a saucepan, bring to a boil, stirring to help the sugar dissolve, and boil to reduce by half. Put all the spices, except the cinnamon and cloves, into a mortar and pound to a coarse mixture, then add to the vinegar with the cloves and cinnamon and let sit for 30 minutes.

3 Pack the cabbage into sterilized jars (*see* page 11) and strain over the vinegar through a nylon strainer. Seal with vinegar-proof lids. Let cool, then refrigerate for two weeks before eating. It keeps for three months in the refrigerator.

teresa's date and apple chutney

Every year the National Trust holds a festival and competition celebrating pickles and chutneys at Barrington Court in Dorset. When I visited in 2010, this was the winning chutney. I wasn't surprised; it has a fabulous flavor, deep, dark, and sweet. The recipe comes from Teresa Hann, who inherited it from her grandmother, and every year she makes pounds of it, usually from windfall apples brought to her by neighbors. Teresa minces the apples, dates, and onions, so they are very fine. The other key thing is that she cooks the fruit without sugar for the first hour. She says sugar hardens the fruit and she wants the chutney to "cook down" well and soften before it goes in. Long, slow cooking is crucial; that is Teresa's top piece of advice for successful chutney making.

Fills 2 (1 pint) jars

10 cooking apples (3¼lb), peeled, cored, and minced, or cut into small chunks
3 onions, minced
3½ cups minced pitted dates
½ tablespoon salt

2 teaspoons ground ginger
2 teaspoons ground cinnamon
½ teaspoon cayenne pepper
2½ cups raw brown sugar
1¼ cups malt vinegar

1 Prepare a boiling-water canner (*see* pages 368–369) and keep the cleaned jars and lids warm.

2 Put all the ingredients into a saucepan except the sugar and half the vinegar. Turn the heat to medium and let cook, stirring every so often. The apples will soon start to release their own juice and provide enough moisture to keep the whole thing going. Reduce the heat to low and cook for an hour, until everything is really soft.

3 Add the sugar and the rest of the vinegar and stir well. Continue to cook, stirring every so often and keeping an eye on it, for another one and a half to two hours. The chutney should be thick, dark, and very soft. It is ready to put up when, if you drag your wooden spoon through it, a slight channel is formed that doesn't immediately fill up. Don't take it too far—you want a moist chutney.

4 Put into warm jars, leaving a ½ inch headspace. Process the filled jars in a boiling-water canner for 10 minutes at sea level (*see* pages 369). Let cool, seal the jars, and label before storing. Leave for at least two weeks before eating and preferably longer. The flavor will get better over time. Refrigerate once opened.

apple, cucumber, and mint pickle

You'll want lamb as you are cooking this (the British nose is so trained to expect lamb with these aromas—mint, vinegar ,and sugar—that you almost think you can smell roasted lamb as well).

Fills 4 (½ pint) jars

2 small onions, halved and
 very thinly sliced
3 cups halved, seeded, and sliced
 cucumbers
2 Granny Smith apples (14oz), peeled,
 cored, and sliced

2 tablespoons salt
2½ cups white wine vinegar
2¾ cups granulated sugar
1 tablespoon mustard seeds
2 small dried red chiles
2 teaspoon white peppercorns
3 sprigs of mint

1 Put the vegetables and fruit in a bowl with the salt. Let sit overnight. Next day, rinse and dry. Put the vinegar in a saucepan with the sugar, mustard seeds, chiles, peppercorns, and mint. Bring to a boil, stirring, reduce the heat, and simmer for a few minutes. Remove from the heat; let sit for 30 minutes.

2 Remove the mint, put in the apple, and bring to a boil. Immediately reduce the heat to low and cook until only just tender. Add the onions and cucumbers and simmer for another minute.

3 Pack the fruit and vegetables into sterilized jars (*see* page 11). Pour the vinegar solution and spices over them. Seal with vinegar-proof lids. This keeps for six months, but refrigerate once opened.

moroccan-spiced apricot chutney

For years, I've made a chicken dish with apricots, honey, and orange flower water. This is that sauce as a chutney. You can omit the flower water, but it lends a touch of the voluptuous east …

Fills 2 (1 pint) jars

4 cups chopped dried apricots
3 cooking apples, peeled, cored, and finely
 chopped
2 tomatoes, chopped
1 onion, finely chopped
1¼ cups white wine vinegar
⅔ cup golden raisins

juice of 1 lemon
juice of 1 orange
1 tablespoon ground ginger
1 cinnamon stick, halved
2¼ teaspoons cayenne pepper
1¼ cups granulated sugar
½ cup honey (preferably orange blossom)
1 teaspoon orange flower water, or to taste

1 Prepare a boiling-water canner (*see* pages 368–369) and keep the cleaned jars and lids warm. Put everything except the honey and flower water into a saucepan and bring to a boil, stirring to help the sugar dissolve. Reduce the heat and cook gently for one and a half hours, stirring so it does not catch.

2 Stir in the honey and cook gently for 15 minutes. Add the flower water, then taste and adjust, if needed. Put into warm jars, leaving a ½ inch headspace. Process the filled jars in a boiling-water canner for 10 minutes at sea level (*see* pages 369). Let cool, seal the jars, and label before storing.

camilla's roast plum and licorice chutney

This chutney—which is very unorthodox in method—is from a fantastic Danish cook called, appropriately, Camilla Plum. I have altered it only slightly. Slow cooking a chutney in the oven produces the richest, deepest flavor. Camilla makes a refrigerator "jam" by the same method (but omits the vinegar, changes the spicing, and adds more sugar, of course). Be sure to adjust the sugar in this chutney to your taste. If you can't find licorice root, you can use the strips of sweet licorice from candy shops; just chop it up and add it with everything else, so it melts. Camilla's book on Nordic food, *The Scandinavian Kitchen*, is the best on the subject, full of unexpected pleasures (and other preserves).

Fills 3 (½ pint) jars
18 plums (2lb)
1 cup white wine or cider vinegar
1 cup red wine
2½ cups granulated or 2¼ cups firmly packed light brown sugar, or to taste
½ tablespoon coriander seeds, crushed

½ tablespoon yellow mustard seeds
1 cinnamon stick, broken in two
3 blades of mace
seeds from 8 cardamom pods, ground
2 red chiles, halved, seeded, and finely sliced
1 inch piece of licorice root, chopped

1 Preheat the oven to 325°F. Halve and pit the plums and put them into a roasting pan (or something similar) with all the other ingredients. The plums have to be able to lie in a single layer. Put into the oven and cook for about 45 minutes. Now have a look and taste. You may need to adjust the sugar (depending on how tart your plums are).

2 Return the dish to the oven and cook until the mixture is glossy and chunks of soft plum are surrounded by a rich, thick syrup; this can take anything from one and a half to three hours, depending on how ripe and juicy your plums are. You need to check every so often to see how your chutney is doing. Remember that sweet syrups thicken more as they cool. If you find that your plums are dark in color (getting overroasted) but you still have too much liquid, drain off most of the liquid and reduce it by boiling, then return it to the plums.

3 Meanwhile, prepare a boiling-water canner (*see* pages 368–369) and keep the cleaned jars and lids warm. Put the plums in the warm jars, leaving a ½ inch headspace. Process the jars in a boiling-water canner for 15 minutes at sea level (*see* pages 369). Let cool, seal the jars, and label before storing.

how to use

This is unlike other chutneys because it is "wet," so it seems more like a sauce. The texture makes it perfect for serving with hot dishes, such as roasted duck legs or roasted pork. Sometimes I even heat it—just gently—before serving.

christmas chutney

You can eat this all year round, but it's nice to have one chutney that you eat only at Christmas. I make it around the same time as the Christmas pudding and the fragrance they both create in the house as they are cooking is wonderful. This is good with all the usual Christmassy fare, cold meats, and cheeses.

Fills 3 (1 pint) jars

⅔ cup dried cranberries

1 cup fresh cranberries

⅔ cup dried sour cherries

⅔ cup chopped pitted dates

1 cup chopped prunes (dried plums)

⅔ cup raisins

⅔ cup golden raisins

4 Pippin apples, peeled, cored, and finely chopped

1¾ cups finely chopped onion

1¾ cups cider vinegar

2¼ cups light brown sugar

½ teaspoon ground ginger

½ teaspoon ground cinnamon

½ teaspoon allspice

2–3 tablespoons brandy or port

1 Put all the ingredients, except the brandy, in a large, heavy saucepan. Bring to a boil and stir to help the sugar dissolve. Reduce the heat to a gentle simmer and cook slowly for about two hours.

2 Meanwhile, prepare a boiling-water canner (*see* pages 368–369) and keep the cleaned jars and lids warm. Try scraping a wooden spoon across the bottom of the pan to check for readiness. It should leave a path that doesn't immediately fill up with vinegar. If so, the chutney is done. (But do make sure your mixture isn't too dry either.)

3 Add the brandy to the hot chutney, and put the mixture immediately in warm, dry, jars, leaving a ½ inch headspace. Process the jars in a boiling-water canner for 15 minutes at sea level (*see* pages 369). Let cool, seal the jars, and label before storing.

Canning preserves for long-term storage

These recipes were originated for the British market, but where appropriate, some of the recipes have been adapted to include the canning process adviced by the United States Food and Drug Administration (USDA). Most recipes can be safely stored in the refrigerator and used within a few weeks or months (see individual recipes for recommendations). However, if you want to safely store certain preserves for a long time—such as some of the jam, pickle, and chutney recipes in this book—you need to processed them in a water bath in a boiling-water canner or pressure canner.

By heating preserves in a boiling-water canner or pressure canner, any potentially dangerous microorganisms, such as molds, yeasts, and bacteria, are destroyed, and the contents are hermetically sealed in—they are airtight. High-acid foods, which includes most fruits, such as apples, apricots, blackberries, gooseberries, lemons, peaches, pears, plums, and sour cherries, as well as pickles and sauerkraut, can be processed in a boiling-water canner at 212°F. Low-acid foods, which includes most vegetables, needs processing in a pressure canner at 240°F. Tomatoes and figs are borderline, but by adding an acidic ingredient, such as vinegar or lemon juice, they can be safely processed in a boiling-water canner.

The recipes suitable for canning in this book are all processed in a boiling-water canner. This process may seem complicated, but once you get started, it will be easy. The main thing to remember is to always follow the directions and keep everything clean.

CANNING EQUIPMENT

If you plan to do a lot of canning, there are a few items you should consider investing in. A boiling-water canner is basically a large enamel pot that comes with lid and a rack with handles; the rack prevents the jars from sitting directly on the bottom of the canner, so that water can circulate underneath them. If you have an electric range, the canner must have a flat bottom (not all do) and it should be no more than 4 inches wider than the heating element.

Instead, you can use a large, stainless steel stockpot or kettle as long as it is 3 inches deeper than the canning jars when set on a rack; you can improvise with a circular cake cooling rack, or you can tie together several screw bands from canning jars. If you use a stockpot, you will also need a jar lifter, which looks like a pair of tongs and are designed to lift and lower jars into the water.

You'll need medium and large, heavy, stainless steel saucepans for cooking the ingredients before canning them. Good-quality ones will provide the best results. Stainless steel is recommended because it won't react with some of the ingredients like other metals, such as copper and aluminum, do.

A few other items will be helpful. A skimming spoon is a large flat spoon with small perforations used to remove scum easily from the surface of the boiling jam. You'll also need a candy thermometer because it is the most accurate way to check the doneness of jams and jellies prepared without pectin.

For jellies, consider getting a jelly bag. This cone-shape bag can be made with cheesecloth or fine nylon mesh. It has strings or long loops at the top so that the bag can be suspended from a frame over a large bowl (make sure to rinse the bowl and bag with boiling water before use). To use one, spoon in the cooked fruit and water and let drip for 3–4 hours, or overnight. Resist the urge to squeeze the bag or the juice will be cloudy. The closer the mesh or weave of the fabric, the clearer the juice will be. If you are new to canning, or not sure how often you will use a jelly bag, improvise with a double-thickness layer of cheesecloth that has been soaked in boiling water, then draped into a large nylon strainer set over a bowl. After use, empty the jelly bag and wash well in hot water, but don't use detergent. Dry thoroughly before storing in a plastic bag.

Cheesecloth and string will come in handy more often than you would think. You can buy cheesecloth at grocery stores and retail stores that sell kitchen supplies. Cut off as much as you need and soak in boiling water for 5 minutes to sterilize before use. Drain and let stand until cool enough to handle. Use to wrap whole spices, or citrus fruit seeds and pith, and tie with string before adding to the pot. Squeeze well at the end of cooking and discard the contents; wash and recycle the cheesecloth, depending on size.

Accuracy is important to make sure you have a good gelling set, so if you plan to get serious about making preserves, invest in kitchen scales, available from stores that sell cookware and kitchen gadgets, for weighing large amounts of fruit and vegetables.

The only recommended type of jar recommended for canning is the mason-style jar that comes with a two-part lid with screw band. It is available in ½ pint, 1 pint, 1½ pints, quart, and ½ gallon sizes, with 1 pint sizes being common. The jars and screw bands can be reused, but the lids should be used only once. The jars used in these recipes are ½ pint or 1 pint sizes. If you use larger jars, the processing times will be different; check with the National Center for Home Food Preservation, which has a Web site providing information based on the USDA recommendations.

CLEANING AND STERILIZING JARS

Always clean empty jars before use and rinse well to remove any detergents, whether by hand or dishwasher. Preheat the jars and keep them warm while the preserves are being made by keeping them submerged in simmering water at 180°F in a stockpot or boiling-water canner. Or put them on a regular cycle in a dishwasher, keeping them in the closed dishwasher until the jars are needed for filling. The lids, but not the screw bands, also need heating in a saucepan of simmering water at 180°F until needed. A magnetic wand—a stick with a magnet on one end—is useful for retrieving lids from hot water.

If jams, jellies, or pickles will be processed in a boiling-water canner for less than 10 minutes, the jars need sterilizing. After cleaning them thoroughly, put the jars, right side up, in a boiling-water canner with the rack in the bottom, then add enough water to have 1 inch above the top of the jars. Bring the water to a boil and boil for 10 minutes, plus 1 minute per every 1,000 feet of elevation. Reduce the heat and keep the jars in the canner until needed, removing one at a time.

the canning process: FILLING THE JARS

Working with one jar at a time, use a jar lifter or large tongs to remove a jar from the water and place it on a protected surface, such as a wooden cutting board or dish towel. Using a funnel, add the preserves to the jar, leaving the headspace indicated in the recipe—this is a gap above the contents, ¼ inch for fruit spreads and ½ inch for tomatoes, chutneys, relishes, and pickles. Too much headspace and the jar won't seal properly; but too little, the contents can overflow. When there are chunks, use a plastic or rubber spatula to stir the contents in the jar to remove any air bubbles that could ruin the preserves.

After filling a jar, remove any drips from the rim and threads of the jar with a damp paper towel, center a lid on the jar, position the screw band, and tighten, following the manufacturer's instructions.

PROCESSING THE JARS

Lower the jars into the boiling-water canner (or pressure canner) and onto the rack, using a jar lifter or tongs. Add enough water to cover the jars by an inch, then cover with a lid and bring to a rolling boil. The length of boiling time depends on the recipe and where you live. The higher the elevation where you are, the lower the temperature at which water boils. If you are using a boiling-water canner, you need to adjust the amount of time the preserves are heated to destroy any microorganisms. The times in the recipes are for sea level, so if you live above 1,000 feet—check with your county cooperative extension office if you are unsure— you need to increase the length of time as inidcated. (If you are using a pressure canner, the gauge will need adjusting—check the manufacturer's instructions.) Turn off the heat, remove the lid, and let rest for 5 minutes before removing the jars.

ALTITUDE ADJUSTMENT TIMES

altitude	boiling water processing time
0–1,000 feet	time given in recipe
1,001–3,000 feet	add 5 minutes
3,001–6,000 feet	add 10 minutes
6,001–8,000 feet	add 15 minutes
8,001–10,000 feet	add 20 minutes

CHECKING THE SEALS AND STORING

Let cool undisturbed for 24 hours. Remove the screw bands (they are no longer needed) and check the seals. At eye level, the lid should look curved down in the center. If the lid springs up when you press down on it, it is not sealed. Store in the refrigerator and use within several days, or reprocess within 24 hours. Most canned preserves can be stored for up to a year if kept in a cool, dark place, between 50°F and 70°F, away from heat or light. Once any jar of preserve is opened, store in the refrigerator.

Do not use a jar if there are any signs of spoilage, including a swelling lid or broken seal, mold, cloudiness, yeast growth, fermentation, siime, or disagreeable ordors. The wisest course of action is to following the old saying, "when in doubt, throw it out."

Index

Acknowledgments

For my Dad, who will eat anything (but particularly loves cured herring), with much love

An Hachette UK Company
www.hachette.co.uk

First published in Great Britain in 2012 by Mitchell Beazley, an imprint of Octopus Publishing Group Limited, Endeavour House, 189 Shaftesbury Avenue, London WC2H 8JY
www.octopusbooks.co.uk

Distributed in the USA by Hachette Book Group USA, 237 Park Avenue, New York NY 10017 USA
www.octopusbooksusa.com

Distributed in Canada by Canadian Manda Group, 165 Dufferin Street, Toronto, Ontario, Canada M6K 3H6

Text © copyright Diana Henry 2012
Photographs © copyright Laura Edwards 2012

The right of Diana Henry to be identified as the Author of this work has been asserted by her in accordance with the Copyright, Designs and Patents Act 1988.

Publisher: Denise Bates
Art Director: Jonathan Christie
Photographer: Laura Edwards
Designer: Miranda Harvey
Editor: Lucy Bannell
Home Economist: Justine Pattinson
Production: Lucy Carter

ISBN 978 1 84533 675 2

Printed and bound in China

All "also try" recipes serve the same number as the main recipe, unless otherwise stated

A lot of people have helped me, taught me new skills, and generously shared their expertise while I've been working on this book. I would particularly like to thank the American food writer Michael Ruhlman. He is a master of charcuterie (his book *Charcuterie*, coauthored with Brian Polcyn, is a magnificent work; you should buy it immediately if you want to go beyond just curing bacon and making duck confit). He was generous with his time and advice, answered questions along the way, and kindly read the chapter on curing and salting.

Nick Selby, from London-based deli Melrose and Morgan, taught me to make marmalade and answered any jamming queries. He also let me use two of his recipes. Please go and buy his Good Morning Breakfast Marmalade if you can't be bothered to make your own.

The wonderful Stephen Harris, chef and co-owner of The Sportsman in Seasalter, let me pester him about various things and eventually gave me his recipe for maple-cured bacon (an achievement on my part because he's far too busy cooking to be bothered writing things down).

Jo Hampson and Georgina Perkins from Smoky Jo's in Shap, Cumbria, UK, taught me a thing or two (or three), answered endless questions, and read the smoking chapter. Thank you guys, you almost made me into a pro.

Roopa Gulati talked to me about Indian chutneys—pretty much every day for about a year—answered every probing e-mail I sent, tested and gathered up recipes, and generally educated me about Indian food. She also supplied some of the best recipes in the book.

Pam Corbin (aka Pam the Jam) at River Cottage helped with questions about pectin and allowed me to use a version of her gorgeous pumpkin achar.

James Swift of Trealy Farm in Wales (where he makes superb charcuterie) helped me to understand the science of his craft.

Chefs Mark Hix and Camilla Plum, and home chutney maker extraordinaire Teresa Hann, kindly gave recipes (and they are the kind of recipes that have entered my core repertoire). Judy Rodgers, chef at the beloved Zuni Café in San Francisco, allowed me to use an amended version of her recipe for pickled onions. (And there's another book you should get for preserves recipes and many other things: *The Zuni Café Cookbook*.)

Julian Henson and Mark Bruce from Henson's salt beef producers talked to me extensively about salt beef (although they wouldn't give me their cure recipe!).

Help on everything from schnapps to shaken red currants came from Signe Johansen, Trine Hahnemann, Camilla Plum, Matt Tebbutt, Alice Hart, Hattie Ellis, Joanna Simon, Bee Wilson, Sally Butcher, Shirley Booth, Kimiko Barber, and Keiko Okawa.

Friends picked fruit and carried loads of it back to London to go into my kettle. I'd especially like to thank Jenny Abbott, Mary Fysh, Fiona Cairns, and Justine Pattison. Thanks too to my fish dealers, Purkis in Muswell Hill, for getting me the fish I needed when I needed it, and Bifulco Butchers for doing the same with meat.

Justine Pattison, Jane Gwillim, and Lauren Spicer were wonderful in the kitchen on photo shoot days, cooking beautiful looking food and joining in the arguments.

Back at base, Denise Bates did what a great publishing director should do: She steered with a light hand, trusting me and designer Miranda Harvey to produce the book we had in our heads, while supporting us every inch of the way. Art director Jonathan Christie did the same. Thank you both for giving us room to run with this.

Finally, and it's a big finally, a trio of people: editor Lucy Bannell, designer Miranda Harvey, and photographer Laura Edwards were with me on this project from beginning to end. They have looked at vast lists of recipes, shortened text, tasted things, shopped with me, argued with me, cropped photos, worried about paper, and raided my cupboards for plates and cloths. They have made this one of the most creatively enjoyable periods of my life. You are, quite simply, a brilliant team. And I thank you from the bottom of my heart.